ALIMENTARY PERFORMANCES

A pea soda. An apple balloon. A cotton candy picnic. A magical *mole*. These are just a handful of examples of mimetic cuisine, a diverse set of culinary practices in which chefs and artists treat food as a means of representation. As theatricalized fine dining and the use of food in theatrical situations both grow in popularity, *Alimentary Performances* traces the origins and implications of food as a mimetic medium, used to imitate, represent, and assume a role in both theatrical and broader performance situations.

Kristin Hunt's rich and wide ranging account of food's growing representational stakes asks:

- What culinary approaches to mimesis can tell us about enduring philosophical debates around knowledge and authenticity
- How the dramaturgy of food within theatres connects with the developing role of theatrical cuisine in restaurant settings
- Ways in which these turns toward culinary mimeticism engender new histories, advance new epistemologies, and enable new modes of multisensory spectatorship and participation

This is an essential study for anyone interested in the intersections between food, theatre, and performance, from fine dining to fan culture and celebrity chefs to the drama of the cookbook.

Kristin Hunt is an Assistant Professor of Film, Dance, and Theatre at Arizona State University, USA.

ALIMENTARY PERFORMANCES

Mimesis, Theatricality, and Cuisine

Kristin Hunt

LONDON AND NEW YORK

First published 2018
by Routledge
2 Park Square, Milton Park, Abingdon, Oxon OX14 4RN

and by Routledge
711 Third Avenue, New York, NY 10017

Routledge is an imprint of the Taylor & Francis Group, an informa business

© 2018 Kristin Hunt

The right of Kristin Hunt to be identified as author of this work has been asserted by her in accordance with sections 77 and 78 of the Copyright, Designs and Patents Act 1988.

All rights reserved. No part of this book may be reprinted or reproduced or utilised in any form or by any electronic, mechanical, or other means, now known or hereafter invented, including photocopying and recording, or in any information storage or retrieval system, without permission in writing from the publishers.

Trademark notice: Product or corporate names may be trademarks or registered trademarks, and are used only for identification and explanation without intent to infringe.

British Library Cataloguing in Publication Data
A catalogue record for this book is available from the British Library

Library of Congress Cataloging in Publication Data
Names: Hunt, Kristin, author.
Title: Alimentary performances : mimesis, theatricality and cuisine / Kristin Hunt.
Description: Abingdon, Oxon ; New York : Routledge, 2018. | Includes bibliographical references and index.
Identifiers: LCCN 2018003983 | ISBN 9781138569690 (hardback) | ISBN 9781138569706 (pbk.) | ISBN 9781351337267 (epub) | ISBN 9781351337250 (mobi/kindle)
Subjects: LCSH: Performance art--United States--History--21st century. | Food in art. | Imitation in art.
Classification: LCC NX650.F64 H86 2018 | DDC 700.973/0905--dc23
LC record available at https://lccn.loc.gov/2018003983

ISBN: 978-1-138-56969-0 (hbk)
ISBN: 978-1-138-56970-6 (pbk)
ISBN: 978-0-203-70415-8 (ebk)

Typeset in Bembo
by Taylor & Francis Books

For Kathy Hunt, who taught me to cook, and for Sally Banes, who taught me to write about it.

CONTENTS

Acknowledgments   *viii*

1 Food, mimesis, and meaning   1
2 The foundations of contemporary mimetic gastronomy   34
3 What's next: Chicago's culture of culinary representation   65
4 Eating a way into house and home: Alimentary performance as resistant strategy   97
5 The proof is in the eating: Mimesis, participation, and embodied knowledge   128

Index   *159*

ACKNOWLEDGMENTS

This book has benefited from the sustained and sustaining influence of the many performers, designers, chefs, scholars, eaters, and collaborators of all kinds who have inspired me over a decade of work in food and performance. Thanks to all the chefs, servers, and restaurateurs who have welcomed me into their kitchens and dining rooms. I owe special thanks to those who offered me extended time in their spaces, including Homaro Cantu and the staff at Moto and iNG; Greg Zanitsch, Will McAvoy, and the staff at Fig Tree; and Ben Goldberg, Erik Anderson, and the staff at Catbird Seat. Thanks to the many artists and scholars who have participated in our American Society for Theatre Research working groups on food and performance, especially my co-convenors Joshua Abrams, Susan Bennett, and Megan Marsh-McGlone. I am indebted to the hundreds of actors, designers, technicians, stage managers, cake artists, dramaturges, and even one production gardener who collaborated with me on the alimentary performances discussed in Chapter 5, as well as the thousands of audience members who attended these productions. Special thanks to scenographer, food designer, and collaborator Leigh Henderson. Thanks to Linda Essig, who provided formative opportunities in alimentary performance. This book was also made possible by generous support from three academic institutions. The University of Wisconsin's Integrated Liberal Studies program and the Department of Theatre and Drama provided performance venues and financial support. My beloved colleagues at Northeastern Illinois University's Department of Communication, Media, and Theatre supported this project with research grants and as collaborators, tasters, and artistic and research partners. The School of Film, Dance, and Theatre at Arizona State University's Herberger Institute for Design and the Arts provided production opportunities and a vital research leave in which to complete the final revisions of this manuscript. I also thank my students at the University of Wisconsin-Madison, Northeastern Illinois University, and Arizona State University for supporting this work. Chapter 5 is derived, in part, from an article published in *Performance Research* on March 22, 2018, available online: https://doi.org/10.1080/13528165.2017.1346943. I am grateful to Richard Gough for his valuable feedback. Thanks to Ben Piggott and the many readers who have provided feedback on this manuscript over the course of its development.

Finally, thanks to Mary McAvoy, who willingly tasted dozens of alimentary first drafts and read many more.

1
FOOD, MIMESIS, AND MEANING

Fried chicken

Cotton candy, okra, mustard (*New Orleans, LA, Square Root, 2016*)

Chef Jason Byl loops a paper cone through a machine that spins hot sugar threads with centrifugal force until he has collected a large pile of fluff. The scent of fried chicken fills the room. Most diners at New Orleans chef Phillip Lopez's Square Root have heard of this dish, a constant on the extensive tasting menu. We watch from perches around the u-shaped countertop as Byl, working in the center of the cooking space, explains that the dish evokes classic flavors of a Southern picnic. He plates a bit of fried chicken cotton candy atop a slice of pickled okra and a dab of mustard. Guests lift fluff with fingers and deposit it on tongues, smiling and nodding to one another: "Tastes like fried chicken!"

Pea popsicle

Fresh peas, canned peas, sugar, lemon (*Madison, WI, Woyzeck, 2013*)

A chorus member, dressed in a leather skullcap with a horsetail hairpiece positioned high on her head, approaches a bank of seats. Audience members recognize her as Horse, one of the carnival characters in tonight's performance of Büchner's Woyzeck. *In her hands is a small silver bowl bearing twenty toothpicks, each of which carries a frozen green ball the size of a pea. As she makes her way along the bank of seating, audience members in the first row reach across the railing and take their treats. "Pea popsicle?" she whispers. Some patrons consult their menus. Some smile and eat, while others grimace and deposit the popsicles in refuse bins. A few add the popsicle to a collection of bites including a single pea, a piece of pea chewing gum, and a pea gummy candy.*

Balloon

Helium, green apple taffy (*Chicago, IL, Alinea, 2013*)

Two diners crane their necks to watch servers gently shepherding a floating dessert down the narrow passage between Alinea's kitchen and its first floor dining room. A few seconds later, the balloons arrive at our table, each inflated with helium and bobbing jauntily atop its fruity candy string, gripped in stainless steel tweezers. "When you're ready, kiss the balloon and inhale. We recommend trying to get it in one breath." We comply, sucking apple taffy into our mouths, chewing and swallowing before talking quietly in squeaky, helium-altered tones.

Mole of fiestas

Roasted beef tenderloin, black bean tamale, braised kale (*Chicago, IL, Cascabel, 2014*)

Patrons seated at balcony tables look down at Rick Bayless, currently chopping cilantro. The celebrity chef's program note calls this play "the story of a meal and a handful of people who pay attention, who open up to where the food can take them." The smell of mole *prepared onstage, redolent with spices and garlic, finally pays off in plates offered to the audience. In ecstatic response to a bite of this same* mole, *a pair of performers engage in an aerial pas de deux, climbing and twirling together around a pole extending vertically from a table at ground level. Meanwhile, audience members dig into their dishes, smelling and tasting chiles, nuts, seeds, herbs, and spices we've seen Bayless working with onstage.*

An introduction to culinary mimeticism

A pea popsicle. An apple balloon. A cotton candy picnic. A magical *mole*. The accounts above trace a few examples of mimetic cuisine, a diverse set of culinary practices in which chefs and artists treat food as a representational medium. In the chapters that follow, I examine moments like these in a study of culinary mimeticism in both fine dining restaurants and avant garde performance spaces, as well as environments that blur the line between the two. While the symbolic functions of food and eating in everyday life are well-established,[1] this study specifically delineates a contemporary turn toward mimetic cookery and mimetic eating, two related phenomena in which chefs and artists intentionally treat food, cooking, and eating as modes of representation. This turn toward culinary mimeticism has manifold philosophical, aesthetic, and practical implications. First, as chefs and artists explore the representational possibilities of food, they challenge longstanding assumptions that cuisine is incapable of conveying mimetic significance. Moreover, in challenging these assumptions, the turn toward culinary mimeticism also signals a shift in understandings of the relationship between the senses and intelligence in both producing knowledge and apprehending meaning. Meanwhile, the burgeoning trend of culinary mimeticism in performance contexts reframes embodied experiences of witnessing performance by focusing audience attention on the proximal senses. Furthermore, while many of the chefs and artists surveyed here work in the relatively exclusive spaces of fine dining restaurants and avant garde performance events, the examples of culinary mimeticism explored in this volume have far-reaching implications. Chefs and artists at the vanguard of culinary mimeticism use alimentary representation to address issues of sustainability, conceive and advocate for new approaches to culinary justice, and reconsider issues of gender, race, and ethnicity in culinary contexts. In light of these implications, this study attends to the immediate material and political stakes of the mimetic turn in cuisine as well as its aesthetic and theoretical impacts by engaging with the discourses, practices, and effects of culinary mimeticism.

Contrary to a limited view of mimesis as synonymous with imitation, this study hews to the more expansive use of the term established in ancient philosophical discourse and reinforced in the work of Walter Benjamin, Michael Taussig, and Elin Diamond, among other mimetic frameworks I discuss below. Following Taussig's concept of mimesis as "the nature that culture uses to create second nature, the faculty to copy, imitate, make models, explore difference, yield into and become Other" (1993, xiii), I use mimesis to denote not only cases of culinary imitation and mimicry, but also culinary representation on a grander scale, including the use of food to evoke stories, spark memories, or communicate ideas. Culinary mimesis may reflect a real time, place, or phenomenon, or it may summon new worlds and ideas to mind, spurring diners or audiences to recognize alternative realities. By this definition, mimetic cookery extends in various forms throughout culinary history, from sculptures carved from ham at Roman Saturnalia to contemporary radish roses and gummy worms. Similarly, popular theatrical dining experiences such as Medieval Times have popularized mimetic eating, casting diners as in-role participants in performance experience. However, for the purposes of this study, I focus specifically on twin developments that have advanced the contemporary theory and practice of culinary mimesis: the advent of mimetic fine dining and the increasingly sophisticated role of culinary mimesis in experimental and avant garde performance contexts.

In the past several decades, theatre artists such as *The Kitchen Show*'s Bobby Baker and *The Last Supper Project*'s Richard Gough have brought renewed critical attention to food as a theatrical medium and design element. Meanwhile, contemporary avant garde chefs like Ferran Adrià and Grant Achatz developed cooking techniques, serving apparatuses, and interaction strategies that position food as a performing object, a representational medium, and a way of thinking about the world. While the resulting cuisine has alternately been referred to as "modernist," "molecular," and "techno-emotional," these techniques and aims also rely upon and revolve around mimesis. Taken together, these experiments in food, performance, and representation have inspired both delight and controversy. Along the way they renew and reconfigure what Plato famously described in book X of the *Republic* as the ancient quarrel between theatre and philosophy (607b), interrogating the role of mimesis in human knowledge and, most critically, its ambiguous status vis-à-vis goodness.

At a time in which relationships between truth and fiction constitute a battlefield in politics, journalism, the sciences, and even education, it is perhaps unsurprising that the concept of mimetic cuisine should inspire both fascination and distrust. For instance, celebrity chef and slow food advocate Alice Waters offered the following critique of Nathan Myhrvold's landmark cookbook, *Modernist Cuisine* (2011): "I am so hungry for the taste of the real that I'm just not able to get into that which doesn't feel real to me. It's a kind of scientific experiment" (Marx 2011). Waters responds largely to the technological innovations described in Myhrvold's text, arguing that new culinary methods transform food from an authentic, satisfying experience into a cerebral, alienating experiment. Taking another approach, food writer Michael Ruhlman critiques *Modernist Cuisine* on the basis of health, asking, "Are we to embrace the ingredients and techniques of modernist cuisine at the very moment industrially processed food is being blamed for many of our national health problems?" (2011). In aligning new cooking practices with disease, Ruhlman draws a connection between avant garde culinary practice and oft-derided convenience foods, suggesting that techniques contemporary chefs use to transform ingredients may also transform food into a dangerous object. Furthermore, this notion of contemporary cuisine as dangerous often connects specifically with critiques of food as a mimetic medium. Spanish chef Santi Santamaria, who famously accused Ferran Adrià of poisoning his guests with food additives, argued that the problem with Adrià's cuisine was its overreaching effort to treat food as a representational medium: "Cooks should not be preoccupied with creating sculptures or painting pictures with their work. A table is not an art gallery" (Govan 2008). Television chef and food science evangelist Alton Brown puts a finer point on the notion of mimetic cuisine as inauthentic, explaining "I just want my food to taste, smell, and feel like food" (Forbes 2011b). For Brown, in order to satisfy, food must exist exclusive of transformation or illusion. Similarly, in an *Epicurious* essay entitled "Why I Hate Molecular Gastronomy," food writer Amy Sherman argues that avant garde cuisine degrades the value of cooking by detaching it from material purposes: "Food, like design, serves a real function. It is not art for art's sake" (2010). Uniting all of these critiques is a concern that avant garde culinary movements transform food from something authentic and good into something tricky and dangerous. Mimetic cuisine, after all, transforms the familiar into something strange, the solid reality of a fried chicken dinner evanescing into the fragility of a chicken skin cotton candy. Along the way, these critics argue, this transformation estranges us from authenticity, goodness, and perhaps our own best interests.

To those without a deep investment in culinary tradition, the criticism of mimetic cuisine collected above may feel overwrought. However, the intensity of these critiques stems from their location within a longstanding and fraught set of concerns about the relationship between mimesis, sensation, knowledge, and goodness. Philosophers from Plato onward have grappled with the problem of mimesis and its relationship to truth. After all, as Benjamin notes, by enabling us to represent one thing through the guise of another, mimesis makes both communication and miscommunication possible (1999). At the same time, food, as a substance essential to life, has often been considered only that: matter itself, its materiality overriding any possibility of other lasting significance. Hence Hegel's famous contention that we "only taste by destroying," rendering food incapable of functioning as an artistic medium (1975, 138). For Hegel, food's meaning persists only during eating, and thus while it may evoke feelings or connect us socially, it is in itself a substance incapable of conveying artistic significance. Therefore, by using food as a mimetic medium, contemporary chefs and artists cross a longstanding boundary between the perceived reality and authenticity of edible matter and the treacherous terrain of ideas. Specifically, mimetic cuisine recontextualizes the relationship between mimesis and the proximal senses, especially in terms of their ability to convey knowledge, meaning, or truth. Carolyn Korsmeyer addresses taste's exclusion from the realm of significance in *Making Sense of Taste: Food and Philosophy* (1999). Korsmeyer points to a critical conjunction of attributes that makes mimetic cuisine a thorny topic; food's ubiquity, practicality, and necessity has often contrasted or complicated its pleasures, especially pleasures that tend toward mimeticism (1999, 223). Yet through exhaustive analysis of the philosophy, science, and culture of food, Korsmeyer carves out space in which to think seriously about food and establishes the necessity of doing so by revaluing not only the proximal senses, but experiences that are fleeting, temporary, or repeated. In doing so, she provides a necessary entrée for examining the relationship between cuisine and mimesis. Building on this work, the present study sheds light on the changing significance of representation in the twenty-first century, the relationship between the sensible and the intelligible, and the experiential epistemologies upon which these developments depend.

This project focuses specifically on culinary and theatrical developments in the late twentieth and early twenty-first centuries. Given my interdisciplinary scope, I draw on multiple resources, both theoretical and experiential, including scholarship on food and the senses; dining experiences; working sessions in contemporary kitchens; experiences as both audience member and creator of alimentary performances; and primary source material from cookbooks to food blogs to trace both the development and the significance of mimetic cuisine in contemporary culture. The questions that guide this inquiry include:

> Under what conditions, and to what ends, does food serve mimetic purposes?
> How might a proximally sensed, embodied understanding of mimesis offer a new perspective on the relationship between representation, meaning, and pleasure?
> How do culinary and theatrical models of mimesis intersect, and how might they be made to intersect?

I address these questions through a series of examinations of mimetic cuisine in restaurants and performance spaces. But first, this chapter maps the philosophical and theoretical ground upon which these investigations unfold. My main contextual strands are threefold. First, I trace the development of philosophical attitudes about mimesis itself, with a special emphasis on the relationship between mimesis, theatricality, knowledge, and goodness. I set the classical philosophers' discussion of the proximal senses, taste especially, alongside debates about representation in order to reveal the ways in which contemporary chefs and theatrical artists have troubled the relationship between performance, meaning, and the senses through the development of culinary practices which challenge longstanding assumptions about the relationship between representation and truth. Second, I set the stage for an examination of culinary mimeticism by mapping boundaries chefs and artists negotiate in the process of using food as a representational medium. In this section, I address ongoing debates in culinary discourse about the nature and value of mimetic cuisine. Finally, I discuss a few influential precursors to contemporary culinary mimeticism, considering Roman mimetic dishes and Escoffier's theatrical banquets as well as theatrical uses of cuisine from ancient tragic festivals to contemporary experimental performance.

On delicious lies: mimesis, cuisine, performance, and philosophy

Mimesis not only underpins much of Western theatrical history but also comprises, to paraphrase German philosopher Walter Benjamin, the most fundamental human faculty (1999). However, much of philosophical discourse associates mimesis with the seemingly objective senses of hearing and, especially, sight, which Aristotle, Kant, and others positioned at the top of the sensory hierarchy. By associating representation and vision, philosophers from Plato onward affirmed the notion that seeing is believing, for good and for ill. Tasting and smelling, on the contrary, have largely remained outside the scope of mimetic discourse. Indeed, philosophers often specifically exclude the sense of taste from the domain of mimesis, and even contemporary culinary philosophers like Elizabeth Telfer question the capacity for taste to convey representational meaning. Yet, from Grant Achatz's representational dishes at Alinea to Rick Bayless's culinary theatre in *Cascabel*, chefs and artists continue to pursue mimetic uses of food. Thus, the imbrication of food and representation in recent decades deserves attention due to its reconfiguration of the relationship between the senses and meaning.

Discourse about mimesis from the eighteenth century onward, driven in part by reductive understandings of Platonic views of mimesis, often treats the concept as synonymous with imitation of nature in the simplest possible sense.[2] Yet as Benjamin, Derrida, and Taussig, among others, have demonstrated, the human mimetic faculty is both more complex and more fundamental than imitation alone.[3] Indeed, the preoccupying presence of mimesis in philosophy indicates its vital role in understanding human experience. While we have tended in modern discourse to associate mimesis with insubstantiality and inauthenticity, even Plato does not dismiss mimesis as wholly worthless or dangerous. In fact, Plato's body of work, especially *Gorgias*, *Phaedo*, the *Symposium*, and the *Republic*, reveals a fascination with mimesis that reflects both its complexity and its centrality in human life. Thus, for the purposes of this book, I employ a definition of mimesis not simply as imitation, but as a diverse set of phenomena involving representation through the evocation of resemblances that have the effect of creating or evoking meaning. Mimetic representation may operate in modes that depend primarily on one or more human senses, may rely completely on nonsensuous means, or may rely on both sensible and intelligible evocation of resemblances. Furthermore, the human mimetic faculty includes not only the evocation of resemblances, but also their recognition. Following classicist Stephen Halliwell's point that "to think about mimesis...is to come up against hard, foundational, and permanently worthwhile questions about artistic meaning, and, ultimately perhaps, about the status of meaning tout court" (2002, 371), this book takes as its starting point the notion that mimesis is fundamentally concerned with the nature of meaning. In their mimetic work, the chefs, scholars, and artists I discuss in this volume explore the meanings of food and eating. They intensify this examination precisely by playing with representation in a sensory field we may previously have considered off limits to such engagement. In order to support a rich working understanding of mimesis, I trace a few of the main historical lines of argument about the relationship between mimesis and culture and connect these ways of understanding the mimetic with philosophical approaches to the senses, especially the sense of taste. Given the extensive body of discourse on mimesis, I focus primarily on mimetic theory that relates to cuisine and theatricality. I begin with discussion of Plato's treatment of food and cooking as it relates to both his distrust of representation and his hierarchy of the senses.

Plato takes up cooking in the *Gorgias*, a dialogue devoted to the nature of rhetoric, specifically because of cooking's association with appearances and its ability to manipulate them. Plato specifically excludes cookery from the arts, referring to it as a practice or routine (462e).[4] But the rationale for this exclusion, which includes a critique of food's mimetic capacity, is of particular interest. Specifically, Plato laments cooking's ability to create an appearance of well-being through the creation of pleasure that may confuse us into thinking of cooking as a kind of medicine (465b). Like a medicine, Plato argues that food enters a body in a state of need and creates a sensation of wholeness or improvement. But this sensation is not to be trusted: the pleasures of the table may lessen our well-being even as salutary medical procedures may produce revulsion. Plato's mistrust of the senses, especially the proximal senses of taste, smell, and touch, doubles his mistrust of representation. Good cooking may trick the body and thus the mind, pleasure itself becoming a dangerous form of imitation. While cooking remains absent from most of Plato's formal discussion of mimesis in the *Republic*, this discussion of the relationship between cooking, pleasure, goodness, and representation clearly connects the two and sets the stage for critiques of mimetic cuisine.

Plato's distrust of culinary pleasure stems in part from the connection between the proximal senses and the body. Socrates argues in *Phaedo* that, if pure reason is to be attained, it is through means outside the senses (64d). The senses engage us in embodied experience, focusing our consciousness on the body and, through experiences of physical pleasure, reinforcing our fear of death and distracting us from reason. This mistrust of the body deeply intertwines with the tendency in classical philosophy to assign rationality to masculinity. Furthermore, the classical association between masculinity, rationality, and objectivity intensifies when viewed alongside the sensory hierarchy that values vision as objective and suspects taste and touch as subjective, compromising, and feminine. As Korsmeyer demonstrates in her review of classical attitudes about the senses, this gendered connection between the proximal senses and embodiment leads both to a comparative lack of attention to taste as well as a presupposition of an opposition between the proximal senses and knowledge (1999, 30–37). The resulting distrust of taste, combined with the possibility of mimesis to create asymmetry between appearance and reality, places culinary mimeticism in particular under heightened suspicion.

However, Plato's concerns about mimesis do not extend equally to all aspects of the term. In the *Republic* Book II, the word *mimetai*, representers or imitators, stands in for artists (373b). In Book III, Socrates sets out to determine whether artists should imitate anything at all (394d), making clear that the task concerns the arts in all their forms specifically because all artists (*mimetai*) traffic in representation. Plato's subsequent differentiation between theatre and other art forms hinges on the senses in that performance involves a more expansive mimesis that convinces through multiple senses at once. In this passage, Plato treats mimesis like a *pharmakon* with the capacity to help or to harm depending on the circumstance and intensity of one's exposure. Specifically, the danger of representation depends not only on the intensity of one's exposure, but also upon the medium through which mimesis occurs. Plato highlights theatre for special critique since it makes human bodies a mimetic medium and thus engages the senses differently than other mimetic art forms. For Plato, theatre simply represents most convincingly; audiences experience a mimeticism that corresponds so well to everyday life that they cannot help but be partly convinced of the truth of the representation.

Given that Plato's concern with mimesis hinges on the senses, the notion of mimetic cuisine, which includes taste, smell, and touch as domains of mimetic play, further complicates the already dangerous terrain of theatrical mimesis. Yet Plato's rejection of theatre in the *Republic* deserves qualification in two ways. First, Plato carefully signals the conditional nature of this rejection, offering room for a defense of poets and of imitation generally. Aristotle, among others, takes up this challenge. This conditionality positions Plato's discussion of mimesis as uniquely vexed, perhaps because Plato is convinced of the significance of the mimetic faculty. Second, Plato pursues his analysis in a representational mode of writing, highlighting his ambivalence about the relationship between representation and truth. Thus Plato positions mimesis as among the most significant human activities, albeit one he distrusts.

In defending mimesis in the *Poetics*, Aristotle opens up a line of thinking critical to understanding mimetic cuisine. For Aristotle, mimesis fundamentally explores what it means to be human. This position is less a rejection of Plato's critique of mimesis than a response to his call for a cogent defense of representation. By focusing on the instrumentality of mimesis, Aristotle thinks differently about its function in culture. Aristotle convincingly argues that mimesis acts upon the rational mind, the emotions, and the body, potentially creating positive physical and mental effects. This approach challenges the notion of insubstantiality leveled both at mimeticism generally and specifically at mimetic cuisine. Still, Aristotle privileges some senses over others as more valid vehicles for representational effects in his famous hierarchy of theatrical elements. In the well-known Aristotelian hierarchy, visual information, specifically that drawn from the dominant visual icon of the playtext, predominates over "gut reactions" stimulated by music or special effects. Here the presumptive equivalence between sight, masculinity, and objectivity again holds sway, positioning visual information as a more appropriate means of conveying representational meaning.

Plato's tempered skepticism about mimesis, performance, and the proximal senses has resonances in more contemporary theatrical theory as well. Twentieth-century artist, activist, and theatre theorist Augusto Boal, who examines mimesis in detail, includes a dig at cookery in his famous critique of Aristotle, arguing that traditional theatre-makers are "no more than cooks of theatrical menus. They study the typical reactions of certain chosen audiences and from there extract conclusions and rules regarding how the perfect work should be written" (1985, 27). This critique of a rote, manipulative, unoriginal theatre recalls Brecht's "culinary theatre," which overstuffs audiences to the point of drowsy and uncritical satiety, numbing them to the possibility of resistance or radical knowledge (1964). Each of these critiques, which connect eating to artifice that leads audiences astray, evokes Plato's original distinction between chef and physician. One induces a manipulative, irrational pleasure while the other improves the body in ways that do not necessarily produce immediate sensory gratification. Reinforcing this longstanding mistrust of bodily pleasure, all three evince deep distrust of mimetic satiety combined with keen awareness of the appeal of sensuous imitation.

While neither Boal nor Brecht dwell on the concept of artist-as-cook, their disdainful remarks on culinary theatre illustrate a pervasive sense of both mimesis and sensory pleasure as central to the operation of oppressive power. They also highlight a distinction, again evocative of Plato, between the domestic cook, who follows a formula, and the professional artist, who innovates. For Boal, to exercise theatrical power with radical impact, an artist must be more than a cook following a recipe. Like Aristotle, Boal relies upon the gendered and classed distinction that continues to separate cook and chef, craftsperson and artist, along the lines of creative productivity. A cook, the term often reserved for women doing unpaid or low-status labor, reproduces recipes. An artist, often a man working in a professional capacity, makes something new. The tendency to distinguish the female cook from the male chef along lines of creativity will haunt much of this text. Moreover, this distinction has ethical implications. Boal exhibits a strong preference for the generative aspect of mimesis, in which the artist creates a representation that exceeds reality, rather than the world-reflecting mimetic view that founds Aristotle's discourse of believability in the *Poetics*.[5] Simply reproducing the world as it is means not only making bad art, but eschewing an ethical responsibility. For Boal, "Theatre is change and not simple presentation of what exists: it is becoming and not being" (1985, 28). In other words, the artist must pay careful attention to the process of mimetically creating a new world that both reflects and transforms the real world in which she finds herself, resisting the alluring sensory pleasures of mimetically reproducing the real world.

What might Plato, Brecht, or Boal make, then, of mimetic cuisine, which also uses the materials of everyday life, and with which human beings interact not only through sight and sound, but through often pleasurable incorporation in the form of smell, taste, touch, and digestion? The critical importance of mimesis outlined above helps explain why contemporary chefs engaged in establishing cooking as an artistic practice have consistently turned to mimetic tactics. Furthermore, the sense of mimesis as manipulation proves foundational to critiques of contemporary mimetic cuisine in two ways. First, the creation of representations often requires manipulation of matter. This concept appears in Aristotle, in which art comprises the manipulation of matter in formal systems that give it structure and allow us to recognize it as something beyond the real or everyday. To be sure, most cooking involves manipulation. Unmanipulated foodstuffs remain raw; chefs on competitive cooking programs like *Chopped* perform "transformations" of ingredients in order to impress judges. But mimetic cuisine goes further, manipulating food in order to evoke other objects, ideas, or emotions. For example, San Francisco chef Dominque Crenn's famous "Walk in the Forest" dish combines many textures of mushrooms with fresh herbs, pine meringue, and basil and pumpernickel soils to evoke not just a literal walk in the forest but transformation, decay, birth, and even fairy tales that take place in forest spaces (Crenn 2015, 79). Second, mimesis, via Boal's construction, becomes a means of manipulation of human beings through the use of structures designed to invite mimetic recognition, and thus acceptance of the representational offer. This recognition is distinct from an acceptance of the representation as real. Instead, as Aristotle argues, we see the representation as likely or comprehensible. This distinction between belief and recognition highlights an intrinsic quality of mimesis that comes to the fore in culinary mimeticism. In many cases, mimesis does not actually deceive. Rather, it delights or confounds us precisely because the representation is incomplete, enabling us to discern the mimetic gesture within the context of an artist's creation. Culinary mimesis, as a multisensory phenomenon that involves examination at close range and in detail rather than willing suspension of disbelief at a distance as in, for instance, realist proscenium theatre, relies upon this incompleteness to engage the eater in active meaning-making. For instance, Grant Achatz's "dry shots" use powdered and dried ingredients to replicate the flavors, but not the textures or visual attributes, of classic food and drink, from piña coladas to pizzas. In these simple courses, the server initiates a mimetic offer in telling the diner the title of the dish, such as "Piña Colada." Even before sliding the powdered ingredients into her mouth, the diner has already begun the process of recognition. In the act of tasting, she extends this mimetic process to the palate, as the ingredients reconstitute, dissolve, and combine to make the powder's reference to the iconic drink legible, but with a difference.

Chefs engaged in culinary mimesis often purposefully intensify this tension between mimetic and non-mimetic aspects of their dishes, as in José Andrés's dish of "real" and "Adrià" olives which places olives alongside Adrià's mimetic spherified olive juice. Here and in the examples I engage in throughout this volume, mimetic resemblances remain essentially and intentionally incomplete, deferred, or interrupted. The relationship between these deferred or incomplete resonances and their referents helps create the rich, and sometimes seemingly dangerous, possibilities of meaning that occur in mimetic cuisine. This new mimetic context invites the diner to experience meaningful pleasure, uniting two aspects of human experience often considered separate. For instance, Square Root's fried chicken cotton candy reproduces the flavors of a picnic in a surprising combination of texture, temperature, and context, inviting contemplation, often in conversation with other diners, about the significance of the original dish in comparison with its mimetic double. Thus culinary mimeticism includes the creation not only of resemblances, but also of critical opportunities to recognize, evaluate, and assess the relationship between representation and reality.

Through this point in the text, I have accepted that cuisine can operate mimetically. However, this notion has inspired a great deal of philosophical debate, a subject to which I return in the next chapter's discussion of Ferran Adrià's philosophy of representation in cuisine. In discussion of the question of the artfulness of cookery, the question of representation becomes a central issue to the notion of cuisine as artistic practice. As Hegel and others have asserted, the materiality of cuisine and the temporally specific features of cooking and eating call into question their ability to do representative work (or play), and thus to constitute art. Since food neither lasts nor can be experienced without being partially consumed, Hegel suggests representation through food does not afford the time and space for contemplation necessary for a representation to be recognized by an audience. Responding to this notion in *Food for Thought: Philosophy and Food* (1996), philosopher Elizabeth Telfer discusses the issue of pleasure in relation to cooking and eating, arguing that ultimately food cannot produce the ongoing pleasure associated with works of literature:

> If I learn a piece of music, see a play, or read a novel, these experiences live in my mind and produce other pleasures – I remember the works and contemplate them again; I see the world in a different way because of them. None of this seems possible with the pleasures of eating and drinking…I can recall flavours and textures, but I cannot contemplate them later or gain a new idea of the world in terms of them.
>
> *(1996, 28)*

While Telfer affords food the possibility of artistic status (albeit a minor art), she argues that the pleasures of food lack the staying power and complexity of the other arts; they do not allow us to imagine the world through them (1996, 59). Telfer's point rests on the mimetic quality considered in the ancient world common to the arts of painting, theatre, music, and literature. For Plato, artists create representations of the world, either the "real" world around us or an imagined world with bearing on our own, and thus open up contemplation about the nature of existence.[6] Telfer thus rejects food as a fully artistic medium based on perceived limitations in its capacity for mimetic action, which tie directly to its materiality and, following Hegel, its destruction during the act of eating.[7] Still, much of contemporary cuisine uses food as a means of representing ideas, stories, emotions, or times and places real or imaginary. In their attempts to elevate cuisine to the artistic status it has often sought and often been denied, contemporary chefs rely on mimesis precisely because representation rests at the core of the relationship between art, life, and meaning.

Walter Benjamin's short essay "On the Mimetic Faculty" (1933) demonstrates that food's instrumentality to life neither conflicts with its mimetic properties nor disqualifies it from other uses. Benjamin makes the useful distinction of dividing mimesis into two related actions: representation (mimetic production) and recognition. Benjamin notes that these two actions play a critical role in nearly all human behavior. Furthermore, Benjamin helpfully teases out the possibility of "nonsensuous similarity" in his example of language's mimetic attributes. One need only think of the imaginary number i to understand how a construct can at the same time exist as an imaginary representation and also a materially relevant and essential feature of the world. Again, Benjamin productively differentiates one attribute of mimesis from another, delineating the possibility of both sensible and intelligible aspects of mimetic recognition. Notably, Benjamin does not observe a hierarchical distinction between these two aspects of mimesis, but rather mourns the loss of complexity of human mimetic engagement (a loss that is both historical and developmental, degrading mimetic action over time but also devaluing the mimetic faculty from childhood into adulthood). Where ancient philosophers most mistrusted mimesis that directly depends on the senses, Benjamin opens the possibility of seeing both the sensed and the imagined qualities of a mimetic experience as fundamental to its existence. The idea that mimesis involves both creation of and recognition of similarity, but that neither necessitates the other, allows Benjamin to include nonsensuous similarity in his mimetic structure, returning to the more complex and capacious version of mimesis presumed by Plato. Taken together, these nuanced views of mimesis illuminate the multiple avenues for cuisine to function mimetically. The act of intended signification on the part of chefs and servers comprises part of a mimetic process, a mimetic offer. But the recognition of similarity that Benjamin identifies as a critical feature of the mimetic faculty in and of itself constitutes mimetic play. Experiencing significance, even without a preceding human intention, itself becomes an exercise of the human mimetic faculty.

With this definition in mind, this book explores the conjunction of explicitly mimetic approaches to cooking with practices of eating that are purposefully attentive to mimesis, treating the two as related phenomena. The mimetic faculty functions in multiple ways in both cuisine and performance. For instance, a dish may evoke an emotion, an association, or a memory by relying on the diner's mimetic faculty of recognition. This recognition then becomes an essential component in the dish. For instance, Achatz uses dishes at his second Chicago restaurant, Next, to evoke emotions, ideas, places, and memories via his semi-scripted interactions between diners, servers, service pieces, and food itself. Next's 2011 "Childhood" menu evoked multiple versions of childhood through a variety of mimetic techniques working together. The menu referenced a contemporary fast-food restaurant with a take on McDonald's Big Mac. It summoned up a seasonal experience in a course entitled "Autumn" in which diners consume the components of a tableside campfire. It represented childhood memory in a "Foie-sting" course presenting foie gras as cake frosting to be licked from a metal beater. Finally, it elicited nostalgia with a dessert course served in a 1980s-era lunchbox. In this menu, mimesis becomes the source of pleasure and knowledge through a combination of recognition, memory, and nostalgia. Through coordinated mimetic manipulation of service, serving-ware, flavors, plating, and the actions of eating, Achatz and executive chef Dave Beran created an experience of eating that invited an extended meditation on childhood. In another mimetic variation, Adrià's aforementioned spherical olives rely on mimesis as a source of pleasure through a purposefully incomplete mimetic process. In each sensory element but one, the olives resemble their traditional counterpart. They taste like olives, look like olives, and are made from olives. However, the texture of the dish surprises through its contradiction of expectations created by the mimetic work of the chef. Furthermore, in both of these cases diners willingly and purposefully experience these dishes with an attentiveness to mimetic recognition.

Chefs themselves have led the way in theorizing the relationship between representation and recognition in cuisine. New York celebrity chef David Chang introduces a theory of reconfiguration and recognition as critical to culinary pleasure in his 2016 *Wired* cover story, "The Unified Theory of Deliciousness." Chang identifies culinary "strange loops," a concept in which a set of flavors and textures recalls something familiar but in a new context, as the foundation of his theory (2016). In doing so he advances a dramaturgical explanation of deliciousness which will prove critical to this book's understanding of culinary mimeticism. Chang argues that true culinary delight hinges on the mimetic action of the chef (manipulating materials to evoke an old concept) and the mimetic recognition of the diner (surprise and recognition mixed together in the act of eating something familiar and strange). The mimetic quality of both acts of dining and the foodstuffs themselves endows them with significance, enables them to evoke memory, and positions them as capable of stimulating new debates about art, meaning, and food. I turn to some of these debates in the next section.

The problem of foam: substance, representation, and culinary meaning

In her 2010 critique of avant garde British chef Heston Blumenthal's "Sound of the Sea" dish, British food writer Rose Prince uses a rhetorical strategy common to skeptics of contemporary mimetic cuisine, critiquing it for both fussiness and a lack of substance. Specifically, Prince calls Blumenthal's dish theatrical. This telling comparison to the theatre rehearses a pseudo-Platonist view of culinary value in which the critic accepts prima facie the idea that cuisine is art but rejects mimetic cuisine as valuable art by establishing its main artistic action as theatrical imitation. As in Plato, theatrical imitation becomes a particularly dangerous species of mimesis, one with special potential to degrade the relationship between experience and knowledge. Since Prince's review constitutes an essential critique of mimetic cuisine, I discuss at length her account of a dinner at The Fat Duck, written in the context of her review of Myrhvold's *Modernist Cuisine*. Prince opens with an expression of delight in a dish of impeccably prepared salmon before her pleasure comes skidding to a halt at the arrival of Blumenthal's famous multisensory mimetic dish, "Sound of the Sea." The dish, a combination of breadcrumb, eel, and seaweed-based edible sand with fresh seafood, lily bulb seashells, and seafood broth foam arranged to visually evoke the sea and served with headphones that allow the diner to listen to ocean sounds, offers the diner a playfully immersive experience of the ocean. For Prince, however, the dish jarred on the nerves. Commenting that the presentation reminded her of cleaning up dog vomit, Prince explains her spirits sank as soon as she spied Blumenthal's culinary seafoam (2010). Calling out both Blumenthal and Adrià for intellectualizing and theatricalizing their work, Prince insists that dishes like these, and techniques extolled by Myhrvold in *Modernist Cuisine*, constitute not pleasurable dining, but "culinary opera" that cannot be taken seriously, no matter how seriously it might take itself. Despite laudatory announcements to the contrary from restaurant critics, Prince confides in her readers that she fervently hopes Adrià and Blumenthal will not truly transform the way we eat and that her local pub will "continue to grill steaks, not transmute them into foaming jelly balls – and my Saturday breakfast will be what it always was" (2010). The review ends with a defiant reassertion of the diner's personal prerogative to enjoy her dinner without the show: "When I want a ticket to laugh, I'll book" (2010).

Prince's critique hinges on boundaries inappropriately crossed, associating Blumenthal's dish, and specifically his use of foam, with a simultaneously over-intellectualized and theatricalized turn in cuisine that inappropriately mixes otherwise worthy but discrete arenas of pleasure: eating, mimesis, and the theatre. The logic of this critique merits careful examination. Prince appreciates the craft of cookery (the perfectly cooked salmon), but rejects the notion of foam as a culinary device, not based on any inartfulness on the part of the chef but rather on the inappropriate or unsatisfying nature of this artful transformation in the context of dining. As performance studies scholar Barbara Kirshenblatt-Gimblett points out, the historical establishment of theatre as an "autonomous art" depended on disentangling food and theatre in a larger project of "cultural work to isolate the senses, create genres of art specific to each, insist on their own autonomy, and cultivate modes of attentiveness that give some senses priority over others" (2007, 71). These careful sensory isolations constitute a firm boundary that Prince sees as inappropriately violated in a way which increases both the dish's mimetic engagement and its potential to disgust diners and defile worthwhile traditions. According to Prince's critique, the chef crosses multiple lines in combining food and non-food, theatre and dining, tradition and innovation, solid and diaphanous, creating an abject rupture of boundaries. These boundary crossings ultimately break the spell of Prince's dinner, stranding her in a border zone between the enjoyment of dining and the enjoyment of theatre as the fun ceases and she withdraws from enthusiastic participation in Blumenthal's interactive meal. Significantly, Prince not only rejects the choice to transform food (liquid into foam, steak into foaming jelly balls) but also the notion of extending mimesis into arenas beyond the theatrical. In doing so, Prince positions Blumenthal and his fellow avant garde chef and collaborator Ferran Adrià as mimetic colonizers of the culinary landscape, aiming to transform the way we eat not only in avant garde restaurants but also at our quotidian breakfasts. Casting doubt on the necessity of such a transformation, she expresses hope that her own dining table will remain unsullied with such pretensions. For Prince, food should remain food while theatre remains theatre. Thus, as a multisensory experience that is at once felt, thought, and sensed in contravention of the hierarchies Kirshenblatt-Gimblett describes, mimetic cuisine trespasses this boundary, necessitating the boundary's reassertion.

In particular, the transformative or imaginative aspect of mimesis, in which representation creates new ideas from old materials, causes a problem here. Blumenthal has attempted a mimetic gesture in which a foodstuff, transformed into foam and added to a plate of seafood, represents an environmental element: seafoam. Prince's concern has partly to do with authenticity; the matter on her plate has, through a mimetic process, transformed into something that is not as it seems. This likeness within unlikeness creates revulsion in an instance of representation come unhinged. What was meant to evoke seafoam instead reads as vomit, rendering the dish and Prince's interaction with it a representational failure. The memory of dog vomit and the desire for a mop overlay, and overshadow, the intended reference.

While her point about the danger of mixing mimesis and the menu is clear, Prince's telling reference to the theatre and specifically culinary opera bears further analysis. It isn't opera Prince is rejecting. Indeed, if she wants to laugh, she's willing to book a ticket. Instead, Prince rejects *culinary* opera. She does not so much devalue the human mimetic faculty as she finds it misplaced in the context of the senses of taste and smell and the act of dining. Her choice of opera as an alternative artistic arena demonstrates the sophistication of her critique, grounding it in a theory of the proper interaction of the senses, knowledge, and representation. Opera serves as an appropriate foil for culinary mimesis precisely because its carefully crafted visual and auditory sensation (linked directly to textual interpretation) and its typical omission of audience/actor interaction keep mimetic representation at a comfortable distance, rather than proximally sensed. By contrast, mimetic cuisine blurs the lines between the phases of mimetic action or the operations of the mimetic faculty on the part of producers (chefs) and consumers (diners), particularly in its use of the proximal senses of taste, touch, and smell. This shift in mimetic action from one sensory paradigm to another (through the increasing inclusion of the proximal senses in mimetic activity) provokes strong reactions precisely because it destabilizes expectations about the relationship between bodies, art, representations, and knowledge.

By crossing boundaries between the sensory and spatial domains in which we expect mimetic action to occur and those in which we might not, theatrical cuisine shocks, delights, and at times disgusts, as in the case of Prince's experience with Blumenthal's foam. Blumenthal, as discussed in greater detail in Chapter 2, stands at the vanguard of mimetic cuisine alongside his collaborator and co-author Ferran Adrià as well as a host of chefs and food scientists around the world who trouble boundaries between art and craft in the advancement of culinary mimesis. As demonstrated by Prince's critique, this boundary crossing has led to vigorous debate about the nature of these innovations. Accordingly, I survey two main strands of gastronomic theory: arts-based approaches to understanding "modernist" cuisine and science-based celebrations and critiques of "molecular" cookery. In the next section I consider these approaches' attitudes toward mimetic cuisine's boundary-crossing properties, but also the ways in which each responds to or depends upon mimesis.

Plate, canvas, stage: locating cuisine as art

The connection Prince identifies between mimetic cuisine and theatricality extends across the work of the chefs discussed here. Contemporary chefs, as well as their reviewers, frequently refer to their work as theatrical. For example, Blumenthal's Fat Duck menu announces his intent to bring "a sense of theatre to the dining experience." Inspired by Blumenthal, small appliance manufacturer Russell Hobbs launched a line of kitchen equipment in May 2011 designed to capitalize on the trend of "kitchen theatre," with the tagline "your kitchen is the stage, and diners the audience" (Which News 2011). Similarly, Chicago chef Grant Achatz describes the table as "a stage where a performance will be carried out" (2008, 44). Taking seriously Prince's idea of culinary mimesis as connected with theatricality provides a helpful framework for food scholars as well as for theatre scholars interested in the complex ways in which theatricality influences contemporary culture. Mimetic cuisine connects directly with theatricality, shifting our focus to the entire event of dining, profitably expanding analysis of cuisine beyond the bounds of the plate. Moreover, analysis of contemporary theatrical cuisine requires a deep engagement with mimesis in order to understand not only individual moments of dialogue, but an entire system of representational play operating in mimetic cuisine as a whole. Chefs like Ferran Adrià, who prefers to refer to his work not as molecular gastronomy but as "techno-emotional cuisine," and Achatz, who arranges his menus at Alinea so that each dish becomes part of an overall emotional arc of the evening's experience, intentionally and explicitly infuse dialogue, conflict, and emotional resonances into the temporally bounded, ephemeral, lived experience of an evening meal.

Despite leading chefs' use of theatrical models for theorizing their work, analytical models that focus largely on the aesthetics of individual plates of food have dominated scholarly explorations of the significance of recent developments in avant garde cookery. Notwithstanding its popularity as a framing device, the plate as boundary of cuisine is itself a relatively recent construct. When Henri Gault, leading proponent of French Nouvelle Cuisine, published his ten-point manifesto rejecting the tradition of Escoffier and Michelin in 1973, he and fellow culinary mavericks like Paul Bocuse upended the Western tradition of elaborate culinary displays and tableside plating, recasting the chef as an artist and the plate as canvas in the model of the Japanese kaiseki tradition to which they responded (McCarron 2017). In insisting on plating foods in the kitchen rather than servers placing food on an empty plate at the table, the Nouvelle Cuisine made the plate the site of the chef's self-assertion as an artist rather than a craftsperson. This idea' of chef-as-artist and plate-as-canvas may explain why the mimetic and theatrical turn in cooking has emerged somewhat more recently than other approaches, in that dishes are often treated as discrete entities, as paintings or poems rather than events.[8] Contemporary thinkers have experimented with evolving plate-based lenses for interpreting avant garde cuisine. For example, Nir Dudek, former line cook, offers a variation on the discrete artwork theory of individual plates in his assertion that "eating is reading" (2008, 54), wherein individual plates and even menus function similarly to poetry, distilling ideas, flavors, experiences, histories, and ingredients into an object for contemplation. This approach attempts to account for culinary representation within individual dishes, yet the complexly mimetic approaches that turn entire menus into representational gestures and performance events in and of themselves necessitate a wider lens.

Heralding the shift from the concept of plate as canvas to a new and more complexly mimetic vocabulary of acts of dining, Cecilia Novero's *Antidiets of the Avant-garde* (2010) traces the connections between modernist movements and cuisine, discussing 1960s Eat Art, the Futurist Cookbook, and Dadaist anti-diets and highlighting connections between the historical and contemporary culinary avant gardes. Novero identifies what she calls "active mimesis" as a trend in avant garde food art (2010, xxii). Focusing on instances of fine artists working with food rather than on restaurants' contexts, Novero frames theatrical uses of food as fundamentally different than dining. For instance, Novero notes that the Italian Futurists' food interventions "were nutritionally impractical, even when supposedly scientifically grounded. It was evident that the diets and the banquets were conceived literally and were theatrically staged, as many reviewers remarked" (2010, 12). Novero's evocation of the theatrical as a point of differentiation from cuisine itself signals the essential role of theatricality in more contemporary culinary experiments. While located firmly within cuisine rather than in the fine arts, edible balloons, oceanic foams, and other mimetic techniques have very little to do with efficacy in terms of nourishment, and much more to do with a theatrical appreciation of the sensory possibilities, surprises, and emotional or intellectual resonances of dining. For instance, Adrià's synthetic olives, composed of chemically spherified olive juice, hinge neither on nutrition nor efficiency. Instead, feeling the pop of the olive-shaped orb in one's mouth, followed by a rush of olive flavored liquid coating the palate, constitutes a theatrical experience driven by mimetic play.

Adrià's olives stand in as one example of the way that the contemporary chefs I discuss, from Grant Achatz to Heston Blumenthal, continually grapple with the fact that, whether or not plating is painting, sculpting, or architecture, dining is acting. To eat is to take action, to consume a product that does not persist in material space after the meal ends, but rather transforms, undergoing incomplete and tenuous incorporation into the diner's body and memory. Dining is a temporally bounded and ephemeral process that leaves few material traces behind. Thus, understanding mimetic cuisine requires different theoretical tools than those we might bring to static forms. Benjamin's theory of incorporation, a lynchpin of Novero's analysis of the avant garde's culinary experiments, provides a useful model for understanding the role of both mimetic production and recognition in the acts of cooking and dining. In describing incorporation, Benjamin explores eating as a potential moment of transformation and reconfiguration of our relationship to a substance during both its preparation and consumption. Incorporative eating, distinguished from an unthinking or mundane consumption of food for sustenance only, is neither a rational process operated by a dispassionate intelligence nor an aesthetic process dictated by culturally specific standards of taste. Contra the notion of eating as reading a plate, Benjamin's notion of incorporation productively expands the concept of eating to include the interaction between its many component processes (e.g. cooking, serving, mastication, digestion, remembering having eaten). This incorporative model of eating does not, for Benjamin, encompass all eating; it is, rather, an alternative or antithesis to mindless or productivity-driven eating-as-assimilation.

Though the notion of attentive eating recurs frequently in theoretical discourses of cuisine, Benjamin's incorporation differs in critical ways from other models of alimentary perception. Elizabeth Telfer draws a distinction between mindless eating and aesthetic eating in *Food for Thought*, describing aesthetic eating as "eating with attention and discernment food which repays attention and discernment" (1996, 57). Extending this notion of attentiveness, Nicola Perullo's *Taste as Experience* (2016) marries biological, cultural, and philosophical studies of taste to promote a view of culinary experience as "embodied knowledge" in which aesthetic experiences of eating become central to the development of wisdom as well as pleasure. Arguing for an aesthetic paradigm of time-limited, proximal, physically engaging alimentary experiences as an overlooked companion to durational, distanced, objective experiences of visual art, Perullo rejects "taste exclusivism" that posits the sense of taste itself as the primary locus of food's meaning. Instead, Perullo offers an alternative vision in which the eater may actively choose to focus attention either on food itself or on its social and commensal context in making meaning. Still Perullo holds with Telfer that food's temporality and ephemerality forecloses the possibility of losing oneself in contemplation, coming unmoored in time as one might in the experience of a novel or painting (2016, 114). Benjamin's theory of incorporation differs substantially from both Telfer and Perullo's visions of aesthetic eating in that it is neither purely rational nor entirely voluntary. For Benjamin, one can indeed lose oneself in an operation of eating that collapses and expands time and memory through an attention to the senses that is akin to intoxication. As Novero describes the process in her thorough discussion of Benjamin's food writing, it is "a dialectical operation leading to a sensory epistemology, grounded in a heightened primeval (early) perception as opposed to both instrumental reason and abstract aesthetic taste" (2010, 92). Specifically, Novero describes incorporation as "an active process of consumption that opens the relation of subject and object to a threshold beyond pure seduction or pure contamination and that rethinks the liminal space between myth and reason, sleep and the waking state. On the thresholds of these dangerous encounters different infra-states of consciousness (and humanity) are enabled to emerge" (2010, 111). In his discussion of the complex sensory epistemologies at play in the act of eating, Benjamin supports a more complex dramaturgical understanding of theatrical dining and dining in theatrical settings by attending not only to the sense of taste, but the interactions between taste, the body, memory, and knowledge at play in processes of cooking and eating. By viewing the actions of cooking, eating, and serving food through this more complex lens, we can simultaneously account not only for food as nourishment, but also for eating as mimetic experience. Not only might we see the plate as a canvas, but also the table as stage, with eating as performance, and dining as acting. This dramaturgical approach to understanding mimetic cuisine, foregrounded in the work of chefs like Blumenthal and Achatz, has emerged alongside and in competition with the scientifically inflected concept of "molecular" cooking, which also inspires its own anti-mimetic backlash.

On food and not-food: Platonic critiques of mimetic alimentary technology

Since Hervé This and Nicholas Kurti coined the term "molecular gastronomy" as a framework for a food science conference in 1988, food scholars have explored its implications, asking what effect the perceived movement of science into food preparation has had on cooking and, in particular, on dining. With chefs using chemicals like calcium carbonate to create seemingly magical spherified liquids and *Top Chef* contestants regularly reaching for liquid nitrogen, it is tempting to see the avant garde cuisine movement springing from an infusion of science and technology into the kitchen. Certainly, food science has enabled the contemporary turn toward culinary mimeticism, but critics often situate science as a new methodology for cooking, with chefs working via a modified scientific method. This supposedly scientific shift leaves diners like Prince complaining of "foam for the sake of foam" in a mode that evokes Shelley's *Frankenstein*, turning a skeptical eye toward innovation for its own sake. Just because we *can* make foam, critics ask, *should* we? In 2011, Alton Brown became a standard-bearer for the now-infamous backlash against "molecular" technique, arguing in his personal blog that such approaches were "not food" and castigating would-be experimenters that culinary foam functions mainly to conceal bad cooking (Forbes 2011a). In his anti-molecular polemic Brown, a well-known proponent for food science, critiques foams and spherification techniques not based on their use of technology per se, but rather the way in which that technology works to mask a lack of culinary skill. The line crossed here is not between science and cuisine. Rather, it's a boundary between food and not-food, violated in the service of representation. Much as Frankenstein crossed a line in bringing life to dead flesh, Brown accuses contemporary chefs of trespassing a moral and professional boundary, blurring the distinction between food and not-food, and, additionally, between good and bad cooking. In this critique, transformation itself is at issue. Furthermore, the transformation in question deceives in a fashion that recalls the philosophical concern that audiences will be led astray by mimesis. As Brown explains: "You can't live on it. It's not food" (Forbes 2011a). Inverting Plato's concern about a well-cooked meal that fools the body into a sense of well-being while simultaneously damaging its health, Brown worries that by transforming ingredients chefs fool diners into mistaking bad cookery for good, and furthermore, into mistaking aesthetic experience for nourishment.

The Platonic tone of Brown's objection, much like Prince's, connects philosophically with the trend toward distrust of processing in general in our food supply, championed by activist Michael Pollan, chef Alice Waters, and other leaders of the slow food, whole food, and locavore movements. A kind of anti-mimetic culinary movement, Pollan's *Food Rules* (2009), which according to his book's promotional materials sprang from his "hunch that the wisdom of our grandparents might have more helpful things to say about how to eat well than the recommendations of science or industry or government" again evokes the Nouvelle Cuisine, in that it too is a manifesto-driven movement to connect the diner with the source of food (Pollan 2011). Arguments about food and health found in books like Pollan's tend to pit complex culinary processing against simple cooking, creating what food scholar Rachel Laudan famously called "culinary luddites" (2001, 36). This all-or-nothing, food-or-not-food approach obscures the ways in which food indeed serves as a nexus for science, art, and everyday life. As the chefs discussed in this study have discovered, eating, as a distinct and ritualized feature of everyday life, provides us interesting opportunities to explore these intersections.

In addition to interrupting the binary between food and not-food, a mimetic frame provides an alternative vantage point on the relationship between innovation and tradition in the field. Instead of seeing the current moment as a debate over whether or not to technologically modernize fine dining, we might conceive of processes like sous vide, anti-griddling, spherification and reverse spherification as scenographic innovations supporting a larger trend toward mimetic play in cooking and eating. To understand the implications of this mode of thinking, one need look no further than New York chef David Chang, often grouped alongside mimetic innovators like Adrià and late Chicago chef Homaro Cantu. Chang's brand of dining, epitomized by his flagship New York restaurant Momofuku (2004), is characterized more by his focus on the evocation of memory and emotion than by high-tech cooking techniques themselves. Chang's colleague, pastry chef Christina Tosi, is also famous for a low-tech mimetic style, inventing nostalgic desserts like corn-flake infused milk and a reimagined version of US home cook birthday staple "funfetti" cake at Tosi's New York casual dining concept and bakery, Milk Bar (2008).[9] Tosi's mimetic desserts playfully reproduce iterations on mass-market foods like boxed birthday cake mixes that diverge from their referents visually, texturally, and contextually but achieve striking sensuous similarity to their familiar "originals" through painstaking replication of flavor. Furthermore, through secondary products like Milk Bar-branded birthday cake lip glosses, manufactured by Glossier in 2017, Tosi reproduces her reproduction, relying once more on flavor as the primary conveyance of mimetic resemblance. Despite their avoidance of techniques associated with molecular gastronomy, most food scholars recognize Chang and Tosi as part of the avant garde cuisine of the moment, indicating that the movement exceeds a drive to innovate through technology and tends also toward a careful, theatrically inclined manipulation of the representational possibilities of cooking and eating. That this manipulation hinges on mimesis is both a source of its appeal and of its controversy, extending beyond the horizon of gastronomy as science.

This is my body: a few predecessors of contemporary mimetic cuisine

As the foregoing discussion demonstrates, the notion of food as a performing object resonates strongly with contemporary food practices, especially since theatrical artists have worked in and through food with a special intensity in the past several decades. However, food has been a medium of play and performance throughout recorded history.[10] Though a brief survey could not possibly account for the many varieties of mimetic cuisine that precede the contemporary turn toward culinary mimeticism, I address a few prominent examples from culinary history in order to track social attitudes toward and historical precedent for the imbrication of food and representation. In establishing the preexisting context for culinary representation, these examples also expose the issues of consumption, identity, desire, health, pleasure, and knowledge that will return to captivate and complicate contemporary culinary mimeticism.

The ancient Roman fondness for culinary mimeticism may help explain the tendency for contemporary chefs, from Grant Achatz to Heston Blumenthal, to restage Roman mimetic feasts. Roman banquets heavily featured dishes that delighted and surprised the wealthy through their transformation of one substance into a mimetic double for another through manipulations of their visual, textural, and alimentary qualities.[11] Petronius's *Satyricon* describes several such mimetic presentations, from birds roasted in pastry "eggs" to landscapes or still-lives constructed of food. Petronius describes one elaborately mimetic banquet, in which a whole roasted pig is presented through a short drama designed to surprise and delight guests. The pig is prepared to look as though the chef forgot to gut it before roasting, which prompts the guests to question and even threaten to torture the chef, who plays along with the ruse before slicing open the pig. When the offending "guts" spill onto the table, the guests are shocked and delighted to see they are actually sausages and puddings (1913, 88–89). Even the use of expensive spices or exotic ingredients, common in imperial Rome, hinged on an imagined mimetic substitution. As Pliny noted, for instance, in his *Natural History*, the wealthy enjoyed eating roasted elephant trunk in part "because it is a bit like eating ivory" (1855, 8.10). A chef might demonstrate his skill by fooling diners into thinking they were eating or drinking something entirely different than the actual ingredients of the dish. Athenaeus, quoting Euphron, discusses an example of food substitution, in which a chef

> took a female turnip, shred it fine
> Into the figure of the delicate fish;
> Then did he pour on oil and savoury salt
> With careful hand in due proportion.
> On that he strew'd twelve grains of poppy seed,
> Food which the Scythians love; then boil'd it all.
> And when the turnip touch'd the royal lips,
> Thus spake the king to the admiring guests:
> "A cook is quite as useful as a poet,
> And quite as wise, and these anchovies show it."
> *(1854, 11)*

So thorough was the Roman taste for mimetic foods that cooks kept on hand bronze forms in the shape of pigs, rabbits, and other animals to enable the shaping of one meat into the form of another, as in the birds fashioned from ham described in Petronius.

The mimetic qualities of Christian communion also emerge in the context of Roman mimetic cuisine.[12] For a contemporary Catholic mass, the belief in transubstantiation literally makes the world different; by believing the bread and wine becomes the body of Christ, the priest and congregation make it so. Conversely, in Protestant traditions that dispense with transubstantiation, the fact of the grape juice and bread remaining as they are in no way diminishes their mimetic power as they perform in place of literal blood and body. We might see the communion ritual as a combination of the world-creating and world-reflecting aspects of mimesis. Transubstantiation creates something new that does not reflect any substance found on Earth; it brings a divine concept into material being. On the other hand, the Protestant version (and other variations eschewing transformation) allows the apprehension of an impossible concept through a mimetic experiential engagement. Note, too, the emphasis on mimetic rather than entirely literal sacrifice. The transition from sacrifice of living animals, whose entrails were imagined to be enjoyed by unseen gods, to the mimetic sacrifice of a represented body, connects with René Girard's discussion of the overall significance of mimesis in the operation of desire and violence (1966). Here culinary mimesis enables the simultaneous celebration and destruction of the other in a ritual context. Further, as Michael Taussig notes and the example of communion helps explain, the mimetic faculty constitutes an extra-logical, sensory avenue for both understanding and influencing the world (1993).

Mimesis also constitutes a critical point of engagement with the relationship between food, health, and pleasure. Fourteenth-century French chef Taillevent, author of the first French cookbook, *La Viander*, focused on the use of spices to move meat from a threatening context (of spoilage) to a pleasing one by disguising its taste. In this use of spices, Taillevent stimulates the debate over mimetic aspects of cooking as either unhealthful maskings of the true nature of ingredients, as in the Nouvelle Cuisine view, or delightful transformations of one substance to another. Yet even the Nouvelle Cuisine's aim to reveal the essential character of a single ingredient through careful cookery ultimately pursues a mimetic goal, reflecting the influence of the highly mimetic Japanese kaiseki tradition on Paul Bocuse and the French chefs of the 1960s (McCarron 2017). After all, enacting a successful representation of the "essence" of, for instance, a carrot, relies on both a successful production of resemblance by the chef and a successful recognition by the diner.

In addition to its implications for notions of health and well-being, culinary mimeticism has long conveyed economic and class distinctions. European courtly banquets from the fifteenth to seventeenth centuries equaled or surpassed the Roman fixation on food as a representational medium, with chefs constructing, according to Kirshenblatt-Gimblett, "a cuisine of signs, a world made edible…discursive food addressed to the senses" (2007, 74). Extending this mimetic fascination beyond the court, nineteenth-century French chef Marie-Antoine Carême began infusing mimetic approaches into the high-class and high-visibility dining of public state dinners and meals at high-end hotel restaurants. Carême's famed elaborate centerpieces made new space for spectacular, scenographic dining that hearkened back to Roman mimetic cuisine, such as the four-foot high marzipan sculpture of a Turkish mosque he constructed for George IV of England in 1817.

Similarly, mimesis plays a significant role in representing the nature of humanity in nineteenth-century culinary writing. Just as Benjamin distinguishes mimesis as the most fundamental skill associated with human intelligence, French gastronome Brillat-Savarin considered taste a "rare perfection of man," distinguishing him from lower species through both physiological development, aesthetic sophistication, and intellectual capacity. His *Physiology of Taste* (1825) represents a major turn toward appreciation of both taste as a sense capable of conveying true knowledge and the conception of mimetic pleasure as part of a diner's experience of eating. Brillat-Savarin first establishes the sense of taste as a viable pathway to knowledge and power before discussing food as a medium of representation itself. Through comparison with birds, fish, and other mammals, he establishes that the human tongue possesses far greater range of motion and ability to register subtle variations in flavor. Similarly, he argues that "gourmandize is the exclusive privilege of man" due to the species' ability to experience food in a way that is complete and embodied:

> As soon as any esculent body is introduced into the mouth it is seized – gas, juice, and all.
> The lips prevent its escape. The teeth take possession of it and crush it. Saliva soaks it; the tongue turns and mashes is, an aspiration forces it toward the throat; the tongue lifts it up to help it slide by; the sense of smell perceives it en route, and it is precipitated into the stomach to undergo ulterior transformations, without the most minute fragment escaping during the whole of this episode. Every drop, every atom has been appreciated.
> *(1854, 23)*

This passage highlights not just human beings' finely developed physical apparatus for tasting, but also a vision of a totality and civility of eating that construes humanity as in possession of special abilities where food is concerned. Note the language of force and control. The diner takes control of the sensory experience of food, seizing, preventing escape, taking possession, forcing, and crushing. At the same time, this construction of the food as expressing some (however faint) desire to escape positions the experience of dining in a colonial model that connects as well with the implicit contrast between the highly mannered, polite notion of appreciating every single atom of food (none has escaped to sully the diner's beard or table) and the violent language of the eating itself.

Finally, Brillat-Savarin, again paralleling Benjamin's concept of mimesis as a source of knowledge, asserts the third element separating human taste from that of other animals: for humans, to quote theatre and performance scholar Susan Bennett, "taste is knowledge" (2015). In asserting the singular perfection of human taste, Brillat-Savarin turns to the human faculty of distinction. Using the concept of connoisseurship as evidence of man's ability to know through taste, Brillat-Savarin asks, "are we not surrounded by experts who can tell the latitude in which any wine ripened as surely as one of Biot's or Arago's disciples can foretell an eclipse?" (1854, 23). In this description of an oenophile's skill, the ability to use one's mimetic faculty of recognition to interpret information by tasting becomes a marker of the physiological, aesthetic, and intellectual predominance of man, leading Brillat-Savarin to "proclaim man the great *gourmand of nature*" (1854, 23). Discerning, for instance, an entire geographic and cultural history within a glass of wine requires a highly trained faculty of recognition in the drinker.[13] The ability to recognize a resemblance between dissimilar objects thus connotes one's superior taste.

By observing these features of food and dining, Brillat-Savarin makes space for Escoffier's revolutionary approach to the event of dining in the early twentieth century. Escoffier's development of the brigade system, a regimented style of restaurant management, was theatrical in its own right, though drawn as well from military culture. This revolution in culinary labor facilitated a carefully managed diner experience predicated on values of surprise and development of the meal as theatrical event, foregrounding the frontstage/backstage divide Erving Goffman would highlight as critical to his dramaturgy of the restaurant (1959). Escoffier's penchant for the mimetic shone through in his tendency to name dishes after celebrities, from Peach Melba (a dish of peaches and cream originally served in a swan ice sculpture, named for opera singer Nellie Melba) to Fraises Sarah (a strawberry and sorbet dessert named for Sarah Bernhardt). Hearkening back to wealthy Romans eating elephant but imagining themselves consuming ivory, these dishes mimetically connected diners with the celebrities for whom they were named.[14]

In addition to innovations in culinary practice, recent developments in food science have also enabled culinary mimesis on a molecular level. For instance, the development of artificial flavors, initiated in the nineteenth century and perfected in the latter half of the twentieth century, made possible a new version of mimetic culinary practice as well as anti-mimetic culinary critique. After chemist Nicolas-Theodore Gobley's discovery of vanillin, the chemical compound most responsible for vanilla's signature flavor, in 1858, multiple methods of synthesizing vanilla flavor rapidly emerged, including a method using tree bark in 1874 (Vidal 2006). Artificial flavors allowed food scientists to use food as a representational medium, for instance transforming oil into a butter substitute through hydrogenization and the addition of diacetyl and acetoin, the chemical compounds responsible for butter's distinct flavor. Following closely on the heels of these discoveries was the development of so-called "fantasy flavors" with no single counterpart in nature, such as cola, invented in 1886 by chemist John Pemberton. As the development of artificial flavors continued, flavor chemists strove to innovate, creating previously unimagined flavors. In an even more mimetically significant turn, the twentieth century saw the development of artificial flavors which have supplanted their natural counterparts, as in the artificial grape and cherry flavors that, to many contemporary palates, signal fruit flavors more clearly than the fruits themselves (Classen et al. 2005, 229). Roald Dahl captures the zeitgeist of fantasy flavors in the mad candy scientist, Willy Wonka, of *Charlie and the Chocolate Factory* (1964). In the 1971 film based on the book, Wonka urges his guests to taste his lickable wallpaper, exclaiming that "The strawberries taste like strawberries! The schnozzberries taste like schnozzberries!" Veruca Salt takes exception: "Snozzberries! Who ever heard of a snozzberry!" Gene Wilder's Wonka takes the petulant child's face in his hand and chides her for her lack of imagination. "We are the music makers, and we are the dreamers of dreams," he scolds.[15] In this scene, Dahl's character anticipates both contemporary skepticism of mimetic cuisine as well as a possible line of defense grounded in mimetic play as vital to artistic and intellectual freedom. These notions of culinary transformation as creativity and the chef as mad scientist/artist will return to found both the practice and criticism of culinary mimeticism in the work of chefs like Heston Blumenthal and Homaro Cantu.

Beyond Wonka, artificial flavors have also played a crucial role in the development of new representational modes based in the proximal senses. Scratch-n-sniff technology, made possible by 3M scientist Gale Madson's invention of microencapsulation in the early 1960s, used artificial scents to replicate "real world" smells in new formats. From Mary Dobson's *Smelly Old History* series, which uses scratch-n-sniff to give readers access to the smells of "Tudor Odours," "Roman Aromas," and "Medieval Muck," to John Waters's "Odorama" scratch-n-sniff cards designed to give viewers of *Polyester* (1981) a scent-enhanced experience of the film, scratch-n-sniff has been put to mimetic uses throughout its history. At the time of this writing, entrepreneurs are bringing scent-based technology into the digital era, introducing devices such as the AromaJet to allow game and website designers to add scents to digital experiences. Meanwhile, mimetic scents find their way to commercial and experimental performance spaces. For instance, Stewart Matthew, Nico Muhly, and Valgeir Sigurdsson teamed with aroma designer Christophe Laudamiel to perform "Green Aria: A ScentOpera" at the Guggenheim Museum in 2009 (Tommasini). In another popular example of olfactory design, Disney theme parks' *Soarin'* films feature artificial scents like evergreen and lemon to evoke California or roses to transport viewers to India (MacDonald 2016). In these examples scent design becomes a means to foreground the artists' focus on mimesis itself. Where a normal Disney film might play only in images, using mimetic means to advance a narrative, *Soarin'* explicitly plays with the nature of sensory representation, highlighting not so much the places it represents as its intriguing technology of representation. Patrons attend not so much out of interest in the specific places represented, but out of interest in the experience of olfactory mimesis.

Much as the artists mentioned above experiment with mimetic scents in commercial and fine art performances, twentieth- and twenty-first-century theatre and performance artists have experimented with returning the experience of eating to the centrality it enjoyed for most of the history of human performance events. While food onstage has a similarly long history, from the animal sacrifices that preceded fifth-century Athenian tragic performance to Andre Antoine's use of real beef carcass in his 1888 production of *The Butchers*, the practice of feeding audience members has also gained ground in both traditional and experimental theatre and performance spaces in the past sixty years. Futurist food experiments and Eat Art projects like Alison Knowles's 1962 *Make a Salad* merged food, cooking, and aesthetic experience in literary and museum contexts. Decades later, Argentinean artist Rirkrit Tiravanija provoked Nicolas Bourriaud's formulation of *Relational Aesthetics* (1998) with works like *pad thai* (1990) and *Untitled (Free)* (1992), in which the artist prepared and served food for gallery and museum visitors. While these practices in and of themselves were often anti-mimetic or uninterested in representation per se, work like Knowles's productively troubled longstanding distinctions between cooking and artistry, both placing cuisine in a fine art context and rupturing gendered boundaries between cooks, chefs, and creators. Meanwhile, theatre artists also pursued new applications of food in performance spaces. New York's Bread and Puppet theatre used bread itself as a social context for theatrical performance, as in the company's 1984 manifesto/recipe, which connects bread and art as two substances that "feed the hungry" (Schumann 1984). Artificial Intelligence's long-running production *Tony n' Tina's Wedding* (1986), originally staged in Greenwich Village and subsequently in Las Vegas, Chicago, Vancouver, and other North

American locations, draws on avant garde performance tactics to create an immersive production that casts audience members as wedding guests, completing the experience with dinner, drinks, dancing, and wedding cake (Benton 1990). More recently, Tooting Arts Club's celebrated 2014 London production of *Sweeney Todd*, now transplanted to New York, offers patrons a pre-show meal of meat and vegetable pies prepared by former White House pastry chef Bill Yosses.

Developing alongside these trends, immersive performance has expanded the sensory framework of a performance event to include proximal senses like taste and touch in addition to sight, smell, or sound. For example, avant garde musician Fast Forward's *Feeding Frenzy*, performed beginning in the late 1990s, marries cooking and musical performance, again recalling Knowles's boundary-breaking treatment of salad-making as a musical score.[16] In a similar vein, Richard Gough's experimental devising project, *The Last Supper Project*, featured a series of ambulatory performance experiences that included multiple opportunities to eat, including a Passover seder positioned as the centerpiece of the event.[17] Lookingglass Theatre and Rick Bayless's *Cascabel*, the subject of a case study in Chapter 4, again plays on the notion of meal-as-event, casting the Chicago celebrity chef as a preternaturally gifted cook whose transcendent *mole* has the ability to call forth magical abilities from the other characters in the play. As audiences dine on Mexican dishes cooked by the chef onstage, they watch the cast perform ecstatic circus acts in response to the taste of the same dishes they are eating.

Just as culinary mimeticism has inspired concern and critique in gastronomic discourse, theatre theorists have also approached the topic with skepticism. In her essay "Theatre as Shopping," Elinor Fuchs connects immersive and alimentary performances such as those described above with consumer culture, articulating a new genre of "shopping play" that, distinct from either Brecht's culinary theatre or from his defamiliarizing alternative, instead aims to "familiarize" theatregoers, "pleasantly suspending" them in an "authentic artificiality" (1996, 140). Fuchs identifies the experiences of choice, consumption, and embodied meaning-making common to immersive productions such as *Tony n' Tina's Wedding* as abolishing "the pedestal of the artistic event – not to gain the critical distance of dialectical inquiry, but to close the distance in what could be called simulacrity" (1996, 138). In this intimate, consuming model of spectatorship Fuchs locates a certain species of pleasure, but also a threat, not only to the theatre's continued existence, but perhaps to goodness itself. Fuchs closes her essay with the haunting image of Blake's apocalyptic rough beast, which in this case slouches toward the proscenium (1996, 143). While the mechanisms of embodied meaning-making Fuchs identifies recur again and again in my analysis, I suggest that a multisensory understanding of knowledge which resists the presumed equivalence between objectivity and distance yields an alternative perspective on culinary mimeticism. In contravention of the notion of objective distance, the chefs and artists I survey instead build an embodied, multisensory mimeticism that hinges precisely on the intimate, consuming, embodied exploration of meaning unique to alimentary performances. Rather than immersing audiences comfortably in a domain of pleasurable simulacrity, I argue that contemporary practitioners of culinary mimeticism instead confront audiences and diners with the challenging yet often pleasurable task of continually sorting out the relationship between representation, recognition, and truth as they experience mimetic cuisine. In a world in which objective assessment of truth seems ever more fraught, practitioners of culinary mimeticism offer an alternative mode of critical engagement in which the subject moves closer, rather than backs away, when confronted with representational complexity.

At the conclusion of *Unmaking Mimesis*, Elin Diamond envisions a critical feminist mimesis founded on incommensurability. This dialectical theatrical mimeticism uses the "nonidentical similar" not to trick a passive viewer, but to "rigorously explore relatedness," cast off old habits, and "imagine differently the dominant cultural norms of representation, embodiment, and pleasure" (1997, 181). While Diamond's vision of mimesis is rooted in the way that theatre "stages our desire to look and keep looking" (1997, 180), I propose that culinary mimeticism importantly stages an additional set of desires. While accommodating the desire to look and to keep looking, culinary mimeticism also brings mimetic experience closer, allowing not only a Brechtian grappling with representation at a distance, but also an embodied desire to eat and have eaten, to consume and to have consumed. This multisensory, critical mimesis literally and figuratively relocates the path of mimetic recognition from the eye to the optic nerve and then the brain to the body writ large, centered in the alimentary canal connecting the mouth to the stomach and onward. Thus instead of a moment of recognition occurring in an instant and at a distance, the alimentary performances explored in this volume offer temporally expansive, embodied, intimate, and subjective experiences of meaning-making, expanding upon the critical mimeticism Diamond envisions by relocating mimetic experience in not just the gazing body, but the consuming one.

The remainder of this text pursues a theoretical and practical examination of this emergent strand of culinary mimeticism. In the chapters that follow, I explore several of the leading practitioners of mimetic cuisine as well as several examples of performance events that reverse the flow of mimesis into culinary contexts, bringing contemporary mimetic frameworks for cooking and eating back into the compass of theatrical events themselves. This book proceeds in three stages. In Chapters 2 and 3, I examine restaurant spaces and the terrain of the chef, unpacking the ways in which two generations of chefs first establish and then expand and trouble the boundaries of contemporary culinary mimeticism. I first explore the roots of the contemporary turn toward culinary mimeticism through an analysis of the culinary and discursive work of Heston Blumenthal and Ferran Adrià in and around the turn of the millennium. Moving into the twenty-first century, I examine the work of two Chicago chefs whose work has influenced the shape of culinary representation in avant garde dining: Grant Achatz and Homaro Cantu. In each of these four chefs' work, I identify two main interventions into the relationship between pleasure and meaning. On the one hand, chefs like Adrià and Achatz use culinary mimeticism as a means of achieving meaningful pleasure by creating something new, treating culinary experience as capable of generating sustaining, inherently significant humanistic and aesthetic engagement. On the other, chefs like Blumenthal and Cantu use representational strategies not only to remake cuisine but also to transform foodsystems and imagine healthier, more just, and more sustainable foodways in both fine dining and everyday contexts. Furthermore, all four chefs unite theatricality, mimesis, and cuisine in the pursuit of the philosophical, aesthetic, and material transformations to which they aspire.

The turn toward culinary mimeticism has occurred not only within fine dining contexts, but across multiple spaces and professions, blurring the line between the domestic and the public, the aesthetic and the everyday, the real and the theatrical. Accordingly, I turn in Chapter 4 to an examination of culinary mimeticism in theatre and performance. Proceeding alongside rather than simply responding to the innovations of chefs and restaurateurs, theatrical and performance artists have pursued parallel engagements with the possibilities of culinary mimeticism. While these engagements extend broadly across popular theatre and performance, I focus my analysis on avant garde and boundary-breaking work in food-based performance in the last sixty years in order to demonstrate these artists' critical role in the advancement of culinary mimeticism and the exploration of the political, social, and economic stakes of culinary representation in performance contexts. In an analysis of Knowles's *Make a Salad* (1962), Carmelita Tropicana's *Chicken Sushi* (1984, 1987), Bobby Baker's *Kitchen Show* (1991) and *How to Shop* (1993), Michael Twitty's plantation performances, and Rick Bayless's *Cascabel* (2014), I examine the ways in which theatre and performance artists use cooking and eating to both subvert and reinforce relationships between mimesis, identity, class, and authenticity discussed in prior chapters. Building on Michael Taussig's notion of mimetic excess, I position alimentary performance as a resistant strategy that uses culinary mimeticism to imagine new ways of living. Through these brief case studies, I analyze multiple ways in which chef/practitioners and artist/cooks have used food as a means of reconsidering the relationship between sensation and meaning, challenging existing gendered, geographic, sensory, and cultural hierarchies in the process.

The chefs and artists surveyed in the prior three chapters establish alimentary experience as a means of uniting pleasure and knowledge, sensation and intelligence, physical action and mimetic recognition. In light of the critical role of embodied experience to culinary mimeticism, the final section of this project draws on my own creative work to offer a perspective on culinary representation grounded in the doing of cooking. In discussing multiple experiments in alimentary performance, I outline multiple means through which food works as a vehicle for performance and meaning as well as a performing object in itself. Through these case studies, I identify four primary modes of operation for mimetic cuisine along with four corresponding mechanisms for mimetic eating, drawing upon the case studies of the prior chapters to provide an initial practical framework aimed at supporting the development of new approaches to the emerging field of alimentary theatrical design and dramaturgy.

Notes

1. For two of the most influential works on culinary symbolism and the social meanings of food and eating, see Claude Lévi-Strauss's *The Raw and the Cooked* (1969) and Mary Douglas's *Implicit Meanings* (1975). For further discussion of the interaction between culinary semiotics and gastro-politics, see Arjun Appadurai's "Gastro-Politics in Hindu South Asia" (1981). For a thorough discussion of the implications of food, cooking, and eating for subjectivity and notions of the self, see Deborah Lupton's *Food, the Body, and the Self* (1996). Finally, Isabelle de Solier's *Food and the Self: Consumption, Production, and Material Culture* (2013) offers an ethnographic study of food production and consumption as a means of self-making in late modern "foodie" culture.
2. For a thorough treatment of ancient philosophy and mimesis, see Halliwell (2002).
3. See for instance, Derrida (1981, Taussig (1993), and Benjamin (1999).
4. The notion of cooking as a routine has been reconsidered often, as in Luce Giard and Michel de Certeau's formulation of "doing-cooking" (1998). Lisa Heldke makes an important intervention in the Platonic tradition of cooking as routine in her feminist reconsideration of cooking as "thoughtful practice," an approach to cooking-as-inquiry that undoes the Platonic split between "head work" and "hand work" and attempts to upend Cartesian distinctions between mind and body (1992, 203–229).
5. My terminology follows from Halliwell's delineation of "world-reflecting" and "world simulating" variations on mimesis in *Aesthetics of Mimesis* (2002).
6. Korsmeyer helpfully reframes the debate about food's status as an art form, refuting the argument against food as a representational medium but arguing that cooking simply "does not have the right history" to constitute a fine art (1999, 144).
7. In *Taste as Experience* (2016), philosopher Nicola Perullo offers a recuperative "lowering strategy" that positions food in the realm of aesthetics while retaining its marginal status vis-à-vis knowledge and intelligence. While Perullo does the important work of broadening the horizons of aesthetic experience to include both contexts of fine dining and everyday eating, my project focuses somewhat differently on the purposeful turn toward treating food as an artistic and representational medium in ways that cross between fine dining, popular, and quotidian contexts.
8. Joshua Abrams's "*Mise-en-plate*: The Scenographic Imagination and the Contemporary Restaurant," blurs the line between these two notions (Abrams 2013).
9. Chang and Tosi have since opened satellite restaurants around the world, most recently installing Momofuku and Milk Bar franchises in Las Vegas's Cosmopolitan hotel.
10. For a wide-ranging discussion of the imbrications of theatre and food, see Dorothy Chansky and Ann Folino White's *Food and Theatre on the World Stage* (2016).
11. As Emily Gowers discusses at length in *The Loaded Table: Representations of Food in Roman Literature* (1993), the Roman fascination with food that surprises also enabled a corresponding fixation on food as a literary and theatrical trope.
12. Communion is one of several examples (with, among others, gummy bears, radish roses, and hamentaschen) Carolyn Korsmeyer uses to refute the claim, from Telfer and others, that food cannot function as a representative medium (1999, 118).
13. But not all of humanity possess either the faculty itself nor the time and resources to develop it. As Brillat-Savarin famously argues, what and how we eat both performs who we are (and are not) and produces who we are. As foodways both represent values and identities and simultaneously produce them, mimetic processes of cooking and dining creating both symbolic and material effects. Thus the act of dining can serve as a means of knowing or producing knowledge, but also a means of producing bodies and embodied practices.
14. For more on this topic, see Folino White (2016).
15. The book's approach to the snozzberry differs slightly. Veruca Salt having already turned into a blueberry after sampling an experimental piece of flavor-changing gum, Mike Teevee queries Wonka insistently about the flavor of a snozzberry. Wonka pretends not to hear him. The contrast between a doubting literalist and a visionary chef-scientist remains clear.

16 For more on *Feeding Frenzy*, see Kirshenblatt-Gimblett (2007).
17 I served as a lighting designer for a *Last Supper* production in Madison, Wisconsin in 2003. Other performances include Amsterdam (1999), Aberystwyth (2000) and Florence (2002).

References

Abrams, Joshua. 2013. "Mise-en-plate: The Scenographic Imagination and the Contemporary Restaurant." *Performance Research* 18(3): 7–14. doi:10.1080/13528165.2013.816464.
Achatz, Grant. 2008. *Alinea*. Toronto: Ten Speed Press.
Appadurai, Arjun. 1981. "Gastro-Politics in Hindu South Asia." *American Ethnologist* 8(3): 494–511. www.jstor.org/stable/644298.
Aristotle. 1967. *Poetics*. Translated by Gerald Else. Ann Arbor: University of Michigan Press.
Athenaeus. 1854. *The Deipnosophists, Or Banquet of the Learned of Athenaeus*. Volume 1. Translated by C.D. Yonge. London: Henry G. Bohn. digital.library.wisc.edu/1711.dl/Literature.AthV1.
Benjamin, Walter. 1999 [1933]. "On the Mimetic Faculty." In *Selected Writings Volume 2, Part 2, 1931–1934*, translated by Edmund Jephcott, edited by Michael W. Jennings, Howard Eiland, and Gary Smith, 720–727. Cambridge: Harvard University Press.
Bennett, Susan. 2015. "'Taste Is Knowledge': Performance and Food at Expo Milano." Working group presentation. "Debating the Steaks: Food, Sustainability, and the Question of Performance." American Society for Theatre Research Annual Conference. Portland, OR.
Benton, Louisa. 1990. "A Marriage Made Off Broadway Takes the Cake." *New York Times*, July 15. www.nytimes.com/1990/07/15/theater/theater-a-marriage-made-off-broadway-takes-the-cake.
Boal, Augusto. 1985 [1974]. *Theatre of the Oppressed*. Translated by Charles A. and Maria-Odilia Leal McBride. New York: TCG.
Bourriaud, Nicolas. 1998. *Relational Aesthetics*. Translated by Simon Pleasance and Fronza Woods with the participation of Mathieu Copeland. Paris: Les Presse Du Reel.
Brecht, Bertolt. 1964 [1930]. "The Modern Theatre is the Epic Theatre." In *Brecht on Theatre: The Development of an Aesthetic*, edited and translated by John Willett, 33–42. New York: Hill and Wang.
Brillat-Savarin, Jean Anthelme. 1854 [1825]. *Physiology of Taste; or, Transcendental Gastronomy*. Translated by Fayette Robinson. Philadelphia: Lindsay and Blakiston.
de Certeau, Michel, Luce Giard, and Pierre Mayol. 1998. *The Practice of Everyday Life, Volume II: Living and Cooking*. Translated by Timothy J. Tomasik. Minneapolis: University of Minnesota Press.
Chang, David. 2016. "The Unified Theory of Deliciousness." *Wired*, July 19. www.wired.com/2016/07/chef-david-chang-on-deliciousness.
Chansky, Dorothy and Ann Folino White. 2016. *Food and Theatre on the World Stage*. New York: Routledge.
Classen, Constance, David Howes, and Anthony Synnott. 2005. "Artificial Flavors." In *The Taste Culture Reader: Experiencing Food and Drink*, edited by Carolyn Korsmeyer, 337–342. Oxford: Berg.
Crenn, Dominique with Karen Liebowitz. 2015. *Atelier Crenn: Metamorphosis of Taste*. Boston: Houghton Mifflin.
Dahl, Roald. 2013 [1964]. *Charlie and the Chocolate Factory*. New York: Penguin.
Dahl, Roald. 2016 [1971]. *Willy Wonka and the Chocolate Factory*. Directed by Mel Stuart. Burbank: Warner Brothers. DVD.
Derrida, Jacques. 1981. "Economimesis" *Diacritics* 11(2): 2–25.

Diamond, Elin. 1997. *Unmaking Mimesis: Essays on Feminism and Theater.* New York: Routledge.
Dobson, Mary. *Smelly Old History.* Multivolume Series. New York: Oxford University Press.
Douglas, Mary. 1975. *Implicit Meanings.* London: Routledge.
Dudek, Nir. 2008. "Reading a Plate." *Gastronomica* 8(2): 51–54.
Folino White, Ann. 2016. "Tasting the Past: Transhistorical Experiences with Food and Celebrity." Working group presentation. "Transplants: Food/Theatre/Performance." American Society for Theatre Research Annual Conference. Minneapolis, MN.
Forbes, Paula. 2011a. "Alton Brown on Molecular Gastronomy: 'It's Not Food.'" *Eater*, July 26. www.eater.com/2011/7/26/6667071/alton-brown-on-molecular-gastronomy-its-not-food.
Forbes, Paula. 2011b. "Alton Brown Still Has Issues With Molecular Gastronomy." *Eater*, August 18. www.eater.com/2011/8/18/6659281/alton-brown-still-has-issues-with-molecular-gastronomy.
Fuchs, Elinor. 1996. *The Death of Character: Perspectives on Theatre After Modernism.* Bloomington: Indiana UP.
Girard, René. 1966 [1961]. *Deceit, Desire, and the Novel.* Translated by Yvonne Freccero. Baltimore: Johns Hopkins UP.
Goffman, Erving. 1959. *The Presentation of Self in Everyday Life.* New York: Doubleday.
Govan, Fiona. 2008. "Famed El Bulli Chef Ferran Adrià Accused of 'Poisoning' His Diners." *The Telegraph*, May 14. www.telegraph.co.uk/news/worldnews/europe/spain/1955806/Famed-El-Bulli-chef-Ferran-Adrià-accused-of-poisoning-his-diners.
Gowers, Emily. 1993. *The Loaded Table: Representations of Food in Roman Literature.* Oxford: Clarendon.
Halliwell, Stephen. 2002. *The Aesthetics of Mimesis: Ancient Texts and Modern Problems.* Princeton: Princeton University Press.
Hegel, Georg Wilhelm Friedrich. 1975 [1835]. *Hegel's Aesthetics: Lectures on Fine Art.* Vol. 1, Translated by T. M. Knox. Oxford: Clarendon.
Heldke, Lisa M. 1992. "Foodmaking as a Thoughtful Practice." In *Cooking, Eating, Thinking: Transformative Philosophies of Food*, edited by Deane W. Curtin and Lisa M. Heldke, 203–229. Bloomington: Indiana University Press.
Kirshenblatt-Gimblett, Barbara. 2007. "Making Sense of Food in Performance: The Table and the Stage." In *The Senses in Performance*, edited by Sally Banes and André Lepecki, 71–89. New York: Routledge.
Korsmeyer, Carolyn. 1999. *Making Sense of Taste: Food and Philosophy.* Ithaca: Cornell University Press.
Laudan, Rachel. 2001. "A Plea for Culinary Modernism: Why We Should Love New, Fast, Processed Food." *Gastronomica* 1(1) (Winter): 36–44.
Lévi-Strauss, Claude. 1969. *The Raw and the Cooked.* Translated by John and Doreen Weightman. New York: Harper and Row.
Lupton, Deborah. 1996. *Food, the Body, and the Self.* London: Sage.
MacDonald, Brandy. 2016. "Disney's rebooted Soarin' ride takes flight over worldwide landmarks." *Los Angeles Times*, June 22. www.latimes.com/travel/themeparks/la-tr-soarin-around-the-world-disney-20160622-snap-story.
Marx, Rebecca. 2011. "Alice Waters Weighs in on Nathan Myhrvold's Modernist Cuisine." *Village Voice*, January 26. www.villagevoice.com/restaurants/alice-waters-weighs-in-on-nathan-myhrvolds-modernist-cuisine-6524285.
McCarron, Meghan. 2017. "The Japanese Origins of Modern Fine Dining." *Eater*, September 7. https://www.eater.com/2017/9/7/16244278/japanese-fine-dining-bocuse-tsuji-kaiseki.
Myhrvold, Nathan. 2011. *Modernist Cuisine: The Art and Science of Cooking.* With Chris Young and Maxime Bilet. Bellevue, WA: The Cooking Lab.

Novero, Cecilia. 2010. *Antidiets of the Avant-garde: From Futurist Cooking to Eat Art.* Minneapolis, MN: University of Minnesota Press.

Perullo, Nicola. 2016. *Taste as Experience: The Philosophy and Aesthetics of Food.* New York: Columbia University Press.

Petronius. 1913. *Satyricon.* In *Petronius, Seneca, Apocolosyntosis*, translated by Michael Heseltine, 1–324. Loeb Classical Library. London: Heinemann.

Plato. 2005 [1961]. *Plato: Collected Dialogues.* Edith Hamilton and Huntington Cairns. Princeton: Princeton University Press.

Pliny the Elder. 1855 [77]. *The Natural History.* Translated by John Bostock and H.T. Riley. London: Taylor and Francis.

Pollan, Michael. 2011 [2009]. *Food Rules: Illustrated Edition.* New York: Penguin. michaelpollan.com/books/food-rules-illustrated-edition.

Prince, Rose. 2010. "A Cookery Book Too Far." *The Daily Telegraph*, September 25. www.telegraph.co.uk/foodanddrink/8023927/Rose-Princes-Saturday-column.

Ruhlman, Michael. 2011. "Cook From It? First Try Lifting It." *New York Times*, March 8. www.nytimes.com/2011/03/09/dining/09modernist.

Schumann, Peter. 1984. "The Why Cheap Art Manifesto." Vermont: Bread and Puppet. breadandpuppet.org/cheap-art/why-cheap-art-manifesto.

Sherman, Amy. 2010. "Why I Hate Molecular Gastronomy." *Epicurious*, September 24. www.epicurious.com/archive/blogs/editor/2010/09/why-i-hate-molecular-gastronomy-1.

de Solier, Isabelle. 2013. *Food and the Self: Consumption, Production, and Material Culture.* London: Bloomsbury.

Taillevent. 1988 [1300]. *The Viander of Taillevent: An Edition of All Extant Manuscripts.* Edited by Terrence Scully. Ottawa: University of Ottawa Press.

Taussig, Michael. 1993. *Mimesis and Alterity: A Particular History of the Senses.* New York: Routledge.

Telfer, Elizabeth. 1996. *Food for Thought: Philosophy and Food.* London: Routledge.

Tommasini, Anthony. 2009. "Opera to Sniff At: A Score Offers Common Scents." *New York Times*, June 1. www.nytimes.com/2009/06/02/arts/music/02scen.

Vidal, J.-P. 2006. "Vanillin." *Kirk-Othmer Encyclopedia of Chemical Technology*. doi:10.1002/0471238961.2201140905191615.a01.pub2.

Which News. 2011. "Heston Blumenthal Effect Causes 'Kitchen Theatre'." *Which?*, May 1. www.which.co.uk/news/2011/05/heston-blumenthal-effect-causes-kitchen-theatre-252265.

2

THE FOUNDATIONS OF CONTEMPORARY MIMETIC GASTRONOMY

"Aceitunas Ferran Adrià"

Spherified green olive juice, assorted whole olives, olive oil
(*Las Vegas, Jaleo, 2016*)

Our server places a small dish before us. Upon it rest eight olives. Four of them jiggle as they absorb the plate's impact upon the table. Their sodium alginate shells retain their liquid interiors until we carefully place them in our mouths and bite down, bursting the membrane and flooding our palates with the flavor of green olive. As we alternate between tasting "real" and "Adrià" olives, a famous country singer walks across a long tabletop nearby. Laughing, he pours a tea-based cocktail directly from a clear teapot into his friends' open mouths as the party cheers him on. A server gently urges him to climb down.

While mimetic approaches to cooking date back at least to the Romans, no living chefs have influenced the development of contemporary mimetic gastronomy more directly than Ferran Adrià and Heston Blumenthal. The scene above recounts a typical moment of dining at Jaleo, a Las Vegas restaurant by Adrià's former apprentice José Andrés, a leading practitioner of culinary mimeticism in his own right. This citational dish of mimetic and real olives, which combines the iconic spherified olives with unadulterated olives to further highlight Adrià's mimetic concept, demonstrates the critical role Adrià has played in defining the stakes of culinary mimeticism for a generation of chefs.[1] A key player in the shift in focus from the French Nouvelle Cuisine to the contemporary avant garde style of fine dining, Adrià first joined the Spanish culinary avant garde led by his mentor Juan Mari Arzak and then pushed cuisine into new territory. Driven by a focus on creativity for its own sake, Adrià has advanced a systematic approach to gastronomy that represents the most substantial theory of cooking of the contemporary era.

Inspiring a vanguard of chefs as well as scientists, entrepreneurs, and artists across a wide spectrum of media and styles, Adrià's poetic and iconoclastic approach to gastronomic innovation both enlivened the contemporary turn toward mimetic cuisine and has driven young chefs to push beyond traditional boundaries of culinary representation.

Meanwhile, even as Adrià's work spurred the acceptance of food as a medium of artistic representation in the elite spaces of the art world, working to the north in the United Kingdom, his collaborator and co-author Heston Blumenthal evangelized culinary mimeticism within popular culture. Through demonstrations, scientific articles, television programs, books, and a growing empire of restaurants, Blumenthal has led the way in popularizing and promoting a scientifically rigorous, playfully mimetic brand of cooking. In addition to his high-profile engagements with food science, including television programs from *Kitchen Chemistry* (2002) to *In Search of Perfection* (2006–2007), Blumenthal also conducted extensive scientific and philosophical exploration of human perception of food. Blumenthal's practical and theoretical explorations of the relationship between pleasure and meaning in cuisine have led him to rethink the dramaturgy of dining.[2] Simultaneously, his interest in mimesis as a means of creating meaningful cuisine has inspired a series of activist interventions into public spaces like hospitals, airports, and schools in addition to the traditional domains of fine dining.

In this chapter, I address Adrià and Blumenthal as leading figures in the struggle to define the philosophical and practical parameters of culinary representation. As these two foundational chefs of the contemporary avant garde explore mimetic aspects of cooking and dining, they also initiate new inquiries into the relationship between sensation and intelligence, between pleasure and meaning, and between food and representation. Each of these inquiries in turn offers insights into the culinary turn in theatre and performance itself. Before embarking on a longer discussion of these chefs' roles in the development of culinary mimeticism, I share a brief snapshot of the experience of dining at their restaurants in order to demonstrate their prominence not only as culinary innovators but as central figures in the debate over the significance of culinary mimeticism.

In 2009, *Washington Post* food critic Blake Gopnik dined at what had been known since 2006 as the best restaurant in the world, Ferran Adrià's elBulli. In his account of the thirty-two-course meal, he highlighted several dishes new to the menu. Among them were mimetic peanuts, which Gopnik described as follows: "Seems to be a peanut, but is a crisp skin filled with a thin peanut cream. 'To be bitten in half,' says the waiter. (Watch for squirts down your shirt.)" (2009). Along with "passion orchid," a passionfruit, yogurt, and saffron crisp which "looks like a flower and tastes like one too," Gopnik's menu also included spherical olives, a solidified olive oil spring, oyster leaf with vinegar dew, spherified beans, citrus air "seafoam," a frozen cocktail shaped as a rose, a jasmine tea pond with nasturtium lily pads, a coconut milk balloon, and a dessert of chocolate roots with black sesame earth, among other mimetic delights (2009). Accepting the meal in the context of mimetic recognition, Gopnik lovingly recounts the representations he mines from even less obviously mimetic dishes, like "Coniferous: The tender tips of pine tree boughs, dipped in rosemary honey, then Maldon salt, served with a yogurt cocktail made with pine-infused gin. Like a walk in the forest, nibbling as you go" (2009). The pleasure and the significance of this meal, Gopnik makes clear, springs from the experience of culinary mimeticism.

Later that same year, prominent food blogger the Ulterior Epicure dined at what was then considered the world's second-best restaurant, Heston Blumenthal's The Fat Duck.[3] A professed "skeptic" of Blumenthal's theatrical cuisine, he expressed delight upon finding the first course of olives was not Adrià's spherified liquid, but natural, "so unadulterated that they still had their pits about them" (Ulterior Epicure 2009). However, the dubious Epicure balked at the "performance art" of a nitrogen-frozen meringue, and alternately enjoyed and critiqued mimetic dishes like parsnip cereal flakes with parsnip milk, the aforementioned "Sound of the Sea," and nitrogen-scrambled bacon and egg ice cream disguised as scrambled eggs. Still, he recounts a moment's pause in response to "Homage to Alain Chapel," a dish of truffled toast, foie gras, quail jelly, pea puree, and langoustine cream served alongside a box of oak moss, oak and pine gelatin sheets, and a scented vapor of oak and pine. Finding himself entranced by the earthy forest experience, the Epicure includes a quizzical evaluation of the source of his enjoyment in which he wonders whether the dish's title, its use of a scented film to transform the palate, or the incorporation of atmospheric scents like oak moss enabled Blumenthal to transport him to the forest. Ultimately, the Epicure decides, it doesn't matter: the dish manages to accomplish its representational effect despite the diner's reservations.

These two reviews indicate the degree to which Adrià and Blumenthal's flagship restaurants, each of which regularly graced lists of the top three restaurants in the world between 2004 and 2010, not only advanced mimetic culinary practices, but also inspired questions about the value of culinary representation. Both of these 2009 menus explore multiple varieties of culinary mimeticism, including evocation of place (two different representations of the forest) as well as multisensory representations in which one foodstuff performs as another (scrambled egg ice cream, chocolate roots, two variations on sea foam). Moreover, each menu intentionally casts gastronomic experience as mimetic in a Benjaminian sense, involving both the articulation and recognition of representations through sensory and nonsensory means. These two menus also offer a snapshot of culinary mimeticism's emergence as an expected feature of haute cuisine experience, whereby mimetic dishes inspire alimentary performances of interpretation, recognition, critical engagement, and embodied knowledge from diners. Accordingly, in the remainder of this chapter, I explore the ways in which, working at the vanguard of this trend, Adrià and Blumenthal define the theoretical and practical parameters for a multisensory culinary mimeticism that expands the terms and scope of mimetic experience in fine art and avant garde contexts and reframes the significance of mimesis in everyday dining.

While neither Adrià nor Blumenthal limit their culinary work to mimetic applications, their cuisine also highlights critical issues in mimetic gastronomy, including but not limited to the parameters within which cooking and eating can convey meaning, the role of labor in culinary representation, problems of excess and waste in avant garde dining, and the significance of theatricality as a dimension of mimetic alimentary experience. While each chef's work stands on its own, I consider Adrià and Blumenthal together for several reasons. First, these two chefs stand at the center of discourse around mimetic culinary theory and practice and have been the most prominently featured chefs in the discussion of the perceived pleasures as well as the reputed dangers of culinary mimesis. Second, their distinctly different approaches to culinary mimeticism establish the terrain against which the next generation of chefs, from Christina Tosi to Grant Achatz, have explored the potential of food as a mimetic medium. Finally, as co-authors of the most influential culinary manifesto of the twenty-first century, these chefs have positioned themselves as philosophical leaders of the culinary avant garde. Before proceeding to an analysis of each chef's culinary discourses and practices, I first examine this foundational culinary document, the 2006 "Statement on the 'New Cookery'," co-authored with US chef Thomas Keller and food scientist Harold McGee.

In defense of culinary representation: the "Statement on the 'New Cookery'"

As a mode of culinary discourse that operates alongside the cookbooks, menus, and reviews that form the backbone of cuisine's discursive archive, the culinary manifesto constitutes a logical starting point for an exploration of contemporary culinary theory. Furthermore, culinary uses of the manifesto form are particularly resonant given the theatricality of contemporary mimetic dining. As theatre scholar Martin Puchner points out, the work of manifesto writing is inherently theatrical in that manifesto writers performatively "occupy the future in an act of prolepsis, of creative anticipation" (2010, 926). Manifesto writers set out a specific program of action; some behaviors and ideas are rejected, while those the manifesto's author imagines into being must fight for the space to come into existence. However, the manifesto also functions as an art form in itself, tending toward the theatrical in dwelling not only on meaning but on its sensory surfaces. Manifesto authors labor to set the scene in the reader or listener's imagination for the conditions of the birth of the futures they imagine. In other words, manifestos push to be performed. Given the manifesto's inherent theatricality, for Puchner, the rhetorical function of these incendiary documents "marks a moment of hesitation, a moment when the manifesto gives up its commitment to absolute efficacy and action, and allows itself to dwell on *theatrics* instead" (2002, 463). Despite its drive to come into being, the manifesto nevertheless lingers over the pleasure of its own irritation and imagination, taking joy in the process of railing against the past and imagining the future. Contemporary chefs' manifesto-cuisine epitomizes Puchner's discussion of the perpetual tension between the forward motion of futurity and the desire to perform the manifesto again and again. Night after night in restaurants like Blumenthal's, diners tuck into dishes that boldly and lovingly deconstruct the history of cuisine, pushing toward the future but also dwelling on the contours and textures of the past. In this manifesto-driven cuisine, chefs create conditions for diners to play out a radical futurity in their dining. As in Benjamin's vision of incorporative experience, this process simultaneously exists in the present, calls up the past, and mimetically creates a vision of the future.

While Adrià, Blumenthal, McGee, and Keller refer to their document as a statement, its brevity, force, and imbrication of the past and the future all place it within the genre of manifesto writing. The choice to compose a culinary manifesto is nothing new, as the history of cuisine is in many ways a history of manifesto movements. Furthermore, many of these historic manifestoes and manifesto-style culinary rebellions also take a position on the role of mimesis in cuisine. For instance, Escoffier's revolutionary *Le Guide Culinaire* (1903) overthrew the notion of culinary convention and modernized both cooking, dining, and the perceived status of chefs by enabling new approaches to culinary mimesis. His revolutionary brigade system enabled the creation of carefully plated dishes meant to be served directly to diners at the table. This innovation overturned prior practice dating back to Carême, carving out space for new forms of culinary transformation and magic founded on an appreciation of mimetic pleasure not only in the form of large visual displays, but also on the smaller scale of the table or plate. Escoffier's creation of dishes named for stars, from Peach Melba (after Nellie Melba) to Fraises Sarah (after Sarah Bernhardt) created a mimetic opportunity to dine with or even as the stars. Three decades later, the 1931 "Manifesto of Futurist Cooking," which art and food critic Charlotte Birnbaum notes bears striking similarities to Adrià's own culinary practice, urged a cuisine that embraced scientific advances in the service of instilling a distinctly mimetic sense of magic into dining (2009). Calling for originality in all dishes and the replacement of traditions like the use of knives and forks with more stimulating and variable dining techniques, the Futurists also demonstrated their ideas in public events like aerobanquets, in which diners ate from airplane-shaped tables, drank from gas cans, and enjoyed dishes designed to evoke the sensation of flight (Novero 2010, 23–24, Sorini and Cutini 2014). In contrast, in the 1973 manifesto published by Gault and Millau, the chefs of the French Nouvelle Cuisine rejected culinary mimesis in favor of simplicity and authenticity, viewing the experience of consuming the pure essence of, for example, a carrot, as healthy not only physically but psychologically. In disavowing brown and white sauces, marinades, fermentation, overcooking, and "cheating" with elaborate presentation, Nouvelle Cuisine adherents, inspired by Japanese kaiseki cuisine, positioned authenticity and processing, specifically techniques aimed at transforming foodstuffs with an aim of representing anything other than the "truth" of ingredients, at opposite ends of a culinary spectrum. From Apicius to Adrià, as chefs and culinary writers have addressed the relationship between creation, imitation, and authenticity they have also of necessity developed new discourses about the implications of mimesis for human well-being.

While the Futurists rejected the past in service of the drive to define cuisine in relation to mimeticism, the Statement authors instead propose to radically reframe culinary practice in order to systematically rethink the relationship between cuisine and representation. Addressing young chefs in particular, Adrià and his co-authors frame the new frontier of gastronomy as a widening of culinary pursuits and a marshaling of new resources. They reinforce this radical openness to both new technology and received wisdom by emphasizing their relationship to history: "This is not a new idea, but a new opportunity. Nearly two centuries ago, Brillat-Savarin wrote that 'the discovery of a new dish does more for human happiness than the discovery of a new star'" (2006, 126). This nod to Brillat-Savarin signals the respect with which Adrià and his peers regard gastronomic history and also the central philosophical focus of the movement, which positions cuisine as a humanistic enterprise equally capable of enhancing human experience and knowledge as the sciences, and perhaps even more so.[4] Accordingly, the authors call for an open exchange of ideas and practices, a citational approach that develops a framework for more rigorous scholarly study of cuisine, and the encouragement of culinary creativity in the service of excellence. As in former Adrià *stagiere* and Copenhagen chef-innovator Rene Redzepi's culinary conferences or culinary scientist Hervé This's Paris seminars on the science of cooking, Adrià and his co-authors mark cuisine as a discipline, attended with intense academic study and international professional exchange.

This reframing of cuisine as a discipline supports a concomitant reframing of culinary philosophy, and specifically of culinary representation. Where the Nouvelle Cuisine treated culinary transformation and gastronomic truth as opposites, Adrià, Blumenthal, and their co-authors extol the virtues of culinary representation, specifically the ability of culinary experience to evoke feelings, memories, ideas, and associations in the mind and body of the diner. The authors express this sense of cuisine's powers of representation most forcefully at the close of the essay, when they imagine a new cookery that takes its place as the most significant of the performing arts due to its ability to engage both the senses and the intellect. It is this sense of a cuisine that impacts bodies and minds, that functions not only sensorily or nutritionally but also as a vehicle for meaning, that the Statement authors set out both to defend and imagine into being. Adrià, Blumenthal, Keller, and McGee aim to correct the record on their gastronomic innovations, which they argue suffer from misrepresentations including a distorting emphasis on the scientific aspects of their culinary research and technique. Rejecting a simplistic association between their cuisine and science, they firmly and famously disavow the label "molecular gastronomy," which they assert describes neither their own cookery nor "indeed any style of cooking" (2006, 127). Rather, they insist, observers have incorrectly fixated on their technological innovation, thereby failing to understand their principle aims and accomplishments. Not a technological or scientific movement at all, the new cookery aims to advance food as a medium capable of creating, conveying, or even constituting meaning itself, rather than a means of achieving either sustenance or pleasure alone.

In laying out the necessary conditions for this culinary advancement, the authors call for "openness to all resources that can help us give pleasure and meaning to people through the medium of food" (2006, 126). This declaration supports the signature outward turn in the contemporary culinary avant garde, urging a bold expansion past the traditional boundaries of cookery and abandoning the notion of secret recipes and proprietary processes. Yet it also, significantly, grounds this shift on two fundamental values: pleasure and meaning. This approach offers a contrast to critiques of mimetic cuisine like Alton Brown's aforementioned derision of foam for foam's sake, which tend to position style and pleasure at one end of a continuum and meaning and authenticity at the other. In Brown's formulation, pleasure, associated both with sensory enjoyment and intellectual play, equates with an absence of substance. Brown symbolically represents the dangers of culinary mimesis through the texture of foam. The unhealthy pleasure of foam is easy, insubstantial, and ephemeral, a self-indulgent trick that distracts from culinary flaws, luring us from substantial engagement with authentic culinary mastery through magical representation of unexpected flavor profiles coupled with a surprising texture. In contrast with this opposition of good and bad pleasures, the Statement authors align meaning and pleasure with one another, opening a space for a meaningful role for mimesis within culinary discourse. If pleasure and meaning travel in the same circles, we need not necessarily look upon pleasure, sensory or not, with suspicion. Indeed, throughout both Adrià and Blumenthal's culinary discourse, meaning becomes, as in Aristotle, a way of inoculating pleasure against charges of danger. Meaningless pleasures may be a temptation to debauchery, but the interaction of pleasure and meaning creates a sense of attentiveness that leads to contemplation, understanding, and a resultant forward motion in human experience. Thus mimetic cuisine becomes, in this formulation, one pathway to culinary progress. By including the experience of representational significance in the sphere of dining, the Statement forwards a vision of meaningful alimentary experience that allows for and even relies upon, rather than discounts, bodily pleasure.

The Statement authors go on to reinforce the connection, rather than opposition, between apprehensible and intelligible aspects of avant garde dining, explicitly linking their cuisine to the performing arts and arguing for the need to create both "delicious and stimulating" dishes (2006, 127). The senses and the mind correspond rather than conflict in this equation. While a Platonic approach to intelligence might construct the senses as a dilution or distraction from the mind, in the authors' calculus, the correspondence between sensation and intelligence becomes an asset to avant garde cuisine. This union of pleasure and meaning situates cuisine as a preeminent performing art since it allows the artist to engage the whole body, including the mind. In this unified view of mind and body, pleasure and meaning function as related rather than divergent phenomena, each essential to the other and both integral to experiences of inherently meaningful cuisine. Still, this approach to pleasure, sensation, and meaning sits uneasily alongside millennia of anti-mimetic discourse linking mimeticism with insubstantiality and inauthenticity, as the critiques of Blumenthal and Adrià's cuisine cited later in this chapter illustrate.

While the "Statement on the 'New Cookery'" addresses misunderstandings and critiques from within culinary discourse, these chefs have also worked to promote understanding of and appreciation for culinary mimeticism in culture at large.

Perhaps no chef has had more impact in this area than Heston Blumenthal, whose efforts to advance popular understandings of avant garde cuisine and culinary mimeticism I discuss in the following section. Through his extensive output of lectures, scientific articles, television programs, and books exploring the potential applications of mimetic cuisine, Blumenthal has effectively countered charges of mimetic superficiality by demonstrating the deep significance mimetic eating can have. Moreover, through extensive study of the means by which humans experience eating, Blumenthal fundamentally shifts understandings of the significance of dining, establishing a common ground for pleasure, meaning, and experience that underpins a thorough engagement with culinary mimeticism in his own work and that of the chefs he has influenced.

Perception is reality: Heston Blumenthal and the dramaturgy of dining

Since his experiments with crab ice cream in the late 1990s, Blumenthal's empirical research into the relationship between the senses, the mind, and perception in dining has built foundational understandings of the dramaturgical aspects of culinary representation. Simultaneously, his popular television programs and books have nurtured an audience for representation in cooking, painstakingly constructing discursive and edible arguments for the historicity, viability, and vitality of culinary mimeticism. A self-taught chef, Blumenthal opened his flagship restaurant, the Fat Duck, in 1995, gaining his first Michelin star in 1999 and shortly thereafter introducing the tasting menu that would gain him world renown. Featuring playfully mimetic dishes like the aforementioned parsnip cereal and milk, Blumenthal's menus mined new and old culinary technologies in an exhaustive engagement with food's capacity to convey both pleasure and meaning. Mind-bending ideas like "Nitro-scrambled egg and bacon ice cream," introduced in 2000, established Blumenthal's reputation for elaborate mimetic dishes. Preparing the ice cream tableside, servers crack egg shells (emptied, cleaned, and stamped with a Fat Duck logo) filled with a bacon and egg custard into a small pan of liquid nitrogen, whipping the mixture into a fluffy yellow ice cream that visually passes as scrambled eggs. The resulting ice cream is plated with caramelized brioche toast, tea jelly, and bacon. This surprising presentation of dessert-as-breakfast-as-dessert delights diners not only in its flavor, temperature, and texture, but in its representational significance. As Blumenthal explains, the dish appeals by treading the "fine line between real and surreal in a way that somehow makes sense" (Blumenthal 2009, 259). Over and over, Blumenthal's dishes explore this active notion of "making sense," a dynamic process of representation in which sensory experience and intellectual engagement combine in playfully incorporative eating. Dishes like these helped make Fat Duck a culinary icon at the vanguard of cuisine. From 2004 to 2012, the Fat Duck would maintain a prominent position alongside elBulli in the World's 50 Best Restaurants top ten, signaling both Blumenthal's prominence and the rising influence of the culinary mimeticism of which he has been a leading example.

As Blumenthal's reputation for culinary mimeticism grew, he developed multiple strategies for edible representation, exploring the full range of a diner's sensory and intellectual capacities to evoke mimetic recognition and, with it, pleasure. Grounded in geography, 2006's "Whisk(e)y Gums" took the diner on a tour from Speyside to Tennessee through a set of whiskey-infused gelatin candies served atop a map of the whiskey-producing regions of the Western hemisphere. The aforementioned "Homage to Alain Chapel" (1999) transported diners on a fanciful journey to the origins of Nouvelle Cuisine as well as a literal experience of the forest floor facilitated by a box of oak moss, a quick-dissolving edible film of oak resin, and an aromatic vapor of oak essential oil. The dish offers guests a multi-sensory experience of the Nouvelle Cuisine's philosophical focus on the local and seasonal. Before consuming the gelee of quail, foie gras parfait, and truffle-buttered toast, the diner smells, sees, touches, and tastes the essence of the oak forest from which these ingredients spring. In contrast, 2004's "Mrs. Marshall's Margaret Coronet" showcases Blumenthal's penchant for representing culinary history. This apple-ginger ice cream cone dusted with apple-vanilla salt pays tribute to the Victorian era chef and inventor who conceived, at the dawn of the twentieth century, of exciting tableside ice cream preparations using liquified gas. As a contemporary treatment of a Victorian recipe, "Mrs. Marshall's Margaret Coronet" serves not only as a mimetic reflection of the past, but also as an edible proof of the vitality of Blumenthal's approach to culinary innovation in the pursuit of meaningful pleasure. Simultaneously evoking culinary history, honoring the scientific contributions of a pioneering female chef, and stimulating pleasure in the here and now, the dessert demonstrates the importance of dramaturgical framing in evoking a fully embodied (intellectual as well as sensible) experience of pleasurable mimetic eating. In the following section, I explore Blumenthal's unique interest in the dramaturgy of pleasure, tracing both the origins of the philosophy that the chef ultimately articulates in the "Statement on the 'New Cookery'" and the implications of Blumenthal's work for both the practice and popular reception of culinary mimeticism.

Pleasures of the table: toward a diner-focused culinary dramaturgy

The *Fat Duck* cookbook begins with an introductory note from Harold McGee highlighting Blumenthal's reputation for employing the scientific method in pursuit of culinary aims. Yet even here, as in the "Statement on the 'New Cookery'," McGee insists that Blumenthal's cooking is not preoccupied with science per se, but rather constitutes a kind of culinary activism that uses science where necessary to advance not only haute cuisine, but food culture in Britain. In line with this interest in food culture as a whole rather than solely the material attributes of food, the book's opening story focuses on the event of dining. A tale of a formative dining experience at L'Oustau de Baumaniere, this opening vignette waxes poetic about the dramaturgy of dining: "more than the extraordinary food they ate that evening, what the boy remembered was the whole open-air theatre of it all" (2009, 17). In describing the impact of that meal, Blumenthal draws a lively contrast between the three-Michelin-starred restaurant, with its elaborate introductory cocktails and its larger-than-life sommelier, and traditional British fine-dining of the mid-1980s, with its stultifying formality and boring repertoire of imported "classics." While the food certainly impressed Blumenthal, the liveliness of the event truly captures his interest. In his recollection, this dinner-as-performance entranced not only the diners but the restaurant staff: "it wasn't just the idea of food as a performance that got to me: it was the unselfconscious pleasure with which everyone – staff and customers alike – played their part" (2009, 23). This interest in dinner as a mutually pleasurable performance led the young Blumenthal to purchase restaurant ranking guides from Michelin and GaultMillau, over which he pored in long study of the service practices as well as the actual edible offerings of the top restaurants in the world. Long before his engagement with the science of flavors, Blumenthal yearned to unlock the secrets of dining as event, seeking out a method for evoking comfort, pleasure, and intellectual and sensory delight in the course of a meal. Even when his interest turned to chef-authored cookbooks a few years later, Blumenthal presciently focused on the scenic, dramaturgical, and performative elements of each chef's recorded practice, gleaning from them a sense of the chef as character and cuisine as culture. This study of the minute as well as the major innovations of preceding chefs paved the way for Blumenthal's attention not only to the details of cooking, but of dining.

An auto-didact who relied on books as the backbone of his culinary education, Blumenthal frames his *Fat Duck* cookbook as a bildungsroman. Significantly, this culinary autobiography suggests that his unique perspective on modern cuisine stems from Blumenthal's access not only to the cookbooks, ingredients, and time necessary to build his skills, but also to early experiences of fine dining. His description of a decade of summers spent eating his way across France, searching for the "subtle attention to detail that – invisibly but effectively – distinguished a great restaurant from a good one" focuses intently on aspects of culinary dramaturgy and design, from cutlery trends to the performative aspects of a server's presentation of a specific dish to a restaurant's architecture or furnishings (2009, 31). These early meals gave Blumenthal a diner's rather than a chef's perspective on fine dining, a perspective that underpins his focus on the diner's perception as critical to the impact of cuisine. Even while collecting "flavour-memories" on these culinary research trips, Blumenthal attends carefully to the discourse of food, its history, its rarity, the care with which it is presented to him, the stories he builds for himself of the meals, and the stories presented to him by servers, chefs, and purveyors: "the B&B owner determined to treat us to his highly prized, unlabelled magnums of Armagnac…. Apparently, the only way to appreciate it was to splash on cupped palms and then rub over face – like aftershave!" (2009, 34). This anecdote, one among a great many, signals Blumenthal's engagement with the dramaturgy of food: the gesture, the social ritual, the accompanying description of the dish, and the accumulation of stories upon stories as the dish is consumed. Food and time link together inextricably, with meals forming the backbone of a dramatic narrative as well as individual dramas understandable either in series or as standalone episodes of Blumenthal's romance with cuisine.

This interest in the dramaturgy of dining guided Blumenthal's early experiments in avant garde cooking. For example, when tasked to present an avant garde cooking technique to a group of food scientists in the late 1990s, Blumenthal chose to create a gel-based dish that allowed the diner to experience four distinct flavors in turn, highlighting both surprise and recognition as critical to the pleasure of a dish (2009, 75). This dramaturgy of eating that depends on surprise, transformation, or reversal of expectation during the process of incorporation has since developed into Blumenthal's famous contrast-based dishes, combining hot and cold temperatures within the same cup of tea or juxtaposing warm crab risotto with a miraculously unmelting crab ice cream. As these examples demonstrate, Blumenthal often reaches for scientific or technological innovation to add emotional, sensory, and intellectual complexity to the diner's alimentary experience. However, in order to evoke surprise, recognition, pleasure, or a sense of progression, Blumenthal argues a chef must attend not only to the dish itself, but also to the dramaturgical frameworks that set a diner's expectations. For instance, 2005's "Hot and Iced Tea" uses its name to prime the diner to recognize the surprising experience of two temperatures of tea within the same glass. It also employs a double-walled serving vessel to insulate the diner's hands from the hot and cold fluid gels, preserving the immediacy of the dish's surprising sensory contrast. Through this attention to detail, Blumenthal designs not only dishes themselves, but dramaturgical frameworks that prime diners for mimetic culinary experience.

Blumenthal first noticed a relationship between expectation and flavor perception in practice at Fat Duck in the mid-1990s. Contemplating diner responses to his early dishes, he discovered that descriptions on menus, the context of the food's presentation, and the creation of expectations before the diner encounters a dish all impact the ultimate ability of the dish not only to please, but to communicate ideas. Blumenthal's focus on diner experience becomes clear in his discussion of the aforementioned crab ice cream, introduced to the Fat Duck menu in the late 1990s. After mixed diner reviews, Blumenthal renamed the savory ice cream "frozen crab bisque" and found that patrons responded far more favorably. Changing the name not only increased sales but also changed how diners perceived the dish, making it seem less sweet. This initial insight led Blumenthal to partner with Firmentech, a Swiss flavor and aroma research company, for more sustained study of food perception (Blumenthal 2009, 69–70). His ensuing research led Blumenthal to the conviction that the most important aspects of a diner's experience, both for the pleasure and also the meaning derived from a dish, are contextual. A few examples from Blumenthal help demonstrate the insights this research enables. For instance, the chef cites an experiment in smell in which identifying an aroma as unwashed socks created revulsion while marking the same aroma as aged cheese resulted in pleasure. In another experiment, sommeliers tasted the same wine differently when it was colored red versus its original white (Friedman 2004). In each case, the initial framing of a sensory stimulus radically transformed individual sensory perceptions, even in highly trained subjects such as sommeliers. Already engaged with mimetic cuisine, Blumenthal's research led him to the conclusion that the dramaturgy of a dish was of greater importance to its representational power than its material attributes. For Blumenthal, "perception is, in effect, reality. As much as any chemical properties of the ingredients and their intermingling, it is the perception of the diner that determines how a food is appreciated" (2009, 71). This notion that the diner's perception, as led by the chef's dramaturgical framing of a dish, constitutes the stage on which the chef truly performs focuses Blumenthal's attention on story, sensory play, and a sustained examination of the possibilities of culinary mimeticism.

More than a student of science, Blumenthal has undertaken experimental research himself in cases in which existing scholarship failed to adequately explain a phenomenon of perception. For example, intrigued by the relationship between expectation, sensation, and perception demonstrated in diner responses to savory ice cream, Blumenthal collaborated with scientists to conduct a series of three experiments with smoked salmon ice cream, serving a savory salmon-flavored product labelled alternatively as ice cream and as a savory mousse. Not only did the researchers find that diners reacted positively to the product labelled as mousse and negatively to it as an ice cream, they also found that perceptions of the dish's saltiness, sweetness, and bitterness changed markedly depending on how the product was labelled (Yeomans et al. 2008). While Blumenthal's research on flavor perception certainly helps cement his credibility as a contributor to food science, it also demonstrates his preoccupation with the dramaturgy of dining as an area worthy of as much interest as flavor pairing, cooking technique, or culinary technology.

Guided by his early recognition of the primacy of perception, Blumenthal has evolved a multi-sensory approach to mimetic dining that manipulates not only the visual elements of a dish but also the flavors, aromas, textures, sounds, and physical actions of eating to create a kaleidoscopic array of representational opportunities. Addressing the senses both individually and in concert, Blumenthal's mimetic dishes stimulate surprising moments of recognition and thus infuse experiences of dining with interconnected pleasure and meaning. Blumenthal describes his sensory innovations in mimetic terms, focusing on the ways in which stimulation of one sense, such as the use of the ocean sounds, the scent of salt, or the tactile sensation of beach sand, could convince the diner of various illusions about flavor and might enhance the diner's ability to experience the "full sensory potential of a dish" (2009, 105). Here the chef distinguishes sensory potential from flavor, envisioning a holistic experience of recognition of an alimentary stimulus rather than simply the chemical impact of a molecule on a palate. The real subject of Blumenthal's experiments, then, is more properly culinary representation itself, and its functions, its effects, and its possibilities especially where food is concerned, than chemistry in particular. This interest manifests in Blumenthal's precise attention to the interaction among the disparate elements of service, presentation, naming conventions, and the multiple sensory elements at play in each of his dishes. In Blumenthal's dramaturgical approach to dining, the chef coordinates each aspect of an alimentary experience to inspire the pleasurable experience of "making sense," in other words, mimetic recognition.

Blumenthal's emphasis on culinary dramaturgy has led to important differentiations between his practice and Adrià's, including his exploration of the impact of sensory input beyond traditional alimentary stimuli on diner perceptions. For instance, while Adrià calls hearing "the least important sense for the act of eating" (Adrià et al. 2008, 464), Blumenthal makes auditory sensation a primary focus of "Sound of the Sea." In conceiving "Sound of the Sea," Blumenthal conducted experiments that indicated listening to specific sounds while eating could sharpen one's sense of taste. In this case, he found that listening to the sound of waves enhanced the taste of oysters in test subjects. The resulting dish is a mimetic representation of the sea made visually compelling by the aforementioned foam, along with tapioca, breadcrumb, and crushed eel sand topped with seafood and edible seaweed. But Blumenthal takes the experience further, providing the diner with an iPod that allows her to listen to the sound of crashing waves while eating. This drive toward verisimilitude confirms both Blumenthal's self-professed theatricality as well as his willingness to use technology as an aid to the accomplishment of culinary representation.

Toward alimentary storytelling: Blumenthal's culinary evangelism

Ultimately, Blumenthal refers to his work at Fat Duck in terms of narrative, arguing that the experience of mimetic recognition exceeds the significance of eating on its own: "In the sense that we cook food and it's served to people, we're a restaurant. But that's not much, is it? The fact is the Fat Duck is about storytelling. I wanted to think about the whole approach of what we do in those terms" (Rayner 2015). Blumenthal has gone on to promote his version of culinary storytelling in elaborate experiments in theatrical dining, famously recorded in popular television programs and books. For example, in a televised series of thirteen "fantastical feasts," a half-dozen of which were also published as a "culinary adventure story" in 2010's *Heston's Fantastical Feasts*, Blumenthal created one-off theatrical meals for small groups of diners. A culinary version of public humanities, the feasts offer complex edible explorations of literary figures and historical contexts. A Roald Dahl–inspired meal included lickable wallpaper and golden tickets. A Carême-inspired fairy tale feast involved a massive edible house, chicken testicle jelly beans, pea shoot beanstalks, and a chicken-skin infused chocolate egg inspired by the story of Jack the giant-killer. In a similar venture, Blumenthal set out to reclaim British cuisine's reputation in a television program and subsequent book, *Historic Heston* (2013). The series casts Blumenthal as a culinary historian, rescuing the reputation of British cuisine by resurrecting historic dishes in new contexts. Many of these dishes, such as the illusionistic Medieval Pome Dorres, a faux apple made of pork, create a double mimetic opportunity for the chef. The Apple of Gold, or Meat Fruit, as Blumenthal renames it, is in itself a mimetic culinary gesture, and Blumenthal's resurrection and recreation of the dish demonstrates the historical basis for culinary mimeticism. At the same time, "Meat Fruit" presents an additional mimetic opportunity. As it is "obvious that what the chef wanted above all was for the apple to be as convincing as possible," Blumenthal sets out to "take advantage of the latest equipment to create meat fruit that the medieval chef could only dream of" (2013, 61). The final "Meat Fruit," which uses mandarin orange gelatin wrapped around a foie gras parfait to evoke an incredibly successful initial visual mimesis of an orange, no doubt created the desired surprise in guests at Blumenthal's London restaurant, Dinner. But the dish goes further. Through Blumenthal's dramaturgical framing, it also constructs an edible argument on behalf of Blumenthal's approach to cuisine. This mimetic orange, composed of elegantly prepared foodstuffs and realized impeccably through the use of contemporary technique merged with historical research, demonstrates that food can convey ideas while also evoking pleasure.

This commitment to culinary representation has driven not only the evolution of the Fat Duck and Dinner, but also Blumenthal's experiments with cuisine outside restaurant contexts. Working in institutional spaces like hospitals and schools, Blumenthal has pushed beyond the confines of the restaurant to demonstrate the potential of culinary mimeticism to serve meaningful purposes. Blumenthal's interest in the transformative power of culinary mimeticism is perhaps best captured in his work with a UK children's hospital using multisensory mimetic cuisine to create positive associations for children reluctant to eat (Highfield 2010). In his hospital menus, Blumenthal deploys mimetic appeals to a single sense, such as the sweet shop-scented balloons, and theatrical presentation techniques, such as liquid nitrogen ice cream created at a child's bedside, to create an overall representation of something on the order of Willy Wonka's workshop. Enticing children to eat, in this approach, has more to do with conjuring a feeling of delight by evoking a combination of positive memory and culinary fantasy than it does with convincing children of the value of healthy eating.

Recorded in the first episode of 2011's *Heston's Mission Impossible*, Blumenthal's advocacy of fun food kicks off with the Herculean task of renovating a hospital menu that is nominally healthful but revolting to young diners. In the episode's opening scenes, the celebrity chef immediately identifies the problem as a lack of pleasure, specifically of fun, drawing the ridicule of the hospital chefs, who argue that menu renovation is not so simple. It's a set piece of manufactured controversy familiar to even occasional viewers of reality television, but the scene also starkly contrasts two culinary philosophies: utilitarian and straightforward versus hedonistic and extravagant. Perhaps unsurprisingly, given his prior experiments with fantastical feasts, Blumenthal's first impulse in proving the skeptical hospital chefs wrong is to mimetically enthrall his young diners. In a bid to prove pleasure connects with nutrition, the chef takes the children to Legoland and serves them a meal designed to prove that culinary fun, treated as inseparable from culinary representation, is essential to enticing children to eat healthy foods. Blumenthal serves a series of vegetables masquerading as sweets, including fennel pastels, beet candy, and a carrot lollipop, each of which the children enjoy before learning their true composition. Responding to the revelation of the foods' vegetable content with joyful expressions of shock and playful retroactive revulsion, the children confirm that mimetic disguise effectively engages them with food. The experience of mimetic trickery is inherently pleasurable, creating a sense of culinary adventure. In an inversion of the Nouvelle Cuisine's reverence for the authenticity of ingredients, this carrot is more than a carrot; it is an experience of emotional and intellectual resonance, attended with surprise and intrigue. The final dish Blumenthal serves the children, his most successful, confirms this notion. The chef uses an anti-griddle to instantaneously freeze exotic ingredients like lychee mousse and mango puree in the convincing shape of a fried egg. The children eagerly dig in, now willing confederates in the mimetic dining experience.

Despite winning over child diners, the program positions adult chefs and administrators as Blumenthal's adversaries. A moment in which Blumenthal shares his famed "Sound of the Sea" with the hospital chefs fills viewers in on Blumenthal's style while driving the challenge home. The chefs are disgusted not only with the dish's seafood-flavored jelly beans but also with the dish's theatrical nature. While Blumenthal wins the chefs over by demonstrating that the sound of the sea does indeed evoke food memories in young diners, the hospital's head of catering remains convinced that his approach to hospital cuisine is unnecessarily convoluted, expensive, and labor intensive. According to the administrator, cooking "on cloud nine" seems far too impractical to implement in a hospital (*Heston's Mission Impossible* 1.1). Yet in the end, Blumenthal's mimetic lunch and dinner menus win over the administration due to their success with young diners. After witnessing children enjoying Blumenthal's "Bet You Can't Eat That" menu, including a stuffed tomato "eyeball," a kiwi-based "snot shake," a passion fruit worm dessert, and a vegetable-based "vomit soup," the formerly reluctant chefs and board members agree that fun in dining is worth the effort after all. Again Blumenthal's work here is doubly mimetic, deploying representational tactics to infuse additional sensory and emotional meaning into his cuisine for his young diners while also staging a televised drama of stodgy rejection and subsequent acceptance of pleasure as a wholesome part of culinary experience.

Perhaps precisely because of this interest in mimetic pleasure, Blumenthal's efforts, however successful, also inspire familiar critiques. For instance, Liz Evans, the chair of the National Nurses Nutrition Group, expressed measured support for Blumenthal's endeavors to improve the taste of hospital food for geriatric patients, layered with a distinction between necessary and excessive culinary experience: "All hospital patients need simple, tasty wholesome food that will stimulate their appetites and promote their recovery. Providing that this is taken into consideration, we wish Mr Blumenthal well" (Dean 2010, 8). The clarification that simplicity and wholesomeness are "all hospital patients need" suggests a concern that Blumenthal's renowned interest in flavor, technique, and technology invites the dangers of excess. But Blumenthal's hospital work aims to offer a powerful counterargument to Evans's underlying assumptions, which treat the nutritional aspects of food as divorced from or even opposed to the emotional and sensory pleasures of dining. Using his high profile as a celebrity chef, Blumenthal advocates for rethinking the supposed opposition between meaning and pleasure, advocating a culinary mimeticism in which each is intensified by the other.

Ferran Adrià and the theory and practice of culinary creativity

As Blumenthal began his exploration of culinary dramaturgy, Ferran Adrià pursued a parallel course in his small fine dining establishment on the Catalan coast, approaching cuisine with an aim of pure creativity. While Adrià's formal pursuit of culinary innovation began in 1987, he developed many of his signature mimetic approaches, from spherical ravioli to deconstructed dishes, in the mid-1990s, just as Blumenthal began developing his own approach to culinary mimeticism. Both chefs began consulting with scientists to further their culinary aims in the 1990s. Though Blumenthal's formal engagements with scientific research predate Adrià's, both chefs have also published work in scientific journals (see for instance Fu et al. 2014, Dermiki et al. 2013). As two of the chefs most responsible for developing this new turn in cooking, Adrià and Blumenthal soon became friends and colleagues. Working in the spirit of open collaboration they espouse in the "Statement on the 'New Cookery'," the two chefs shared cooking techniques. For instance, Adrià's use of soda siphons to create whipped cream and culinary foams inspired Blumenthal's pioneering nitrogen-frozen desserts, such as his nitrogen-frozen green tea mousse, in 2001 (Blumenthal 2009, 135). Moreover, each chef worked diligently to develop practical and theoretical understandings of the nature of gastronomic creativity, culinary representation, and alimentary experience. While Blumenthal has worked largely in the public eye, bringing culinary representation to hospital trays and television screens, Adrià's focus on pure creativity garnered the attention of the elite art world. After over a decade of collaboration with artists and multiple exhibits of his working methods, service pieces, and photographs of his dishes in major museums, Adrià became the first chef ever featured in the twelfth international documenta art exhibition in 2007. Given his position as a pioneering chef whose early experiments inspired even his co-authors in the "Statement on the 'New Cookery'," I turn now to an extended discussion of Adrià's culinary philosophy and practice.

Like Blumenthal, Adrià's culinary innovations are both expansive and critical to the development of culinary mimeticism. During his tenure as head chef at elBulli from 1987 to 2011, Adrià positioned creativity itself as the driving force behind his gastronomic practice and relied upon the concept of total art to bring all aspects of human experience within the compass of the chef's aesthetic vision, a move Joshua Abrams describes as the creation of a culinary *gesamtkunstwerk* (Abrams 2013, 14). Famous for his iconoclastic approach to culinary technique, Adrià's technological innovations often, perhaps understandably, dominate narratives about his work. Still, the chef's development of theories of human experience that reconsider the relationship between sensation and intelligence are of as great a significance to a wide array of scientific, humanistic, and creative disciplines. Though his work has implications across these areas of inquiry and beyond, for the purposes of this study

I approach Adrià as a gastronomic artist and philosopher who influenced a generation of chefs to think creatively about all aspects of cuisine. I examine two critical aspects of Adrià's body of work as they relate to the mimetic turn in contemporary cuisine: his articulation of a creativity-driven culinary philosophy and his exploration of dining as a performance event. In each aspect of his work, from his initial experiments at elBulli to his latest restaurant venture, Heart Ibiza, a collaboration with Cirque du Soleil, Adrià reconfigures the relationship between sensation and intelligence, and thus pleasure and meaning, by proving food a medium capable of conveying representational significance.

On creativity and not copying: mimesis and meaning in Adrià's culinary philosophy

In tracing the origin of his transformation from a traditional chef to the uncontested leader of the culinary avant garde, Adrià consistently references a line from French chef Jacques Maximin: "creativity means not copying."[5] The exhortation not to copy, significant enough to Adrià that his meticulous catalog of elBulli dishes begins in 1987, the date when he put away his cookbooks and began developing new recipes, establishes the centrality of creativity in Adrià's cuisine. His devotion to this simple adage underpins most of Adrià's culinary theory and practice. As a necessary outgrowth of this turn toward creativity, Adrià developed both a discourse of cuisine and the notion of cuisine as a mode of discourse. Driven by a mantra that distinguishes originality from copying without denigrating mimesis, Adrià ushered avant garde culinary practice into a new era of experimentation with gastronomy as a creative and communicative medium.

The choice to focus primarily on creativity led Adrià to construct not only a theory of cuisine, but a theory of culinary creativity. Recognizing his contributions to the field of creativity, a 2007 *Journal of Organizational Behaviors* article identified Adrià as an "institutional entrepreneur," specifically noting his innovation in the discourse surrounding cookery as a driving force behind the new wave in contemporary avant garde cuisine (Svejenova et al. 2007). Adrià, the authors argue, transformed modern cuisine by shifting his focus from reproducing high-quality classic recipes to specifically cultivating creativity, a process that led, significantly, to theoretical engagement with the processes, products, and outcomes of cooking. Adrià's interest in creativity led him to close elBulli for a six-month creative development period each year. During this focused period of creative practice, Adrià and his team worked on flavors, textures, techniques, and service for multiple dishes at once. Beginning with an idea, Adrià's staff worked with a range of creative techniques, including free association, adaptation, deconstruction, and minimalism, as well as a dish's visual, structural, or technological attributes, to begin developing new recipes (Adrià 2009). Each creative period involved research on multiple ideas simultaneously, creating a synergistic exploration of culinary possibilities. Examining technology, chefs invented new tools and serviceware like scent spoons and spherification rigs while also searching the shelves of hardware stores to find existing tools to put to new purposes, like the electric screwdrivers they used to create the "sweet olive oil spring" mentioned at the opening of this chapter. Exploring flavor, chefs pored over the archive of elBulli's previous dishes while also searching out novel ingredients from foodways around the world. Before tackling a prototype dish to be tested against initial diner experience, elBulli chefs conducted extensive tests, discussion, and analysis, recorded in the restaurant's creative archives. Each final elBulli dish, carefully photographed at each state of its development, also joined the extensive archive. Thus the drive toward creativity, founded in the notion of "not copying," led Adrià to create a massive archive of culinary innovation, delineating multiple processes for devising new culinary techniques and applications. This systematic exploration of culinary creativity, undertaken simultaneously with Harold McGee and Hervé This's investigations into the science of cooking and Blumenthal's experiments in alimentary perception, provided the necessary conditions for the dissemination of ideas that helped nurture the contemporary gastronomic avant garde. Moreover, Adrià's vision of cooking as a creative enterprise led him to a deep exploration of the nature of culinary representation.

Adrià's distinction between creativity and copying helps stake out the territory of contemporary culinary representation. In defining culinary creativity, Adrià distinguishes between a solely imitative approach and an innovative technique which generates something new, seeing the former as a stepping stone to the latter. At the first level of a chef's development stands the culinary repertoire, a set of dishes that chefs learn to execute and against which their skills may be judged by critics and diners. Chefs distinguish their mastery of technique, at least at first, by imitating the masters who came before. Yet Adrià casts prolonged repetition of the culinary repertoire as a scourge to creativity, arguing "years of recreating and copying create culinary 'baggage'" (Adrià et al. 2008, 519). Contrary to the notion that culinary mimeticism betrays a superficial focus on surfaces, Adrià positions representation as the antidote to culinary stagnation, a way to deepen chefs' and diners' engagement with cuisine. After achieving mastery of the culinary repertoire, Adrià identifies a new level of achievement: creativity. The creative chef pursues the development of culinary practices rooted not in flawless reproduction, but in ability to communicate ideas and evoke emotions through the use of unique and new ingredients, techniques, preparations, and presentations (Adrià et al. 2008, 136–137). Thus while Adrià resists imitation per se, mimetic reproduction and recognition stands as a necessary engagement for chefs at every level of their development, as well as a signifier of their developing culinary abilities. It is precisely the chef's ability to bring technique, ingredients, and ideas together to create new meanings and evoke other times, places, and memories that signifies mastery.

In addition to its significance in evaluating a chef's abilities, Adrià has positioned representation as a central part of the creative exchange between chefs, servers, and diners. This engagement proves central not only to the notion of cooking as an art, but as a form of meaning-making. Adrià has repeatedly asserted that cooking functions as a mode of discourse: "Cooking is a language through which all the following properties may be expressed: harmony, creativity, happiness, beauty, poetry, complexity, magic, humour, provocation, and culture" (Hamilton and Todolí 2009, 281). In casting cooking as its own language, Adrià draws another important distinction: cuisine is not merely like art, but rather is its own art form, with its own representational mechanisms. Adrià has repeatedly resisted any suggestion that he personally transformed cooking from a craft into an art, arguing instead that he recognized the significance of creativity to culinary art, seeing something that had always been present (Svejenova et al. 2007, 554). This assertion of cuisine as always artful reveals a key feature of Adrià's culinary discourse. Where critics of mimetic cuisine may decry its movement away from everyday contexts of eating, Adrià reverses that flow, asserting that meaningful alimentary experience always stems from the same creativity that motivates his approach to cooking. Adrià addresses the relationship between quotidian and artful cookery in his assertion that "gastronomy begins when the primary necessity – to feed oneself – ceases. It is from this realization that conscious pleasure is born" (Adrià et al. 2008, 147). This "conscious pleasure" depends upon a transition from simple necessity to purposeful creativity, enabling a higher form of eating, an engagement with food beyond sustenance. In other words, just as a chef must master culinary repertoire on the way to true creativity, Adrià argues the diner should already be sustained before meaningful gastronomy is possible.

In describing the necessary conditions for this meaningful gastronomy, Adrià also links food and knowledge, noting that "there is another pleasure possible, particularly with avant-garde cooking: reasoning, the ability to intersect, to compare, to detect elements that are not simply sensory – the sense of humor, of play, deceit, 'decontextualisation', creative innovation" (Jouary 2011, 147). In Adrià's culinary philosophy, sensory information travels alongside intelligible and philosophical insight, initiating a pleasure which exceeds the physical even as it springs from it. Adrià rejects any real distinction between the five traditional senses and the intellect, classifying intellectual pleasure as a "sixth sense" (including, for example, memory, recognition, surprise, contemplation, and other reactions to gastronomic experience as sensory reactions) (Adrià et al. 2008, 320–321). This intellectual pleasure corresponds with Benjaminian recognition, uniting the mimetic faculty with the senses as a fundamentally embodied experience. Noting "our capacity to think is what makes us most different from animals," Adrià seizes on intellectual engagement as the most significant aspect of human activity before staking a claim to cooking and eating as means of achieving uniquely embodied forms of knowledge (Jouary 2011, 147). In this Platonic pleasure beyond pleasure, Adrià does not promote a sensory epistemology, but rather an epistemology of gastronomy.

Because this model of alimentary knowledge depends on pleasures such as surprise and recognition, Adrià's model of gastronomic epistemology also requires a split between diner and chef, creation and consumption, in which the chef-artist crafts a culinary representation for a diner who brings all of her sensory, intellectual, and emotional capabilities to bear in the experience of mimetic eating. For Adrià, the chef is styled as an "emitter," using his judgment and knowledge of cuisine, as well as his creativity, to generate new dishes. The server becomes a "transmitter," controlling the timing of the event and conveying both technical instructions for dining, culinary dramaturgy, and emotional content that nurtures the chef's desired social atmosphere throughout the meal. The diner, on the other hand, becomes a "receptor," a term that implies a certain passivity but also a sense of the eater as an essential part of the language of cooking. The chef completes his culinary ambitions in the diner/receptor's experience of his work. If the diner leaves transformed, with memories of the event of dining that persist, the chef succeeds (Adrià et al. 2008, 320).[6] This notion of culinary experience that merges pleasure, communication, and transformation helps explain the significance of mimesis in Adrià's culinary theory.

While against copying per se, Adrià's model of culinary creativity insists that cuisine must innovate within its own historical, technical, and discursive frameworks. In fact, he positions cuisine as a discursive system in which creativity depends on mimetic play rather than total originality itself: "Since the innovative creator is aware that everything already exists in some form, thanks to his knowledge he will be able to access what very few people see, and to offer something new ... he will open a breach through which new possibilities can be foreseen" (Parasecoli 2001, 68). In this model of culinary creativity, the chef relies on understanding of culinary history in order to enable a creative rupture. This process of intimately understanding the logic of a dish, cuisine, or process before "opening a breach" recalls Adrià's famous preoccupation with deconstruction, a notion he originally borrowed from architectural discourse but which he also acknowledges as connected to Derridean philosophy.

By popularizing culinary deconstruction, still a major influence on international avant garde gastronomy, Adrià infused theory into cuisine in a way that surpassed prior efforts, tearing open just the sort of breach he considered a gateway toward truly creative cuisine. Adrià has explained his understanding of deconstruction in some detail, elaborating both its relationship to Derrida's concept and also its dependency on representation and illusion (see for example Adrià et al. 2008; Jouary 2011). For Adrià, deconstruction is something like a culinary language game, in which a classic referent is destabilized through a manipulation of one or more of its typical attributes (temperature or texture, for instance) while its essential flavor persists or intensifies. This culinary play with an original recipe/referent bears a familial resemblance to the Derridean practice of deconstructive reading of texts: the sorting out of an internal logic, flipping of expectations, construction of a new logic, and even the creation of a new reading that may be similarly deconstructed. Culinary deconstruction is also similarly derided in some quarters as superficial, overly intellectual, mocking, or inherently damaging to cuisine (see for example Dunlop 2013). Still, the process of eating a deconstructed dish demonstrates the operation of Adrià's collaboration between chef, server, and diner in creating meaningful alimentary experience. As the dish is served and eaten, a short drama ensues. First, the chef and server facilitate the development of a diner's expectations, which usually hinge upon hearing the name of the dish and seeing it on the serving vessel. Then, in eating, the diner experiences a planned peripity, a shocking reversal of expectations, or an edible anagnorisis as they discover something they knew all along but which they now experience in a shocking new light. This delight depends on illusion in two ways. First, the real relationship with the referent dish must be disguised or made surprising. Second, the dish must recognizably recall the original referent even as it upends its logic. For instance, Adrià's famous deconstructed Spanish omelet reproduces the ingredients and flavors of a classic dish in a way that creates immediate recognition in diners, but rethinks the composition, textures, arrangement, and presentation of the dish. The resulting sherry glass filled with layers of potato foam, pureed onion, egg sabayon, and fried potato crumbs both surprises diners with something new and reminds them of a familar referent. Conversely, Adrià's spherified olives at first look "real," only to be revealed as "fakes" when they burst in the mouth. As soon as this initial reversal pierces the diner's awareness, the second reversal occurs as the diner realizes that the flavor of the spherified olive is more intense than their prior experience of "real" olives. Furthermore, this process of deconstruction may restart again and again. For instance, José Andrés deconstructed spherified olives in his aforementioned appetizer of "Adrià" olives. In this dish, diners test the "real" against the "deconstructed" dish and again throw the logic of the construction into a new and surprising relationship. The diner's mimetic faculty, the ability to recognize both the mimetic context of the dish and to interpret its representational offer, becomes a crucial factor in both the meaning and the pleasure of the experience of eating.

Adrià's deconstructive technique represents one of several means by which he has influenced the theory of gastronomy. However, deconstruction stands as an iconic example of his theory in its aim to destabilize a diner's culinary expectations to create a new experience. For some diners, this experience even calls to mind the creation of a new world. A sense of elBulli's union of pleasure and meaning pervades accounts by the artists, critics, and dignitaries who dined at elBulli's "documenta table" in 2007. Among the most intriguing responses was architect Aldo Duelli's, which emphasized the mimetic aspects of the experience as key to its mystical and captivating quality, which Duelli indicated far outlasted the momentary pleasure of the meal: "I'm still not quite back from the long journey. I see myself seated at elBulli in my thoughts almost every day…It's a world of its own, a little parallel world that is related to what we know, but which is nonetheless incomparable" (Hamilton and Todolí 2009, 144). Duelli's experience of elBulli is of a strikingly effective culinary mimesis. Though nothing physical is left of it after the meal ends, this meal constructs an imaginary reality that is both immaterial and unforgettable for the diner. This imaginary world, for Duelli, shares distinct elements with a Platonic vision of imitation, but reverses the narrative of Plato's allegory of the cave. Instead of moving away from representation and into truth, Duelli describes an intimate, embodied mimesis that leaves him knowing the world better than ever before: "I felt like a blind man who thought he had been seeing clearly … The raspberry fondant with wasabi and raspberry vinegar is not a raspberry dish – it's an experience of the 'idea,' the 'essence' of raspberry. You could not eat a raspberry in a more intense, pure or direct way" (Hamilton and Todolí

2009, 147). This transcendent description of a raspberry suggests that, while for Plato imitation may threaten the purity of an ideal through the degrading process of material reproduction, in the hands of an innovative chef, mimetic repetition enhances the meaning of alimentary experience by focusing a diner on the immediate embodied knowledge produced by culinary mimesis. Duelli declares "I've eaten at elBulli and the world is no longer what it was" (2009, 147). Like Plato's famous subject exiting the cave and seeing the real world for the first time, the diner newly recognizes his own inability to comprehend the world prior to dining at elBulli. Adrià's raspberry has transformed the world by making it apprehensible to him, connecting him with a truth he could otherwise never have conceived.

This notion of a world transformed through new culinary experience pervades commentary on Adrià's work, both positive and negative. For enthusiasts, Adrià blew open the barriers of culinary experience. For detractors, he ruined a generation of chefs. Fellow Spanish chef Santi Santamaria went so far as to accuse Adrià of poisoning his guests with the chemicals used in his famous deconstructions, arguing that elBulli's food aimed to "impress rather than satisfy" (Govan 2008). An anonymous British chef, after comparing a photomontage of elBulli dishes on display at a London art gallery to an abortion, opined to art blogger Fuschia Dunlop that "He's fucked it all up," meaning that Adrià had destroyed the profession by persuading a generation of chefs to leave behind traditional cookery (Dunlop 2013). Perhaps in defense against these well-known critiques, an almost compulsive delineation of the relationship between transcendent innovation and superficial imitation pervades diner accounts of elBulli. Painter and critic Adrian Serle, for instance, treats imitation as a *pharmakon* in his discussion of his meal. Comparing Adrià to Picasso and lesser chefs to derivative later Cubists, Serle argues that imitation in the wrong hands can go "horribly wrong" (Hamilton and Todolí 2009, 65). But skilled and judicious innovators can imitate safely, Serle suggests, as he praises a series of gelatinized bites of water that represent entire cultures (Thailand, Japan, and Mexico), marveling that "with each mouthful, you savour an entire culinary tradition" (Hamilton and Todolí 2009, 70). This discourse of gustatory power mirrors and intensifies Brillat-Savarin's image of the all-consuming, all-knowing body of the imperial gastronome: Adrià and his guest become eaters of worlds as Serle narrates them swallowing entire cultures whole. Serle's sense of whirling disorientation that triggers critical engagement with alimentary experience, a bewilderment created in part by the mimetic power of this culinary work, leads many of the documenta observers to cast Adrià as a special case, a virtuoso capable of doing more with food than his peers. In his own account, artist Richard Hamilton revisits the challenges that have plagued the cuisine-as-art conversation throughout philosophy. Like many critics who analyze chefs at the mimetic vanguard, he threads the needle, considering Adrià an exceptional chef who defies categories. His nearest artistic analogue, Hamilton suggests, might be Duchamp. Acknowledging that "definitions are not helpful in determining Adrià's area of competence," Hamilton decides that nevertheless Adrià is a de facto artist by virtue of his inclusion in documenta 12 (2009, 50). Hamilton quickly zeroes in on theatre as the form able to analogize Adrià's scope, aesthetic complexity, and attention to temporal elements like the flow of patron experience, the repetition of themes, and the dramaturgical arrangement of courses in a system that Hamilton calls a "language of food" (2009, 50) to be staged in elBulli, a "theatre of its own making" (2009, 57). Yet while the theatre becomes a means of contextualizing Adrià's genius in Hamilton's account, elBulli's theatricality also spurred one of the most common sets of critiques levied at Adrià's food: insubstantiality, a lack of seriousness, and, notably, waste.

Cuisine as collaborative art: on waste, theatricality, ephemerality, and artful labor

The question of waste, the concern that labor, capital, and resources (foodstuffs themselves, most prominently) might be better used elsewhere, or that the largesses of dining-as-art cannot be justified in a world of famine and lack, arises immediately in connection with Adrià's work. Philosopher Jean-Paul Jouary, in the introduction to his text on the chef's work, defends Adrià's cuisine on the basis of humanistic significance, arguing that despite the pressing concerns of war, famine, declining natural resources, and growing inequality, human life derives its meaning from cultural experiences that create "multiple possibilities of shared pleasure" (Jouary 2011, 14). The expense and ephemerality of avant garde dining necessitates this disclaimer, spurring Jouary's reference to famine and the waste of resources. elBulli in particular indulged in well-documented wastefulness in its insistence on perfection. Accounts of imperfect food tossed into the trash litter the pages of Lisa Abend's account of labor at elBulli in *The Sorcerer's Apprentices* (2011), for instance, as the journalist narrates the immense pressure on the restaurant's unpaid *stagieres*. However, something beyond this concern over waste motivates the urge to justify avant garde cuisine. For instance, Blumenthal handily defeats critics of his hospital menus on the basis of his cuisine's efficacy; the results justify the effort. Rather, the collision of food and art requires defense, specifically defense of aesthetic and sensory pleasures for their own sake. Adrià's cuisine, an example of cooking-as-art for art's sake, provides us a chance to see, especially in its theatricality, culinary mimeticism's dependence on visible labor as a performed unproductivity, an inefficiency that is, nevertheless, meaningful on its own terms. This performance of waste and excess, of artful inefficiency, both requires philosophical justification and simultaneously disavows that justification in a reinforcement of its performance of inherent meaningfulness. The dishes of elBulli, which use food as a means of representation, must walk this fine line in order to reconcile the chef's commitment to a sense of representation as deeply meaningful with his insistence on proximal sensory experience as inherently valuable.

While tension between sensory pleasure, the everyday acts of eating and cooking, and the human mimetic faculty may come to the fore in Adrià's cuisine, they're also long-established in philosophies of taste and culture. As geographer Yi-Fu Tuan suggests, the combination of food and art may "make any thinking person uneasy" since "in these activities, biological imperatives are worrisomely joined to sensual delight, the killing and evisceration of living things to art, animality to the claims of culture, taste (a process in the mouth's cavern) to that refined achievement known as 'good taste'" (2005, 227). For Adrià, this uneasy relation between pleasure and destruction is resolved in creativity, the development of something new that reframes waste as sacrifice in service of a meaningful goal. Since Adrià's goal is creation itself, his cuisine cannot be justified in terms of external effects on society quite as easily as Blumenthal's carrot lollipop. Adrià's food does not entice sick children to eat their vegetables. It simply shows a few quite privileged diners new worlds. Thus defending Adrià's brand of culinary mimeticism against charges of wastefulness necessitates a defense of cuisine as art. Moreover, Adrià's artful cuisine does not align with the material, tangible arts of painting or even poetry, but with the ephemeral forms of performance. Yet while Prince critiques culinary opera as a scourge on cuisine, it is through affiliation with the performing arts that Adrià establishes his cuisine's ethical basis. Through this emphasis on theatricality, Adrià positions culinary mimeticism as valuable precisely *because* of its ephemerality, collectivity, and irreproducibility, each of which reinforce the sense of mimetic alimentary experience as generative of an embodied knowledge that is otherwise inaccessible.

Though he also likened his work to poetry and to filmmaking, Adrià often turned to the theatre in articulating his vision of culinary artistry. For instance, Adrià refers to the five phases of a tasting menu as acts and the unoccupied restaurant as an empty stage (Adrià et al. 2008, 5).[7] In part, it is the collective nature of contemporary mimetic cuisine, which demands meticulous work from a brigade of chefs and an army of servers, that grounds Adrià's interest in theatricality. Using the model of the theatre, Adrià conceives of a collective creative effort that yields ephemeral but meaningful work, rebutting critiques that his cuisine is inherently wasteful. This notion of collective creation as the heart of what makes a dining experience artful recurs often in diners' reflections on elBulli, as in documenta 12 participant Helga Bender-Wolanski's observation that the experience of the meal evokes "a workshop in the Middle Ages or in the Renaissance, where the project came from one person, but the complete work of art was achieved when many worked on it" (Hamilton and Todolí 2009, 186). In this collaborative and theatrical definition of culinary labor, the individual creative genius animates many cooks, servers, and diners working synergistically to enliven the artwork. Furthermore, the significance of the event lies in the meticulous creative labor invested in the meal as much as in its temporality or interactivity. Documenta guest Marleine Chedraoui reinforces this notion in her comment that each dish "lets you guess at the abundance of decisions that have gone into them, from the ingredients and their combination, the procedures corresponding to their preparation, to the waiters' instructions on how to eat them" (Hamilton and Todolí 2009, 159). Thus a diner's sense of the meaning of the event springs in part from the awareness that her own lengthy experience is but the tip of a larger iceberg of thought and care on the part of a team of creative laborers. The tantalizing relationship between this massive outlay of effort, the incredibly thin financial margin of the endeavor, and the ephemerality of the experience, so famously hard to completely recount, comes together in an alchemical process to frame the diner's subjective experience as artful in itself.

The importance of Adrià's theatrical style in priming patrons to experience dining as artful pervades the vast archive of diner responses to elBulli. Ephemerality becomes a critical factor in establishing the value of both theatrical performance and mimetic dining. It's not that diners cannot remember eating. Rather, each individual act of eating is fleeting and cannot be experienced exactly the same way over and over, rendering the immediate experience of eating valuable while distinguishing the act of dining from the critical reflection it inspires, which extends into the future. Adrià highlights the importance of this ephemeral alimentary experience in his *Nature* interview, using theatricality to explain the subjectivity of dining: "I'm expressing myself and everyone perceives it in a different way, like a piece of theatre. Each person takes away something new" (Adrià 2009, 267). Continuing on the theme of subjectivity, Adrià implies a common necessity of experiential knowledge between theatre, cuisine, and science, arguing that "It's not possible to grasp our work without seeing it for yourself – it would be like trying to describe eating an Amazonian fruit you've never tried" (Adrià 2009, 267). Here Adrià carefully differentiates between culinary memory and culinary experience, each of which informs but remains distinct from the other, by positioning embodied experience as the *sine qua non* of culinary knowledge.

Adrià reinforced this emphasis on ephemeral, embodied experience by keeping track of each dish consumed by each elBulli patron and ensuring that no diner ate the same meal twice. Since each year's menu, created during the annual development period and continually adjusted over the course of the six-month active season, closed at the end of the year never to be repeated, the experience of elBulli evoked a theatrical season, with each year's themes and explorations different from those before and after. In turn, Adrià's seasonal closures gave elBulli menus a temporal specificity that evoked the seasonal timing of the Japanese kaiseki cuisine that helped inspire his culinary style (Adrià 2012).[8] For instance, due to its sensitivity to humidity, "Pineapple paper tramontana with Parmesan," could only be prepared when the tramontana, a seasonal dry wind, blew in from the north (Adrià et al. 2008, 103). Thus both through the specificity of its individual dishes and the commitment to remake the menu each year, elBulli's menus remained distinct from not only other restaurants, but from those of each preceding day, week, month, or year. At elBulli, each experience of eating was thus, literally, unrepeatable. This emphasis on each meal's impermanence foregrounds the restaurant's unique relationship to time and space, situating elBulli as a version of Foucault's heterotopia (Foucault 1986). The restaurant, like the theatre or the library, opens again and again onto new experience. Like both of these famous examples, elBulli invited those who visit to travel without moving, experiencing other places and times, and in some cases entirely new worlds, through the embodied exercise of their mental, sensory, and affective mimetic faculties. Moreover, in Adrià's model, the restaurant exceeds the theatre or the library in its ability to evoke other times or places, real or imaginary, by engaging the entire body and mind. Thus, Adrià's creativity-driven, theatrical mimeticism melds the sensory and the intelligible to create a transcendent awareness that persists not despite but because of its immediacy and ephemerality: a uniquely alimentary insight. Perhaps one source of Adrià's appeal to philosophers is precisely this investment in tasting as knowledge, a phenomenon often considered either impossible or unlikely.

elBulli and after

Throughout his pioneering work at elBulli, Adrià's overall project explores the complex terrain of creating sensory resemblances in order to conjure meaning, interpretation, and memory, and thus is deeply imbricated with culinary mimeticism and with the critical possibilities of a multisensory, embodied mimesis. Even at the level of the individual dish, mimetic approaches to cuisine remained important to Adrià at elBulli and beyond. His final menu upon the restaurant's closing in 2011 featured multiple mimetic dishes, including:

> A rose shaped of thinly sliced apple flesh served with "apple essence" spheres
> "Mimetic peanuts," a crispy peanut praline and peanut oil shell filled with multiple flavors
> Spherical olives
> Crispy soy matches with a gold leaf head that mimetically recreated the smell of a freshly-struck match
> "Bones" of shaved iced tea

These variations on some of the restaurant's most famous (and most-imitated) culinary experiments communicate the centrality of mimetic practice to not just elBulli, but to Adrià's culinary project. Prominently positioned among the restaurant's final forty-nine courses, they serve as representational touchstones that return the diner, again and again, to the vital fact of food's capability to conjure meanings, inspire new insights, and in doing so challenge any perceived firm division between sensation, emotion, and intelligence. And in their adventurous, boundary-pushing exploration of food's representational capacities, they forecast Adrià's later career as a culinary researcher.

Just as Blumenthal has pursued culinary innovation in surprising spaces, Adrià's endeavors since the closing of elBulli have expanded his research into creativity while freeing himself from the constraints of restaurants. In 2016 he opened an exhibit of his work alongside the art of fellow Spanish iconoclast Salvador Dalí at Florida's Gulf Coast Museum (Chua-Eoan 2016).[9] Meanwhile, elBulliLab, in conjunction with the elBulli Foundation, partners with chefs, Nobel laureates, creativity experts, the wealthy, and corporations like Dom Perignon to create culinary research and host events exploring the nature of creativity and cuisine (Stein 2015). Adrià's investment in creativity as a driving force behind all operations in his culinary empire has continued to draw attention far beyond traditional culinary discourse, from *Time* magazine (Luscombe 2014), to *Nature* (Adrià 2009), to the *Economist* ("Bulli for Him" 2014). Of course, the chef who said "creativity comes first; then comes the customer" also continues to pursue culinary innovation (Capdevila et al. 2015). Heart Ibiza, a collaboration between Ferran and Albert Adrià and Guy Laliberté, founder of Cirque du Soleil, opened in summer 2015 in the Ibiza Grand Hotel to great expectations (Ebeling 2016, Husa 2017). The restaurant pairs Adrià's cuisine and Cirque-style performance; Adrià's famous caipirinha sorbet is still served in a frozen lime, but at Heart may include a tableside magic show or an offering of a raw oyster served atop a live costumed mermaid reclining in an ice bath. Yet another venture, the still-developing Bullipedia, aims to collect an online compendium of culinary knowledge. As this book goes to press, construction is ongoing to transform the restaurant site of elBulli into elBulli1846, a research lab and gallery named for the number of dishes archived in elBulli's catalog of dishes (also the year of Escoffier's birth). Though the lab will not offer dining in a conventional sense, it will open approximately twenty times a year for culinary "experiences," often reserved for donors.

Adrià speaks of elBulli's transformation from restaurant to research space in terms of freedom. Specifically, Adrià foresees avoiding the repetition that he sees as antithetical to creativity, in which "artisanal reproduction" overshadows the thrill of pure creativity. Working outside the limitation of the restaurant, however, the chef becomes free to create outside the context of repetition or reproduction (Abend 2017). Thus, while Blumenthal's eater-centered approach to culinary innovation inspires a search for new kinds of diners, from hospital patients to airline passengers, Adrià's focus has shifted further from the context of everyday eating toward a more concentrated engagement with food itself. Interestingly, as Adrià's focus has shifted from running elBulli to exploring gastronomic creativity outside the confines of a restaurant structure, he has also shifted his discourse on labor. Fetishized photos of repetitive labor were a mainstay of representations of elBulli, with chefs meticulously cleaning glasses, arranging rocks, or painstakingly making yuba. In investing each meal with this attention to detail, these images suggest, the staff at elBulli make the restaurant an artful space. But Adrià's discourse of culinary creativity has evolved. From the standpoint of pure creativity rather than the subjective experience of the diner, the labor of executing the same dish for multiple customers over multiple evenings becomes a waste, siphoning away energy that could better be spent on innovating new dishes and techniques. By recontextualizing his work as culinary research, Adrià again reframes the significance of culinary labor. Just as his prior work constructed culinary labor as a collaborative art that enables a critical reflection on life itself, in his latest projects Adrià delineates a new category of pure culinary research, intensive creative work that advances the larger project of human creativity outside the context of sustenance entirely.

Beyond elBulli: toward the next generation of mimetic chefs

As their recent work demonstrates, both Adrià and Blumenthal have continued to explore the possibilities of mimetic cookery by moving outside the domain of the traditional restaurant. While they operate more squarely within popular culture, Blumenthal's fantastical feasts and hospital meals function similarly to Adrià's culinary research experiences. Each serves as a means of pushing beyond the boundaries of tables, plates, and social convention to examine the possibilities of culinary communication, creation, and transformation in new environments. Together, Adrià and Blumenthal's work represents the breadth of early approaches to culinary mimeticism, working in scientific and artistic contexts, and in popular and elite spaces, to develop a wide range of practical and theoretical approaches to uniting pleasure and meaning in culinary representation. In turn, the Chicago area chefs I discuss in the next chapter have transformed the culture of their restaurants to allow new culinary horizons to appear. In doing so, they changed the culinary landscape of one of the US's major metropolitan areas, developing a culture of mimetic cuisine that extends culinary mimeticism further, from fine dining to everyday contexts.

Notes

1 Andrés is only one of many chefs to produce elBulli homages on their own menus. Grant Achatz's Next Restaurant famously produced an entire menu of Adrià's dishes for 2012's elBulli menu. During his stint at Nashville's theatrical restaurant Catbird Seat, chef Erik Anderson included both savory (porcini and parmesan) and sweet (mocha) variations of elBulli's mimetic oreo (the original was flavored with olive).
2 Erving Goffman establishes a dramaturgical framework for understanding restaurant service and dining in *The Presentation of Self in Everyday Life* (1959). For a contemporary approach that expands upon this notion, see Joshua Abrams's discussion of the dramaturgy of avant garde dining (Abrams 2013). My usage of the term "dramaturgy" references a chef's intentional design of the social conventions of service, including not only server, chef, and diner interactivity but also instructions for eating, contextualizing information for individual dishes, menu design, and additional framing meant to influence diner expectations and perceptions, such as the use of sonic stimulus in Blumenthal's "Sound of the Sea."
3 Though his reviews were, at the time, strictly anonymous, the Ulterior Epicure, Bonjwing Lee, later revealed his identity in an interview with *Eater* (Ulla 2011).
4 Respect for culinary ancestors pervades each chef's work. Heston Blumenthal's *Fat Duck Cookbook* reads as a tale of culinary education, recounting the chef's initial intensive study of the cookbooks of the masters. Similarly, Adrià lists among his primary influences *El Practico*, the classic Spanish cooking manual deeply influenced, in turn, by Escoffier (Adrià et al. 2008, 32).
5 This statement is so pivotal to his development that Adrià marks the occasion of Maximin's famous statement, at an Escoffier foundation dinner in Cannes, in an entry for 1987 on the elBulli history section of his website (see www.elbulli.com/historia).
6 This notion of transmission may lack the complexity of Blumenthal's dramaturgical awareness of the relationship of expectation and meaning, but it's worth noting that Adrià himself included a more substantial feedback system in his kitchen table experience. With a characteristically methodical approach, Adrià referred to the use of the kitchen table as an observation experience for the chefs, who could adjust dishes based on their impressions of the success of each dish for kitchen table diners.
7 This reference recalls Peter Brook's empty space, a fitting resonance given the two innovators' similar interests in transformation, collaboration, and reinvention of the classics. As with Brook, one of Adrià's most profound innovations, aside from the food, involved rethinking the significance of the physical apparatus of the event.

8 Beyond acknowledging its influence on his own culinary style, Adrià cites kaiseki as a foundational influence on all Western haute cuisine. Grant Achatz's Next restaurant also highlighted kaiseki in 2012's "Kyoto" menu, discussed in Chapter 3. For more discussion of this influence, which has often been elided by emphasis on French trends like the Nouvelle Cuisine, themselves also indebted to kaiseki, see Brenner and Busico (2007) and McCarron (2017).
9 Dalí was also a resident of the Costa Brava near elBulli's location in Roses, Spain.

References

Abend, Lisa. 2011. *The Sorcerer's Apprentices: A Season in the Kitchen at Ferran Adrià's elBulli*. New York: Simon and Schuster.

Abend, Lisa. 2017. "How Ferran Adrià Took elBulli from Great Restaurant to Culinary Innovation Lab." *Newsweek*, April 22. www.newsweek.com/ferran-Adrià-elbulli-restaurants-cooking-and-food-food-culinary-arts-588146.

Abrams, Joshua. 2013. "Mise-en-plate: The scenographic imagination and the contemporary restaurant." *Performance Research* 18(3): 7–14. doi:10.1080/13528165.2013.816464.

Adrià, Ferran. 2009. "Q & A: Chemistry in the Kitchen." Interview by Jascha Hoffman. *Nature* 475(15): 267.

Adrià, Ferran. 2012 [2006]. Foreword. *Kaiseki: The Exquisite Cuisine of Kyoto's Kikunoi Restaurant*. Yoshihiro Murata. New York: Kodansha International.

Adrià, Ferran, Heston Blumenthal, Thomas Keller, and Harold McGee. 2006. "Statement on the 'New Cookery.'" *The Guardian*. Reprinted in Blumenthal, Heston. 2009 [2008]. *The Fat Duck Cookbook*: 126–127. London: Bloomsbury.

Adrià, Ferran, Juli Soler, and Albert Adrià. 2008. *A Day at elBulli: An insight into the ideas, methods, and creativity of Ferran Adrià*. London: Phaidon.

Birnbaum, Charlotte. 2009. "Alimentary School: Charlotte Birnbaum on Ferran Adrià and Futurist Cooking." *Artforum International* 48(2): 111–112.

Blumenthal, Heston. 2009 [2008]. *The Fat Duck Cookbook*. London: Bloomsbury.

Blumenthal, Heston. 2010. *Heston's Fantastical Feasts*. London: Bloomsbury.

Blumenthal, Heston. 2013. *Historic Heston Blumenthal*. London: Bloomsbury.

Brenner, Leslie and Michalene Busico. 2007. "Eating the Seasons." *Los Angeles Times*, May 15. articles.latimes.com/2007/may/16/food/fo-kaiseki16.

"Bulli for Him; Ferran Adrià." 2014. *Economist* 410(8878): 79.

Capdevila, Ignasi, Patrick Cohendet, and Laurent Simon. 2015. "Establishing New Codes for Creativity through Haute Cuisine: The Case of Ferran Adrià and elBulli." *Technology Innovation and Management Review* 5(7): 25–33.

Chua-Eoan, Howard. 2016. "Rock Star Chef Ferran Adrià Says Chefs Should Not Be Rock Stars." *Bloomberg*, September 15. www.bloomberg.com/news/articles/2016-09-15/rock-star-chef-ferran-Adrià-says-chefs-should-not-be-rock-stars.

Dean, Erin. 2010. "Heston's Helping Hand to Hospital Food Study." *Nursing Standard* 24(36): 8.

Dermiki, Maria, Rana Mounayar, Chutipapha Suwankanit, Jennifer Scott, Orla B. Kennedy, Donald S. Mottram, Margot A. Gosney, Heston Blumenthal, and Lisa Methven. 2013. "Maximising Umami Taste in Meat Using Natural Ingredients: Effects on Chemistry, Sensory Perception and Hedonic Liking in Young and Old Consumers." *Journal of the Science of Food and Agriculture* 93(13): 3312–3332.

Dunlop, Fuchsia. 2013. "ElBulli: Ferran Adrià and the Art of Food." July 10. www.fuchsiadunlop.com/el-bulli-ferran-Adrià-and-the-art-of-food.

Ebeling, Olivia. 2016. "An Immersive Food Fantasy at Heart Ibiza." *Essential Ibiza*, September 15. http://www.essentialibiza.com/news/an-immersive-food-fantasy-at-heart-ibiza/.

Escoffier, Georges Auguste. 2011 [1903]. *Le Guide Culinaire.* Translated by H. L. Cracknell and R. J. Kaufmann. New York: Wiley.
Foucault, Michel. 1986. "Of Other Spaces." Trans. Jay Miskowiec. *Diacritics* 16(1): 22–27. www.jstor.org/stable/464648.
Friedman, Amanda Moslé. 2004. "Heston Blumenthal: Sense and Sensibility Ingredients for Success." *Nation's Restaurant News,* August 16: 50.
Fu, Haohao, Yingzhe Liu, Ferran Adrià, Xueguang Shao, Wensheng Cai, and Christophe Chipot. 2014. "From Material Science to Avant-Garde Cuisine. The Art of Shaping Liquids into Spheres." *The Journal of Physical Chemistry* 118: 11747–11756. doi:10.1021/jp508841p.
Goffman, Erving. 1959. *The Presentation of Self in Everyday Life.* New York: Doubleday.
Gopnik, Blake. 2009. "Palate vs Palette: Avant-Garde Cuisine as Contemporary Art." *Washington Post,* September 23. www.washingtonpost.com/wp-dyn/content/article/2009/09/22/AR2009092200778.
Govan, Fiona. 2008. "Famed El Bulli Chef Ferran Adrià Accused of 'Poisoning' His Diners." *The Telegraph,* May 14. www.telegraph.co.uk/news/worldnews/europe/spain/1955806/Famed-El-Bulli-chef-Ferran-Adrià-accused-of-poisoning-his-diners.
Hamilton, Richard and Vicente Todolí, eds. 2009. *Food for Thought, Thought for Food.* Barcelona: Actar.
Heston's Mission Impossible. 2011. "NHS/Alder Hey Children's Hospital." Season 1, Episode 1. Produced by Jessica Honeyball. Cineworld.
Highfield, Roger. 2010. "Sweet Smelling Balloons Plus Jellyfish and Chips – Welcome to Heston Blumenthal's World." *New Scientist* 206(2763): 23.
Husa, Anders. 2017. "Heart Ibiza: The Greatest Show on Earth." *Foodie Stories.* https://andershusa.com/heart-ibiza-greatest-show-on-earth-ferran-Adrià-cirque-du-soleil-estrella-damm.
In Search of Perfection. 2006–2007. Executive Producer Gary Hunter. BBC Two.
Jouary, Jean-Paul with Ferran Adrià. 2011. *Ferran Adrià and elBulli: The Art, the Philosophy, the Gastronomy.* New York: Overlook.
Kitchen Chemistry with Heston Blumenthal. 2002. Discovery UK.
Luscombe, Belinda. 2014. "Ten Questions." *Time,* June 2: 60.
McCarron, Meghan. 2017. "The Japanese Origins of Modern Fine Dining." *Eater,* September 7. www.eater.com/2017/9/7/16244278/japanese-fine-dining-bocuse-tsuji-kaiseki.
Novero, Cecilia. 2010. *Antidiets of the Avant-garde: From Futurist Cooking to Eat Art.* Minneapolis, MN: University of Minnesota Press.
Parasecoli, Fabio. 2001. "Deconstructing Soup: Ferran Adrià's Culinary Challenges." *Gastronomica* 1(1): 60–73.
Puchner, Martin. 2002. "Manifesto = Theatre." *Theatre Journal* 54(3): 449–465. doi:10.1353/tj.2002.0095.
Puchner, Martin. 2010. "It's Not Over ('Til It's Over)." *New Literary History* 41(4): 915–928. www.jstor.org/stable/23012713.
Rayner, Jay. 2015. "Heston Blumenthal Interview: The Fat Duck Flies Again." *The Guardian,* August 23. www.theguardian.com/lifeandstyle/2015/aug/23/the-fat-duck-flies-again-heston-blumenthal.
Sorini, Alex Revelli, and Susanna Cutini. 2014. "Dining with Marinetti: The Manifesto of Futurist Cuisine." *Fine Dining Lovers,* February 15. www.finedininglovers.com/stories/futurism-cuisine-manifesto-dining-marinetti.
Stein, Sadie. 2015. "The Remarkable Ambition and Chaos of Ferran Adrià's ElBulli Lab." *Bon Appetit,* May 14. www.bonappetit.com/people/chefs/article/el-bulli-lab-ferran-Adrià.
Svejenova, Silviya, Carmelo Mazza, and Marcel Planellas. 2007. "Cooking up Change in Haute Cuisine: Ferran Adrià as an Institutional Entrepreneur." *Journal of Organizational Behavior* 28(5): 539–561. www.jstor.org/stable/30162577.

Tuan, Yi-Fu. 2005. "Pleasures of the Proximate Senses: Eating, Taste, and Culture." In *The Taste Culture Reader: Experiencing Food and Drink*, edited by Carolyn Korsmeyer, 226–234. New York: Berg.
Ulla, Gabe. 2011. "The Ulterior Epicure Finally Reveals His Identity." *Eater*, September 19. www.eater.com/2011/9/19/6649893/the-ulterior-epicure-finally-reveals-his-identity.
Ulterior Epicure. 2009. "M to the G." Review of The Fat Duck, London. January 25. ulteriorepicure.com/2009/01/25/review-m-to-the-g/.
Yeomans, Martin R., Lucy Chambers, Heston Blumenthal, and Anthony Blake. 2008. "The Role of Expectancy in Sensory and Hedonic Evaluation: The Case of Smoked Salmon Ice-cream." *Food Quality and Preference* 19(6): 565–573. doi:10.1016/j.foodqual.2008.02.009.

3

WHAT'S NEXT

Chicago's culture of culinary representation

Tire D'Erable

Maple taffy, snow, maple twig (*Chicago, IL, Next Restaurant: The Hunt, 2013*)

Our server deposits a metal trough atop our deerskin table covering. It's filled to the brim with icy snow, a reminder of the Midwestern winter from which we're just emerging into spring. Drizzling a thin stream of maple-bourbon taffy over the snow, the server invites us to use twigs to roll small lollipops of the candy. As we do, we reminisce about childhood experiences of snow ice cream. Two Southerners, we imagine never-experienced trips to maple sugar shacks, dipping fresh twigs into boiling sap to steal a taste of sweet syrup. We wonder: is this what Northern winters taste like?

Having laid out the international roots of contemporary mimetic cuisine in the preceding chapter, I turn to a close study of emergent trends in culinary representation. As the scene above indicates, a new generation of chefs have both embraced and advanced the representational thrust of Adrià and Blumenthal's avant garde cuisine, pushing further into the realm of theatrically mimetic dining. This chapter examines the work of two Chicago chefs at the vanguard of culinary mimeticism in the US: Grant Achatz's representational innovations at Aviary, Alinea, and Next and the late Homaru Cantu's futuristically mimetic work at Moto and iNG. While these chefs' mimetic tactics link their work through a particular collection of techniques, their interventions also coalesce around the project of educating the public about the value of culinary mimeticism. However, each chef pursues this project with different aims. For Achatz, a constellation of Chicago restaurants creates space to establish the chef as artist and the restaurant as a mimetic construct. Meanwhile, for Cantu, culinary mimeticism enabled an experimental exploration of the relationship between food, art, economics, and science, transforming perceptions of food in order to change the world for the better.

Even as they push beyond global trends in culinary representation, these chefs' mimetic cuisine also reflects a representational terroir unique to Chicago, a site famous not only for culinary innovation, but also for its significance to the labor movement; its vibrant theatre culture; and its religious, ethnic, and racial diversity. In the US's famed "second city," which prides itself on its broad shoulders and gritty authenticity, these avant garde chefs tread the line between authenticity and artifice to create a dining culture that uniquely reflects local preoccupations. The construct of the celebrity chef stands as one critical feature of Chicago's representational landscape. In their development of the celebrity chef construct, Cantu and Achatz each, in their own ways, emulate their former boss, the late Charlie Trotter. A juggernaut of the Chicago fine dining scene from the late 1980s until his death in 2013, Trotter helped usher in the era of the chef as performer in his creation of the "kitchen table" experience, in which patrons dine inside a restaurant's working kitchen.[1] The theatrical and pedagogical tendencies of this 1989 innovation not only reverberate through Cantu and Achatz's work in their emphasis on pedagogy and theatricality as elements of the dining experience, but also in their focus on highly coordinated, beautiful displays of culinary labor. In each chef's restaurants, diners experience not only performances of service, cooking, and dining, but also a representation of the contemporary chef himself. Before discussing Cantu and Achatz's unique approaches to culinary representation, I briefly sketch Trotter's role in defining Chicago's fine dining landscape in order to demonstrate the ways in which his erstwhile apprentices reshaped it.

At the kitchen table: the foundations of Chicago's theatrical cuisine

Trotter's decision to install a "kitchen table" in his eponymous Chicago restaurant in 1989 not only kicked off a fine-dining trend that continues around the country today, but also positioned Chicago as a primary US site of theatrical cuisine. Working in the hometown of improv master Viola Spolin, Charlie Trotter advanced a theatrical approach to cuisine driven by a vision of improvisation as key to creativity. The landmark chef, mentor to Cantu and other innovators (notably Graham Elliot, another Chicago chef with an affinity for mimetic experimentation), shared Adrià's emphasis on innovation as synonymous with excellence, but with a strikingly different inspiration. Where Adrià proceeds from Maximin's "not copying," Trotter's impulse to creativity sprang from divergent influences, including Winston Churchill, Miles Davis, and John Coltrane. Devoted to the pursuit of virtuosic improvisation, Trotter displayed a framed quote from Churchill in his staff dining room: "To improve is to change; to be perfect is to change often" (Kamholz 2013), highlighting what he saw as a crucial connection between mastery and change. Discussing Davis and Coltrane as an inspiration for his culinary style, Trotter expanded on this connection in a 2003 interview: "When I think of Coltrane, or of Miles Davis, they never played a song the same way twice.... To cook like that, one must know combinations, one must have a true knowledge of food to be in the moment…. that's when cuisine is truly exciting" (Iannolo 2003). Thus unlike Adrià's methodical creativity, pursued systematically over long periods of development, for Trotter innovation revealed itself in improvisation, an exploration of spontaneous change that demonstrates an artist's mastery of his form. While both chefs eschewed copying, Trotter famously developed and served a different menu daily, where Adrià preferred to implement a new repertoire each season. This relentless drive to demonstrate mastery through perpetual and often spontaneous reinvention reverberates through both Achatz and Cantu's careers as well.

In addition to his focus on theatricality and improvisation, Trotter also imbued Chicago culinary culture with a unique penchant for innovation that helped put Trotter, and Chicago, on the map as a culinary trendsetter. The history of Trotter's abounds with bold moves, leaps of faith, and prescient strokes of genius. For instance, Trotter's focus on fresh, carefully sourced ingredients, which led to the elimination of walk-in coolers in his restaurant in a 1995 renovation, anticipated the locavore movement long before chef and food writer Jessica Prentice coined the term in 2007. Trotter also led the way in establishing the degustation menu as the hallmark of US fine dining, was the first US chef to offer a vegetarian tasting menu, and even added a raw menu in the late 1990s (Martin 2012). While the culinary avant garde had largely moved on before his death in 2013, as Chicago magazine restaurant critic Jeff Ruby put it, "In the Mount Rushmore of Chicago, his face would probably be up there" (Rudoren 2012). Again, Cantu and Achatz, each famous for entrepreneurial innovation, from Cantu's patented culinary techniques to Achatz's pioneering approach to ticket-based dining, have extended and intensified Trotter's legacy.

Finally, the famously mercurial chef imbued Chicago culinary culture with an uncompromising approach to avant garde dining as pedagogy, in which the chef pushes diners beyond their comfort zone toward new ideas. Trotter's aggressive style, reflected in his love of Ayn Rand's school of radical individualism and his unstinting embrace of cooking as a capitalist enterprise, perhaps explains his rejection of the old notion that the customer is always right: "It's easy to give the guest what he or she wants. The real challenge lies in figuring out what they don't even know they want, and then 'crushing them' with something way beyond their expectations" (Iannolo 2003). The idea of crushing a patron with innovation contrasts sharply with Trotter's reputation for sumptuous service. His generosity with guests became an integral part of dining in the restaurant, and Trotter's became synonymous with experience design upon the publication of his seminal text, *Lessons in Service from Charlie Trotter* (Lawler 2001). On my own visits to Trotter's, the chef personally escorted me through the kitchen, despite my status as a student with no standing in the culinary world, taking time to pause chefs during their work and have them explain specific procedures and recipes in which I expressed an interest. Similarly, Trotter's humanitarian and charitable work, which won him the James Beard Humanitarian of the Year award in 2012, reflected his sense, following culinary hero Fernand Pont, that cuisine required "generosity and hugeness of heart" (Iannolo 2003). The combination of a relentless pursuit of personal excellence, a violently competitive individualism, and risky improvisational innovation, coexisting alongside a surprising depth of generosity and commitment to the common good, carries over in the work of both Achatz and Cantu, the chefs who would wrest the mantle of culinary dominance from him in the process of constructing their own strands of culinary innovation. In doing so they would reframe Chicago cuisine while maintaining the focus on celebrity and theatricality that Trotter helped make central to local fine dining culture. Where Trotter heightened the theatricality and exclusivity of fine dining through the device of the kitchen table, Cantu and Achatz would rethink the very notion of dining by embracing culinary mimeticism. As they built their own restaurant empires, these two young Chicago chefs further established the city as a hotbed of dining innovation, paving the way for new ventures pushing the bounds of culinary representation.

Grant Achatz and the staging of Chicago cuisine

Though today his name is synonymous with Chicago, Achatz's culinary story begins with a sojourn away from the Midwest. After working with the famously demanding Trotter for a scant eight weeks in 1995, the young chef abruptly left the windy city. Landing in California at Thomas Keller's French Laundry, Achatz found an intellectual and emotional home with a chef known for culinary innovation. Keller, who would become one of Adrià and Blumenthal's co-authors in the "Statement on the 'New Cookery'," had already built a reputation for punningly mimetic dishes, particularly ones that combine related ingredients in new ways. For example, Keller's famed "Oysters and Pearls" mimetically combines real oysters and oyster-flavored tapioca pearls suspended in sabayon. Similarly, his multi-sensory "Coffee and Doughnuts" pairs cinnamon-sugar doughnuts with a cappuccino semifreddo served in a coffee cup with a smoldering cinnamon stick, contrasting the expected temperature of hot coffee and the solidity of a frozen dessert. Achatz excelled in French Laundry's creative environment, and Keller arranged a *stage* at elBulli for his young protégé in 2000 (Achatz 2011). During his time in Spain, the young sous chef was overwhelmed by the novelty of Adrià's approach to cuisine, both in his experience dining at elBulli and later, working in Adrià's kitchen. Achatz describes a culinary space unlike any he had ever worked in before, in which chefs used new tools and techniques, working with a precision and intensity that made them look, to the astonished young chef, more like jewelers than conventional cooks (Achatz 2010). This visit to the elBulli kitchen, with its unexpected sights, smells, and ways of conceiving of culinary labor, convinced Achatz of the significance of Adrià's reinvention of cuisine. Inspired by his *stage* with Adrià, Achatz would go on to expand and rethink Keller's playful culinary mimeticism, as well as the technological, aesthetic, and scenographic innovation he encountered at elBulli. He would return to Chicago to do so. Launching his flagship restaurant, Alinea, just blocks away from Trotter's, Achatz rethought his former boss's innovations in dining, starting with the kitchen table. While Trotter offered a theatrical experience for a select few, Achatz exploded the conventions of dining in order to extend that theatricality throughout the entire restaurant, creating not just a performance of culinary labor, but a performance of dining that stimulates thought, emotion, and the diner's capacity for mimetic recognition.

Though a growing culinary empire, Achatz ultimately established an approach to culinary mimeticism in which the entire event of dining becomes a means of conveying aesthetic, intellectual, and emotional significance. As in Adrià's culinary philosophy, for Achatz, the ability to represent ideas, emotions, and geographies through food positions avant garde cuisine as art. As his fame continues to grow, Achatz has used new ventures to stake out territory in the expanding domain of mimetic cuisine, cementing his status at the forefront of US culinary innovation. Before exploring these later innovations, I begin with Alinea, the chef's flagship restaurant. In discussing the landmark Chicago restaurant, I detail Achatz's initial development of representational strategies that both respond to and advance the approaches to culinary mimeticism introduced by Adrià, Keller, and Blumenthal.

Toward alimentary performance: Alinea's edible events

After establishing himself as a local culinary celebrity at Evanston "Progressive French" restaurant Trio, Achatz found himself, thanks to an investment from frequent diner Nick Kokonas, with the opportunity to open his own space with a simple directive to "fulfill his vision" (Achatz 2011). Opening in 2005, Alinea quickly became a critical success. *Gourmet* magazine declared Alinea the best restaurant in the US in 2006 (Reichl 2006), and it joined the prestigious World's Fifty Best list in 2007. This immediate critical acclaim reflected Achatz's status as the US chef elevating avant garde cuisine to new heights, especially in his development of new theatrical tactics for culinary representation. Where Blumenthal focused on the dramaturgy of individual dishes, generating surprise, delight, and recognition through mimetic contrast and contextual framing, Alinea pushed the dramaturgy of dining further. Joined together within the Alinea tasting menu, each individual dish becomes a part of a larger theatrical experience, one which relies on culinary representation of ideas, memories, and sensations in order to evoke an emotional arc for the diner. The restaurant's premise, described by Kokonas in a 2006 interview with *Crain's Chicago Business*, is inherently representational and specifically theatrical: "'It's theater,' he says. 'It's buying a ticket to a show.' And the dishes themselves aren't merely food on a plate, he adds, but carry an intellectual concept, like Samuel Beckett's play, *Waiting for Godot*" (Scheffler 2006). Kokonas's reference to Beckett signals the partners' twin intentions. First, Alinea aims to establish Achatz as a serious artist. Second, Alinea pushes the generic conventions not only of culinary art, but of the culinary avant garde. In pursuing these goals, Alinea became a critical step in Achatz's ultimate development of a complexly representational theatrical cuisine. For the purposes of this volume, I focus my attention on the aspects of Alinea that resonate most with culinary mimeticism, including the restaurant's dramaturgical management of service, theatrical staging of eating, scenographic treatment of the table as stage, culinary representation of emotional content, and performances of culinary labor. But first, I frame these ideas with a discussion of Achatz's distinctive approach to culinary discourse, which both builds an audience for his alimentary performances and also establishes the chef as an avant garde culinary artist.

Kokonas and Achatz established Alinea within the context of Achatz's growing fame, thanks in part to a dedicated social media following Achatz cultivated beginning in 2003. Through the Society for Culinary Arts and Letters eGullet forums, Achatz, then relatively unknown at age twenty-five, discussed his developing approach to cuisine. In freewheeling conversations with fellow chefs and gastronomes, Achatz debated recipes and flavor profiles along with philosophies of taste, dining, and culinary art. Simultaneously, the chef articulated a focus on cooking and eating as a meaning-making creative endeavor rather than an experience focused exclusively on either sensation or sustenance. For example, in 2003, Achatz responded to a forum poster's question about whether experiments in flavor combination, textural variation, and unusual serviceware were "intellectualizing" food and thus removing it from a visceral context of consumption, pleasure, and sustenance. In his reply, the chef described his goals as theatrical and artistic, drawing a connection between the intellect and pleasure:

> the more we intellectualize, the closer to my goal we are. We are crossing the line of "a meal" or "dinner" and moving into the realm of entertainment: in the forms of theater, education, discussion, visible [sic] art. The overall experience becomes so fulfilling on so many different levels it could become the ultimate form of recreation.
>
> *(Achatz 2003)*

The metaphor of crossing a line haunts both Achatz and Kokonas's discourse of Alinea. Kokonas, for example, explained the venture as a break from restaurant norms: "This will be different. It's not really a restaurant. It's going to be more like a performance-art [sic] theatre, something that no one in this country has done before" (Achatz 2011, 189). This focus on disruptive innovation certainly built interest in the young chef's new venture. Yet, like Adrià, Achatz aimed to do more than disrupt culinary discourse. Instead, the chef used new modes of communication, especially social media, to support a vision of dining as a meaningful performance event.

Continuing his exploration of culinary philosophy and technique on eGullet, Achatz opened a set of dedicated threads for conversation about "The Alinea Project" in 2004. Generating culinary buzz well before the restaurant's preview meals, this conversation also advanced Achatz's development of celebrity chef status by positioning him as an artist on the vanguard of cuisine. The chef and his collaborators posted frequently in these moderated forums, fielding questions from enthusiasts and sharing reports on Alinea's development. Throughout these discussions, Achatz grounded both creative and practical decisions in culinary philosophy. For instance, the chef debated the importance of culinary originality with forum posters in a discussion of his design of a dehydrated creme brulee globe. The crisp sugar sphere, which took weeks to develop, turned out to be similar to José Andrés's "caramel light bulb," written up in *Food and Wine* and ultimately brought to Achatz's attention by Kokonas (Tep et al. 2004; Kokonas 2004). The chef soon announced his decision to scrap the dish, sparking a conversation about the role of originality in cuisine (Achatz 2004). This digital conversation, which previewed the restaurant's philosophy, dishes, and even the design of its furniture, logo, and serviceware, also generated its own mimetic drive as forum posters fantasized about encountering the thing they'd read about in an edible, experiential mode. Thus even before its doors opened, Achtaz established Alinea as an artistic project, driven by a rigorous pursuit of meaningful alimentary experience and rooted in performance.

In addition to the preoccupation with culinary mimesis that has pervaded the restaurant's discourse since its founding, Alinea also focused on representation in its menu, approach to service, and design of individual dishes. Though its 2005 opening featured multiple menus, including a longer twenty-eight-course Tour and a shorter twelve-course Tasting, the restaurant subsequently streamlined to a single menu of eighteen to twenty-two courses, which changed four times a year in rhythm with the seasons.[2] In these lengthy menus, Achatz created a performance of cooking and eating that combines culinary representation and ludic experience in a long form act of dining, a style culinary critic Ruth Reichl calls "a carnival of food…food as performance, food as surprise" (2014). After a pre-opening visit, *Food and Wine* writer Pete Wells was so taken with Alinea that he speculated the restaurant might be the best in the US two months in advance of its opening. Wells's preview, which expresses exhaustion with farm-to-table restaurants' "reverence for seasonal produce," hails Achatz's theatrical mimeticism as an antidote for market-driven boredom (2005a). Wells highlights a crucial feature of Achatz's cuisine in his description of a typical Alinea dish, an atomizer that the diner uses to spritz his palate with a distilled essence of shrimp cocktail. Narrating the process by which he reluctantly enacts this unfamiliar instruction, Wells first notes the slight embarrassment involved in squirting a fine spray of liquid into his mouth in a fine dining restaurant. Yet as soon as this initial emotion becomes known, it's replaced with a new experience of wonder. Bewildered, Wells describes individual flavors of shrimp, horseradish, and tomato appearing on his palate in succession before a "crystallizing" moment of recognition in which they cohere in his awareness as a shrimp cocktail. Surprised at the pleasure of this experience, Wells finds himself wondering whether the sensation is an illusion enabled by artificial flavors. On the contrary, he assures us, the restaurant has distilled these flavors "by honest means" (Wells 2005a). In this participatory dish, the chef intentionally provokes a series of emotions in the diner, from disorientation and even embarrassment to surprise, relief, pleasure, recognition, and finally a new and quickly resolved confusion. The dish both is and is not shrimp cocktail, a paradox the server stands at the ready to resolve, explaining after the diner has spritzed his palate the "honest means" involved in stewing and then concentrating the ingredients for atomization. Thus, while Adrià developed the notion of intellectual pleasure as a sixth sense, Achatz prioritizes on a seventh, affective, dimension of dining whereby emotional responses operate in concert with sensory and intellectual ones.

This commitment to stimulating emotional responses from diners defined Alinea's early innovations in culinary mimeticism, grounding Achatz's cuisine in theatricality as a means of provoking affective experiences of eating. In an interview during the early days of Alinea, Achatz explains that he wishes to evoke a wide range of emotions in the diner, asking "How can we change emotion through the mechanics of eating? Sometimes, quite honestly, we want diners to feel confronted, if that makes their hearts beat faster, if that helps them take note of the moment" (Wells 2005a). Conceiving of the meal as a unified performance event, Achatz remade fine dining in a way that recalls the chef's own sense of disorientation and disbelief upon entering Adrià's reimagined kitchen for the first time. This vision of dining as an emotional activity led Achatz to treat the entire event of dinner as a linked series of affective experiences, beginning with the diner's entry into the restaurant. Upon entering Alinea, early diners traversed a long hallway featuring no apparent entry into the dining space. Nearing the kinetic sculpture at the end of the hall,[3] guests triggered a motion sensor that automatically opened a set of doors in the left side of the hallway, surprising the first-time guest and delighting repeat patrons who witnessed fellow diners' enjoyment (or paying off the hopes of diners who read about this effect in advance).

This pattern of confusion, recognition, and resolution, which unfolds before diners have tasted a single bite of food, also foreshadows Alinea's pedagogical approach to service. Situated at the leading edge of the culinary turn toward mimeticism, Achatz's project necessitates the education of diners into a new way of eating. Recalling Benjamin's point that the human ability to learn is inextricable from mimesis, Alinea deploys a process of representation and recognition to facilitate this learning. First, using surprising presentation styles, visual trickery, or unusual modes of eating, Achatz sets up both pleasurable and challenging moments of confusion and surprise. Then, as in Wells's description of "shrimp cocktail," the diner experiences a moment of recognition that invites him to critically reflect upon his prior emotional, intellectual, and sensory conflict. This recognition functions pedagogically as well as emotionally, as diners contemplate the meaning of their experience and develop new expectations for future dishes. Indeed, Achatz described Alinea's mission in pedagogical terms in 2003, arguing that the project was moving cuisine into the realms of "theater, education, discussion... art." Moreover, in this edible introduction to culinary representation, both servers and diners become performers in their own right.

In keeping with its tendency toward theatricality, Alinea also extends Adrià's notion of artful culinary labor. During the lengthy meal, servers function as actors assisting in the creation of narrative and guides to the diner's experience. Simultaneously, diners become performers themselves, executing the event of dining with the guidance of the server. For example, Achatz's "Black Truffle Explosion" requires the server to play a trick on the diner. The server places a bottomless dish before the diner, showing the black wood of the table through the dish's hollow bottom and labeling it a truffle sauce. Next, he lifts the dish from the table to reveal the ruse: there's nothing there. Finally, he nestles within the hollow dish a spoon cradling the single raviolo, explaining to the diner-audience that the black truffle emulsion is hidden inside the pasta. Before giving the diner license to eat, the server first urges him to consume the dish in a single bite, relating the cautionary tale of a prior diner's erroneous performance. Attempting to eat decorously in small bites, the hapless victim burst the raviolo, spraying the emulsion across the table and soaking his clothing. The restaurant, the server explains, would hate to see the diner embarrassed. Here the server functions as an actor, executing a scripted visual joke, before the diner himself takes on the risky proposition of exploding the raviolo in his mouth, observed by an audience of fellow patrons. By highlighting the risks of the dish, Achatz infuses the performance of dining with emotional stakes; one can eat this dish successfully, but one may also fail by ignoring the server's instructions. The possibility of a mistake both focuses the diner's attention on the present, educates him about how to experience Achatz's participatory cuisine, and frames dining itself as performance. Furthermore, in "Black Truffle Explosion" and dishes like it, diners become performers and audience members simultaneously. We watch the same act repeated by those seated at other tables, delighting in the slight variations that occur in the repeated behavior of performing a script, in this case the execution of the dish's service instructions. Staff carefully rehearse their interactions with diners in order to ensure the successful execution of each dish, but the delight of the performance is in the variations that emerge. For instance, guests must often work with custom serviceware to execute the performance of a dish. When instructed to suck a combination of hibiscus, vanilla, and bubblegum tapioca from a lexan tube at the start of a course, dining companions face a choice. They are instructed to try to suck the contents of the tube out in one fell swoop but given license to be delicate if they prefer. Any choice the diner makes serves the dish's purpose here; success, failure, and everything in between each become an interesting new performance of eating.

In addition to casting both diner and server as performers, Alinea's cuisine also employs scenographic effects that intensify the delights of mimetic culinary experience by treating food as a performing object. Service pieces designed by Crucial Detail's Martin Kastner invest each dish with unique kinetic properties. For example, a wire serving piece called the peacock suspends single bites of food in a network of wire rods so that it quivers before the diner's eyes like a living thing. The bow, a metal tightrope, holds small dishes suspended in the air like acrobats, swinging and swaying until the diner plucks them with her fingers. These and dozens of other custom serving devices transform both dishes and diners into performers. Furthermore, this scenographic approach to plating theatricalizes the meal, priming the diner to experience a menu as a set of scenes, each inspiring new moments of recognition, surprise, memory, and incorporative reverie.

In addition to these unconventional service pieces, perhaps the best example of Alinea's approach to culinary scenography are the restaurant's edible centerpieces, in which ingredients treated as sculptural elements evolve over the course of the meal before being transformed and consumed later in the evening. As with the aforementioned transmutation of server into actor, these edible centerpieces rethink a conventional aspect of fine dining by adding new representational weight to an otherwise mundane element of a meal. These centerpieces transform ingredients into mimetic reference points by casting them first as sculptures, then as spurs to theatrical tableside cooking. For example, on one visit to Alinea, our server presented us with sheets of thinly sliced Kobe beef, frozen with liquid nitrogen and displayed in a wooden framework as a centerpiece. As the night progressed, the meat thawed, collapsing in a carefully timed process that left it limp just before the tableside arrival of a superheated rock, on which the beef was quickly seared and served. As diners contemplate the visual, textural, and olfactory qualities of the sculptural ingredient before them, watching it transform over time, Achatz invites them to anticipate the object's transformation from visual art to culinary ingredient to edible art. Robert Edmond Jones famously suggested that scenery performs by creating a "sense of expectancy" before actors ever set foot onstage (1987, 71–72). Similarly, in Alinea's edible centerpieces, food performs as both scenery and actor in turn, helping diners envision their upcoming experience before metamorphosing again in the rhythm of the progression of alimentary scenes throughout the evening. Moreover, the edible centerpiece allows a striking feature of Alinea's service to come to the fore, in which servers' artful labor becomes part of the enjoyment and significance of a dish.

Alinea's more recent menus have further explored this notion of artful labor. Most significant among these dishes is Achatz's development of large-format desserts constructed by the chef atop the table in view of the diners. "Chocolate Mat" offers a fascinating look at Alinea's perspective on the relationship between culinary labor, art, and the relation among the two, which coalesces through the mechanism of culinary mimesis. The dessert, which varies in ingredients and flavor profile, makes use of a silicone sheet placed over the dining table for service. This covering both protects the table and causes the dish's sauces, which the chef ladles in swoops and drips delicately from spoons, to metamorphose from organic shapes into circles and rectangles (due to capillary action as sauces of different density respond to tiny indentations in the mat). Moreover, the mat performs mimetically as a canvas during the chef's preparation, reflecting Achatz's aforementioned interest in food as visual art. The event begins similarly to many tableside food presentations, replicating and recontextualizing tableside guacamole or flambéing. The chef sets up a collection of small bowls and spoons as well as an edible centerpiece (for instance, an orb of white or dark chocolate filled with mignardises or a nitrogen-frozen mousse). Setting the centerpiece on the table, he begins working with sauces, focused and mostly silent, except for brief descriptions of each plated element, while the diners watch and, often, film the action. On a visit in which Achatz prepared our dessert, this process took several minutes. As he worked, I wondered if it would be fair to speak to the chef. I opted to remain silent. This urge toward silence seems common, and indicates the degree to which the chef's performed labor itself becomes part of the incorporative process of experiencing the dish. As he finished plating, Achatz asked "are you ready?" When we agreed, the chef lifted the orb and dropped it onto the table, smashing it to reveal an array of mignardises inside. We thanked the chef and he returned to the kitchen. A few moments later, we watched with interest as the chef plated the dish once more for another table seated fifteen minutes after us.

What's at stake in this performance of dessert construction/deconstruction? First, Achatz explodes the popular concept of the plate as canvas, expanding beyond the bounds of conventional cuisine in a literal way. But the dish does more than play with cuisine's physical boundaries; it also expands the territory of culinary representation. Bringing the celebrity chef into the dining room, Achatz deconstructs Charlie Trotter's kitchen table innovation. Instead of watching chefs prepare food inside the kitchen, we have the chance to see Achatz himself made part of the service of our meal. It's not only the dessert that one consumes in this dish, but also the chef's performed labor. We are certainly aware that pre-service labor enables this performance of culinary artistry, but at the same time the work Achatz performs reframes culinary labor as an artistic product. Labor, in this case the labor of culinary artmaking, becomes a representational element of the dessert. Like Warhol or Pollock, by positioning his artmaking as performance, Achatz becomes a living, breathing artistic project as well.

As one of the most prominent of the generation of chefs to follow Adrià, Keller, and Blumenthal in the development of new approaches to contemporary cooking and dining, Achatz has advanced the discourses and practices of culinary mimeticism in multiple related endeavors. In the case of Alinea, Achatz drives the energy of culinary innovation from the kitchen to the dining room, rethinking the event of dining from the tabletop upwards. In his next two ventures, Next Restaurant and the Aviary bar, Achatz would push Chicago's fine dining culture toward the vanguard of culinary mimeticism, redoubling his focus on theatricality as a means of investing dining with representational significance.

Up next: Staging the mimetic restaurant

While Alinea pioneered the chef's distinctively theatrical approach to mimetic cuisine, Achatz's second Chicago restaurant, Next, intensifies Achatz's representational aims, imagining a restaurant that performs as a theatre. Founded in 2011, this second collaboration between Achatz and Nick Kokonas, first helmed by chef Dave Beran and led as of this writing by chef Jenner Tomaska, operates on a theatrical business model. A degustation-driven restaurant, Next's menus change in a rhythm evocative of a theatre's season of plays, with a new concept replacing the old every three to four months. Patrons purchase tickets either for a single dinner or an entire season of menus (typically three menus per season)[4] from an online box office, priced according to the desirability and status associated with the dining time, in advance.[5] Each menu takes as its point of departure a specific time, place, or state of being, transporting patrons into the past, the future, other lands, or imaginary geographies. From an exploration of contemporary Thai street food to Apicius's Rome to the concept of childhood, each Next menu opens on a new vista. In its representation of other times and places, Next exemplifies Foucault's heterotopic "placeless place" (1986, 27), unchanging in its own physical qualities but opening onto new locations again and again. In the pages that follow, I discuss several of Next's menus in order to chronicle the restaurant's evolving approaches to culinary representation, from the historical to the geographical to the imaginary.

In addition to bolstering the restaurant's appeal for the culinary elite, Achatz's choice of Paris 1906, or "Escoffier at the Ritz," as the inaugural Next menu reflects the restaurant's trademark mimeticism in its irreverent but painstaking representation of culinary history.[6] In a moment of loving re-creation, the menu signals Achatz's complex awareness of his own reliance on Escoffier's legacy while also positioning the chef as a visionary prepared to drive the field into new territory. Like Escoffier, who revolutionized luxury dining after teaming up with hotelier Cesar Ritz to create experiences of performed and incorporated luxury for the upper class, Achatz and his partners' new restaurant innovates with an intensely theatrical model for fine dining. Achatz's innovations, from ticketed dining to elaborate shifting menus, recall Escoffier's own radical changes in fine dining practice, including the institution of the brigade system and the designation of the five "mother" sauces. In concert with Ritz, Escoffier extended his interest in the harmonious orchestration of the event of dining outwards onto patron experience, offering the rich and famous fêtes featuring exotic foods paired with ostentatious entertainments, set-pieces, and lighting schemes that rivaled Jonsonian courtly masques. Thus the choice of "Paris: 1906" as Next's inaugural menu announced Achatz's intent to both revive and supplant this tradition, offering a tightly controlled and yet cheekily self-aware performance of luxury that both hearkens back to Escoffier and simultaneously attempts to push beyond his legacy.

The Paris tasting menu revisited Escoffier's *Le Guide Culinaire*, reimagining but also lovingly recreating the work of the father of modern French cuisine. Each of the dishes of "Paris: 1906" actively gestured backward to Escoffier, with servers explaining the chef's original approach before describing how Next reconstructed or reimagined it for today's diners. Achatz recreated many of Escoffier's classic recipes, refining or modernizing the dish's presentation while maintaining a sense of historical detail. For example, Achatz faithfully executed Escoffier's original recipe for pheasant, including the use of an antique duck press to create a tableside sauce, but added an over-the-top pheasant claw garnish which the diner must remove in order to consume the dish. Here, Achatz and Beran restaged a classic dish but at the same time violently forced it into the realm of art by inviting the diner into a strongly theatrical mode of consumption. This boldly reimagined dish reads like Achatz's pheasant-claw/middle finger to the notion of slavish devotion to culinary tradition even as it celebrates and re-presents that tradition to diners. The pheasant claw's multiple representational registers are as important as the deliciously executed meat and sauces, as the chef invites diners to make sense of complex layers of historical research, contemporary reimagination, and immediate sensory stimulus. Both a reenactment and a revision, "Paris: 1906" simultaneously exists in the present, calls up the past, and mimetically enlivens a vision of the future.

While "Paris: 1906" exemplified Next's penchant for representing culinary history, 2012's "Sicily" offered an iconic experience of the restaurant's uniquely heterotopic travel-in-place. Recalling Blumenthal's realization that a diner's expectations are of paramount importance to her experience of a dish, "Sicily" relied on not only food, but place settings, servingware, and dramaturgical materials to conjure a feeling of travel without moving. Upon arrival at the restaurant, patrons were greeted with a wax-sealed envelope containing quotations about Sicily from Goethe and Hemingway. This opening gesture, which uses the words of literary outsiders to describe a poetic impression of Sicily, reinforced the sense of patron as tourist by casting diners as prospective visitors to the island, at once not quite there and simultaneously transported. The restaurant thus introduces itself as a representation of Sicily distinct from the actual island. We have yet to visit, the greeting suggests, and much as aficionados of travel writing, we may even prefer the performance of landscape that the meal we are about to consume will provide us. Instead, recalling Roland Barthes's discussion of travel narratives as mythology (2012), "Next: Sicily" deploys signs of the region in order to represent a mythical place for us to read ourselves into. We are foreigners invited to imagine travel across this landscape, with signposts to remind us that we've made it to an imaginary geography recognizable as the Sicily of our dreams, even and perhaps especially if we've never visited the island in the first place. As in Foucault's description of the heterotopia as "space of illusion that exposes every real space ... as still more illusory" (1986, 27), Next evokes a feeling of Sicilian authenticity that hinges on other mythic constructions rather than the place itself.

Pursuing this heterotopic representation of Sicily scenographically, the restaurant employed rustic serving dishes and a family-style presentation meant to support a sense of dining within the home of a Sicilian grandmother. Eschewing contemporary technique, Beran and Achatz also chose to use traditional cooking methods for the menu, including a charcoal grill set up in the alley beyond the restaurant. *Chicago Tribune* food writer Phil Vettel hailed the move as a performance of authenticity: "it's not enough for the Next staff simply to cook Italian; it has to cook as Italians" (Vettel 2012). In Vettel's formulation, the chefs mimetically perform as the mythic grandmother who serves as inspiration for the menu's dishes. This imagined grandmother, referenced by the servers but never actually present, works as one of Barthes's mythic meta-signs; her invocation is a sign of respect for a rustic, feminine, and homespun labor of love that we may see as emblematic of Sicily. Vettel situates this mimetic reproduction of home cookery as a risky form of culinary honesty: "The masters of food manipulation are staking their reputations on a menu that repudiates manipulation in favor of simplicity and purity" (2012). In this performance of honesty Next exemplifies yet another attribute of Foucault's heterotopia, the ability to create "another real space, as perfect, meticulous, and well-arranged as ours is disordered, ill-conceived, and in a sketchy state" (1986, 27). Yet despite this rigorous pursuit of a Sicilian culinary technique that values purity rather than manipulation, "Sicily" constitutes one of the most mimetically complex menus in Next's history, conjuring a rustic Sicilian-ness within the still-present conventions of US fine dining. For instance, the mythic grandmother played contrastingly against the polished, crisp, youthful, and often masculine labor that occurred just outside the space of the table. This absent yet signified rusticity continually contrasted with the carefully choreographed rhythm of service, with up to five servers coordinating their actions to deliver courses simultaneously to all patrons at a table.

Much of the experience of "Sicily," in fact, played upon the relationship between artifice and authenticity. Narrating the tradition, technique, and philosophy informing each dish, highly skilled servers delivered courses of Sicilian street foods, then dishes of exotic seafood and house-made pasta, then braised pork with slow-cooked tomato sauce, and finally an array of traditional Italian desserts like a cassata displayed family style before being plated. The server, noting our interest, divulged winkingly that the showpiece display cake was in fact made of frosted Styrofoam, leaning into rather than denying the evening's mimetic delights. My eavesdropping revealed a theme among most diners' experience of the meal: a focus on the food's authenticity and the restaurant's performance of place through its serviceware, cuisine, and plating style. Diners at the next table enthused, "We are in Sicily," noting in passing that they had never visited the island. Still, they insisted, recognizing the meal's accurate depiction of the locale felt effortless. Returning to the menu-as-travelogue, it's possible that this meal might feel more acutely Sicilian than a meal in Sicily itself for Next diners, since it endeavors to perform Sicilian mythos for its patrons in a way that the place might not bother to.

Indeed, patrons' desire for an inchoate experience of authenticity deeply informs Next's appeal. Rather than demanding literal experiences of other times and places, patrons expect what can best be described as an authentic theatricality, in which Next evokes the quality of a place, time, or feeling without fully transporting the diner, who looks through the frame of the table to a representation of a time, place, and culture. In this construction, there is no rigid fourth wall convention. Rather, the joy in dining is traversing the boundary between the mimetic dining presentation and one's own embodied experiences and memories. For example, in contrast to evocation of a mythic Italian authenticity in "Sicily," for 2011's "Childhood" menu, Achatz used food to both mimic experiences of childhood and provoke specific memories in diners. In addition to the aforementioned "foie-sting" licked from metal beaters and a course served in 1980s-style lunchboxes, a sweet potato pie dish looked like a campfire and burned with the associated smells, fostering both a literal resemblance to a campfire and also a feeling of community at the table. This social, visual, and olfactory evocation of campfire aimed to spark recognition even in those who may have never experienced a campfire directly. An entirely new representation of campfireness, this dish exemplifies and clarifies the possibilities of culinary mimesis that pushes beyond imitation to the creation of something new. Diners don't recognize the sweet potato pie campfire merely as a reflection of a memory, nor as a reflection of reality. Instead the eater recognizes the dish's offer, through the representation of many sensory signifiers of the social event of communal dining around a campfire, of an aestheticized nostalgia for an event many associate with childhood. Those with memories of campfires are invited to transform and re-perform that memory, seeing what they find this time. And even if they have no personal memory on which to draw, Next nonetheless invites diners to performatively explore nostalgia.

Over its first seven seasons, Next has continued to refine its approach to representing other times and places, deepening its engagement with culinary philosophy along the way. True to his tendency to educate diners into appreciation of mimetic technique, Achatz's introductory text for 2017's "Ancient Rome" menu made a historical argument that mimesis has a long shadow in culinary practice and discourse. He closed his welcome note with Athenaeus of Naucratis's line from *Deipnosophistae*: "We can thus see the similarity between the cook and the poet. Art lies in the imagination." In quoting Athenaeus's third century record of dinner conversations among the Greek learned elite, which vies with Apicius for the title of world's oldest cookbook, Achatz not only demonstrated his devotion to culinary discourse, but also the depth of his own culinary philosophy's roots. "Next: Ancient Rome" mimetically recreated historic recipes associated with an ancient elite who, Achatz stipulated in his introduction, "considered the plate to be a blank canvas, and his ingredients the means by which he could apply color and shape." In doing so, Next asserted its imaginative culinary prerogative, simultaneously educating skeptical audiences with this dramaturgical device and providing enthusiastic diners a historical basis for the alimentary performance they are about to enjoy.

"Ancient Rome" offered a new twist on Next's emphasis on travel in place, inviting diners to enjoy a form of culinary archaeology by serving over a dozen dishes inspired directly by Apicius's loose descriptions of dishes and preparation techniques in *On Cooking*. Intensifying the dramaturgical bent of earlier menus, each table at "Ancient Rome" featured a copy of a critical edition of Apicius's text. The menu noted the Latin name and page number for each dish, inviting guests to read the dish's original description as they ate their way through courses accented with Roman flavors like liquamen, olive, lovage, garum, and fennel. "Ancient Rome" revisited the technique of "Paris: 1906," lovingly innovating upon a classic text, intensifying the experience by inviting the diner herself to indulge in the same culinary research that informed the menu design. Since the gulf between ancient Roman palates and our own is particularly large, the device of the tableside culinary compendium allowed the diner to literally see the logic of Achatz and Tomaska's menu. At the same time, browsing the edition of Apicius helped diners comprehend the impossibility of complete reproduction of a Roman original, highlighting the tantalizingly large challenge the chefs faced and rendering diners confederates in imaginatively conjuring a Rome they could not fully access. In keeping with the notion of the imaginative chef inscribed on its welcome note, "Ancient Rome" worked as an imaginative reenactment, not a literal one.

In addition to the philosophical approach exemplified in "Next: Ancient Rome," menus like the aforementioned "Childhood" and 2017's "Hollywood" explore congruencies between mimesis and play. "Hollywood" featured playful devices like a short film script narrating two mysterious new diners visiting Next for the first time and a red-carpet style photo session for patrons as they entered the restaurant, catering to film fans with intricate references to popular films. For instance, "*The Breakfast Club*" bento box included a white bread sandwich made of mimetic aerated cheese semifreddo "bread" and rutabaga "cheese" alongside a watermelon gazpacho "pixie stick" and a nigiri of mushrooms. Each element of this dish visually replicates a food item eaten by the film's characters while surprising the diner with unexpected ingredients, textures, and flavors. By priming diners to both mimetically recognize and simultaneously perform as characters from *The Breakfast Club*, "Hollywood" emphasized the connection between incorporation, illusion, and joy. As my companion and I ate our way through this menu, moments of recognition inspired playful reenactments of films referenced in the menu. Some of these reenactments were physical, as in the "Horror" dish, which required the diner to stab a spherified beet sauce and splatter blood red liquid across the plate. Others were verbal, as in a recitation of favorite lines from Quentin Tarantino's ouvre inspired by the "*Pulp Fiction*" course, a play on the filmmaker's oft-referenced Big Kahuna Burger. In this dish, representation and participation merged and reinforced one another, extending the chef's culinary references backward through memory and forward into new alimentary performances.

In addition to offering unique opportunities for experimentation with multiple modes of culinary mimeticism, Next's short-run menus also generate a heightened sense of scarcity and demand. Reflecting on the "Paris" menu, Vettel opined that "the 7,000 or so diners who manage to experience 'Paris 1906' will have bragging rights for a lifetime" (2011). 2012 season tickets sold out in less than ten seconds (Lande 2012), and prime Friday and Saturday night tables remain difficult to acquire for virtually every menu. Coupled with Vettel's notion of bragging rights, in which guests compete for an unrepeatable culinary experience, this consistent demand highlights the economic dimensions of mimetic cuisine. At Next, dinner becomes a hot ticket on par with a sold out performance, desirable both in terms of the ephemeral pleasures of the event itself as well as the cultural capital of having been there for something special. The economic impacts of Achatz's culinary empire are evident in the transformation of Chicago's Fulton Market, home to both Next and its sister restaurants, Aviary and Roister. A typical night for patrons able to meet the challenge of scoring tickets involves a trip through the rapidly gentrifying streets of this remnant of Chicago's historic meatpacking district. In Next's early seasons, the air of Fulton Market oozed with the umami of discarded seafood. As this book goes to press, Fulton Market has become a culinary hotspot, with patrons lined up to score a table at Duck Duck Goat, the latest venture from celebrity chef Stephanie Izard, or to claim a spot at the bar of Achatz's new casual concept, Roister. A new Google office building overlooks the restaurant complex, and wide sidewalks are under construction to accommodate increased foot traffic.

Construction permits proliferate in the windows of empty warehouse spaces. As I walked Fulton Market before my June 2017 visit to "Next: Hollywood," I noticed that someone had scrawled "yuppies suck" over one such notice. Less costly than a meal at Alinea or seats at many of the touring Broadway productions housed a short distance away in the theatre district, a dinner at Next has rarely qualified as the most expensive ticket in town. Still, even before reaching the restaurant, diners already embody a privileged status: possessed of the time and technological savvy to acquire tickets, enjoying mimetic cuisine even as a few remaining night laborers move boxes of carcasses with forklifts nearby.

Aviary's conspicuous theatrical consumption

Before experiencing the main event at Next, patrons might stop for drinks at Achatz's Aviary bar, a highly theatrical venue in its own right. In keeping with the chef's flair for both entrepreneurship and innovation, Aviary extends Achatz's engagement with the theatrical event of dining while also investing considerable attention to the continued advancement of mimetic cuisine. Heralded as a top Chicago venue upon its opening in 2011, Aviary aimed to bring a culinary sensibility to Chicago drinking culture. Entering an already-competitive scene, featuring internationally acclaimed bartenders including Mike Ryan, then heading the bar program at Sable, and Stephen Cole, of Violet Hour and Barrelhouse Flat, Aviary's approach to cocktail service foregrounded theatrical experience even as it eschewed traditional elements of bar service such as counter seating. Signaling its iconoclasm, Aviary even discarded the term "bartender" in favor of "cocktail chef" until Charles Joly, taking over for original lead cocktail chef Craig Schoettler, insisted on reclaiming the term. As with the eGullet launch of Alinea in 2005, Achatz, Schoettler, and staffer Micah Melton (now Aviary's head chef) teased the Aviary menu well in advance of its opening, using web-based video to showcase their experiments in spherification (a spherified Gin and Tonic that has been an on-again, off-again menu feature), ice variations including the "In the Rocks" cocktail I discuss below, and other innovations in serviceware, ingredients, and preparation methods. Furthermore, mimetic techniques abound, from spherification to the use of additional sensory detail such as aroma to convey dramaturgical information and scenographic serving pieces such as bunsen burners, antique tea kettles, treasure chests, and even performative devices like a Viking-style drinking horn for a cocktail commemorating Next's "The Hunt" menu.

This focus on transforming traditional bar conventions manifests in both mimetic drinks and a highly theatrical style of service. Consider the following snapshot of service I experienced on a visit to Aviary soon after its opening in 2011: A waiter delivers our drinks, and we learn my companion's cocktail includes exactly one thousand spheres of cinnamon-infused ice. Incredibly, my beverage is more elaborate. The server places a chunk of oak barrel on the table, lighting a small fire in an indentation in the wood before extinguishing it with my overturned glass. A flask of liquor emptied into the still-smoking vessel takes on an almost electric tang of campfire. My partner and I glance around the room at other patrons, watching the display of our drinks being served, consulting their menus to ascertain which cocktails we ordered. In the next moment, our eyes wander to a couple seated across from us as they learn how to use a slingshot to crack the egg-shaped ice that contains their reimagined Old Fashioned into a specially made glass designed to collect the shards of the ice sphere. My companion and I return to conversation, continually scanning our peripheral vision for performances of new drinks as we strategize about what to order next.

As the aforementioned description suggests, cocktail service at Achatz's Aviary takes the typical performance of bartending and intensifies it, crafting a theatrical event designed to maximize the performed elements of the presentation and consumption of drinks. Beverages are prepared in the cocktail kitchen rather than at a traditional bar, enabling a highly visible and theatricalized tableside dispensing of libations, usually including an element of participation. Near the standing tables, the kitchen remains visible just beyond a screen of gridded metal known as the birdcage; no additional real backstage area exists for prep other than the bar's ice kitchen and storage space. Aviary's staff work almost completely within the view of patrons, largely in silence. As much as a theatrical expression of cocktail consumption, Aviary is also a performance of service, and therefore of a tightly controlled repertoire of bodily and affective labor. In addition to its treatment of staff as performers, Aviary also positions diners in multiple theatrical contexts. As the evening unfolds, patrons become audiences for servers and fellow customers, as well as performers in a cocktail theatre event for those around them. The bar is strategically located adjacent to Next, with a small porthole window allowing Aviary customers a glimpse of the restaurant's ongoing pattern of service, reinforcing the sense of Next and Aviary as separate spaces within a larger culinary performing arts center. Next patrons often stop in for drinks and are escorted through this door to their dinners, creating a performance of exclusivity and access for those who witness drinkers whisked to their next, more exclusive, engagement. A distinctive performance of cultural capital pervades the experience: patrons in the standing-room-only area can peek through the wireframe birdcage to witness a select few enjoying an elaborate sequence of cocktails and food at the Aviary "Kitchen Table." Meanwhile, staff usher those with tickets into the bar's main seating area or convey special guests downstairs to the Office, Aviary's exclusive speakeasy. Just as Next intensifies the perceived value of its menus by emphasizing their ephemerality and exclusivity, separating diners into those who were there and those who missed an experience, Aviary offers multiple levels of experience, each rarer and more exclusive than the next. This purposeful inclusion of multiple opportunities to serve as both performer and audience member, each operating in different registers of class and distinction, is crucial to understanding the multilayered mimeticism of Alinea, Next, and Aviary. Just as drinks, dishes, menus, and serviceware perform together in the mimetic evocation of relationships, representations, emotions, and ideas, within the relational context of these restaurants, diners and servers also play multiple roles in the unfolding mimetic experience.

Even as Aviary highlights the value of embodied experiences of culinary mimeticism in exclusive contexts like the Office, the bar also participates in the mimetic trend of culinary closet drama that offers home chefs a chance to manufacture a mimetic reproduction of exclusive restaurants. The trend of reproducing restaurant dishes in detail at home entered full swing in the second decade of the twenty-first century, when lifestyle bloggers became famous by cooking their way through complex texts like the *Alinea* cookbook. Allen Hemberger, the most famous Alinea completist, would go on to publish a book about his experience (Hemberger 2014). As of this writing, Hemberger has partnered with Achatz and Kokonas to produce the Kickstarter-supported *Aviary Cocktail Book*, coming full circle from culinary outsider to insider through a lengthy performance of culinary reproduction. Custom serviceware designed by Martin Kastner, such as the Porthole, which sandwiches cocktail ingredients between circular plates of glass to display a long-term infusion drunk in small sips so the patron can experience a change in color and flavor over time, are available for purchase online and have spread to homes and bars across the country. Using Hemberger's book and servingware purchased from Kastner's Crucial Detail website, aspiring cocktail chefs will be able to create facsimiles of Aviary standbys. Continuing this trend of textual reproduction that enables mimetic culinary reenactments by home chefs, Achatz's Next restaurant also dabbled in publishing e-books of recipes for their menus, complete with plating instructions. This turn toward the cookbook as closet drama reinforces the mimetic thrust of Achatz's empire, inviting would-be diners in far-flung locales or those without the means to invest several hundred dollars in a dinner for two to instead imagine an Alinea meal into being or even, through an immense expenditure of time, labor, and money, create a reproduction of one at home.

Aviary's engagement with mimetic innovation has also inspired its own mimetic backlash, most prominently in television comedy *Parks and Recreation*'s 2013 episode "Two Parties," which pokes fun at "molecular mixology." The episode features a bachelor party at high-end bar "Essence," a parodic version of Aviary in which high concept drinks like whiskey-infused lotion and a beer served in the form of cotton candy prompt acerbic libertarian Ron Swanson to ask if "this entire establishment is a practical joke of some kind" (2013). While Swanson's critique echoes familiar notions of mimetic cuisine as insubstantial and unserious, it also demonstrates Achatz's widespread culinary influence, which in the episode threatens to transform the nature of the everyday bachelor party. Furthermore, these developments also highlight the shift from visual mimesis, which represents at a distance, to a multisensory mimeticism that spurs critical reflection on the nature of embodied knowledge and its relationship to representation.

Like Adrià and Blumenthal, Achatz has continued to pursue new approaches to culinary representation, pushing outside of the boundaries of Chicago and of the restaurant itself in the process. Achatz opened a New York franchise of Aviary in the Mandarin Oriental hotel in late 2017, offering new riffs on Aviary cocktails including a coffee-infused Manhattan accompanied by the aroma of everything bagel. In 2016, Achatz and Kokonas opened a reinvented, completely redesigned flagship that *Eater*'s Sarah Freeman aptly called "Alinea 2.0" (Freeman 2016). Returning to Achatz's initial interest in evoking emotional responses from diners, this new Alinea offers three possible experiences, ranging from a more affordable short menu to a longer experience that "combines a dozen or so courses (always in unexpected forms) with performance art, and service that borders on choreography" (Vettel 2016). Moreover, the new menu further foregrounds mimetic dishes. "Vanilla," a dish of dried beef cut to visually resemble vanilla beans and flavored with vanilla, chili, and soy, uses culinary mimesis to challenge the diner not to believe his eyes. "Spiced Orange Explosion" deploys a similar contrast between visual mimesis and alimentary surprise, encapsulating orange tea in a saffron shell that uncannily mimics an orange. While Achatz's famed tabletop dessert and edible helium balloon remain staples of the menu, new additions include visits to the kitchen, with scene changes occurring in the main dining space while guests take turns shaking their own cocktails backstage. In Alinea 2.0, Achatz's interest in theatricality comes full circle, transforming his flagship restaurant into a self-described experience of performance art. This progression from mimetic dishes to mimetic culinary experience writ large also grounds the work of Achatz's colleague, Homaro Cantu, whose restaurants stood just steps from Next and Aviary.

Homaro Cantu: mimetic cuisine as theatrical pedagogy

The late Homaro Cantu's two restaurants, Moto and iNG (short for Imagining New Gastronomy), operated in counterpoint to Achatz's Chicago restaurant empire. Moving on parallel courses, Cantu and Achatz took different approaches to culinary mimeticism despite each building restaurants steeped in high technology, mimetic cookery, and theatrical dining. Both chefs apprenticed for Chicago luminary Charlie Trotter, Cantu going on to serve as Trotter's sous chef. Just as Achatz's bar chefs at Aviary have risen to national prominence for their theatrical cocktails, Cantu's sous and executive chefs at Moto, Chris Jones and Richie Farina, extolled the virtues of culinary mimesis as prominent contestants on the ninth season of popular culinary competition program *Top Chef* (2011–2012). While Achatz rethought the tasting menu as a series of affective experiences, Cantu reimagined the materiality of the menu, designing edible menus that are both a dramaturgical tool and a mimetic dish in and of themselves (Verbeek 2015). The same 2006 issue of *Gourmet* that named Alinea the best restaurant in the US featured a cover photo of Cantu taking a bite of one such edible menu.

His peers recognized Cantu as a culinary futurist. Achatz, for instance, told *Eater* magazine that Cantu was a critical player in moving the industry forward: "He's so relentless and so confident, with a lack of care about what anybody thinks about him. You need those people in every industry in order for that industry to go further" (Caro 2012). Indeed, the most distinct difference between the two chefs lay in Cantu's interest in futurity for its own sake, versus Achatz's stronger affinity for artfully designing the diner's emotional experience. Unlike Achatz, who bristles at the notion of cooking-as-science, Cantu embraced the concept, citing Stephen

Hawking as one of his culinary inspirations (Battaglia 2008). Cantu's focus on futurity itself led to the other great distinction between the two Chicago innovators' business practices. While Achatz embraced an open-source ethos for cuisine, Cantu took the opposite tack. The chef patented multiple culinary innovations, including the aforementioned edible paper, which he described as a method for creating mimetic "substitute food items" (Cantu 2006). In order to protect proprietary innovations, he required a legal nondisclosure agreement from visitors to his kitchen.[7] Cantu's use of a printed statement of copyright on his edible paper cotton candy even inspired a *Food and Wine* article on the concept of culinary plagiarism (Wells 2015b). These critical divergences between Cantu and his culinary contemporaries notwithstanding, his career offers an important vantage point on culinary mimeticism's implications for contemporary foodways outside fine dining contexts. While his work also reveled in high art discourse and aesthetic play, Cantu's two main restaurants more directly connected the flights of fancy of avant garde cuisine with impacts on economic, social, and political issues beyond the restaurant, aiming at changing the world by changing our understanding of both food and cooking.

Cantu's two most prominent restaurants, the longer-lived and higher-end Moto and the more economically accessible iNG, were located next door to one another on the same Fulton Market block where Achatz and Kokonas would later open Next and Aviary.[8] Moto (2004–2016), Cantu's flagship, thoroughly embraced the theatrically scientific feel of molecular gastronomy, nurturing a vision of Cantu as a mad scientist. Moto's famously mimetic dishes often relied upon the chef's innovations in culinary technique and technology to carry off their illusions. For instance, Cantu's Magritte-style sushi, wrapped in the chef's copyrighted edible paper imprinted with images of sushi, used his innovative process for printing with vegetable inks to create mimetic sushi. As food writer Nir Dudek points out, the process of eating these rolls is itself mimetic: "Like actors in a play, we are actually eating a reference to sushi, making us mere representations of people eating sushi" (2008, 54). However, Dudek's notion of reduction to "mere representation" belies the complexity of Cantu's expansive mimetic practice. Cantu's mimetic creations, like his Cuban sandwich made in the shape of a cigar, create a twofold sense of mimetic delight in the diner. First the dish acts for the diner, in this case a kale-wrapped cylinder of braised pork playing the role of cigar in ashtray. Then, the mimetic flow reverses and the dish delights again as it is consumed, performing a perfect impression of a familiar food despite its unfamiliar guise. In each case, the presentation of the dish foregrounds its representational aspects alongside its technological innovations, from the sushi dish's use of edible printing to the cigar's use of modernist technique to transform a Cuban spice blend into "cigar ash."

Earning both praise for its experience of "dinner theatre on a plate" and raised eyebrows for catering to "a trend-conscious crowd," Moto quickly entered the Chicago culinary elite (Bernstein 2005). In 2006, Adrià himself visited, declaring Cantu a chef with the capacity "to find out what is the limit – what is cooking" (Reingold 2006). Cantu's dishes earned him national media coverage, patents, overtures from NASA and SpaceX, and, in 2012, a Michelin star. Described by New York chef Wylie Dufresne as "an inventor who accidentally ended up as a chef," Cantu devoted much of his time at Moto to developing new techniques from laser-cooked fish to the aforementioned "edible surfaces." Jennifer Reingold describes one application of this technology, a surf and turf dish featured on the 2006 menu Cantu served Adrià: "Accompanying the dish was a sketch inspired by M.C. Escher, the mind-bending surrealist, depicting a sea that morphs into a sky. "And please eat the drawing," a server would say. "It's flavored on the top like a bird and on the bottom like a sea" (Reingold 2006). This bifurcated edible sketch is an apt metaphor for Cantu's two-pronged mimetic project to both push the frontiers of culinary representation and transform everyday dining. While Cantu's edible surfaces opened a new frontier for culinary representation, the chef also advocated for their use as an inexpensive, shelf-stable food technology with applications from space exploration to military logistics to the fight against world hunger (Wells 2015c). Expanding Cantu's futuristic culinary empire, the chef's more affordable concept, iNG (2011–2014), similarly focused on new applications of science and technology aimed not only at enhanced restaurant experiences, but a new way of seeing food. ING's exploration of culinary applications for *synsepalum dulcificum*, a West African fruit commonly known as the miracle berry, that temporarily blocks taste receptors that sense bitterness or sourness, exemplified Cantu's interest in developing mimetic culinary techniques that aimed to transform the entire concept of cooking and eating.

While I devote much of the remainder of this chapter to an extended discussion of Cantu's use of the miracle berry, I first explore the chef's approach to culinary mimeticism as a means of changing the world. In his 2011 TED talk with collaborator Ben Roche, viewed nearly one million times since it was featured on the program's website, Cantu discusses his approach to transformational cuisine, or "cooking as alchemy." In a freewheeling review of some of his greatest hits, Cantu puts the principles of culinary luddism on the defensive by demonstrating the virtues of mimetic cuisine. The talk's blurb succinctly describes Cantu's culinary concerns while also reinforcing the controversy surrounding mimetic cuisine: "beyond the fun and flavor-tripping, there's a serious intent: Can we use new food technology for good?" (Cantu and Roche 2011). By way of answering this question, Cantu takes his audience through a progression of mimetic delights. First comes his famous printed sushi, made of edible ink and paper that looks like a two-dimensional image of sushi and tastes like the "real thing." The chefs then discuss evolutions of mimetic cookery, from "real" food paired with photographic printed versions of the same dish to vegan beef made of beets, corn, and barley, the main ingredients common in cattle feed. Referencing its origins in the foodstuffs that cows themselves consume, chefs describe this mimetic meat as, through a transitive culinary process, as close to "real" beef as anyone could wish: it looks, tastes, and is composed of the same materials as meat (Cantu and Roche 2011). In this pitch for mimetic meat, in contrast to the TED introduction, Cantu is not so much moving "beyond the fun" as he is interested in moving "beyond the food." Inverting his famed edible photo of a cow, which used edible ink technology to give diners a mimetic impression of filet mignon, this mimetic foodstuff performs as a burger but omits the cow.[9] In replicating hamburger that creates less waste, Cantu casts mimetic technique as a way of remaking global foodways entirely by rethinking associative relationships between plant and animal matter. Through the mimetic magic tricks of Cantu's "culinary alchemy," the chef articulates a goal of radically reconfiguring what counts as food, and having fun doing so. For Cantu, it's not only fun to transform our food. It's also essential to transform our ways of thinking, seeing, tasting, and doing cooking in order to survive on a changing planet.

Cantu assiduously promoted his culinary innovations as meaningful, pleasurable, and useful. Culinary mimesis, he argued, would reduce the need for wasteful food transit, decreasing the energy required to bring a plate of food to the table. Similarly, Cantu advocated "food recycling," transforming a single overabundant foodstuff to create multiple different dishes, as a way to tackle world hunger by reducing food waste. Not content to reduce the food miles or waste profile of specific ingredients through mimetic substitution, Cantu continued to trouble the issue of excess inherent in fine dining, using his restaurants as a laboratory for experiments aimed at developing more sustainable foodways such as the development of an in-house aeroponic farm that cut food costs, reduced food waste, and minimized the restaurant's carbon footprint. Ultimately, Cantu managed to reframe the problem in his experiments with the miracle berry, moving his explorations of culinary representation outside the context of food altogether and into transformations of the diner herself.

Fake food for real change: the miracle berry and Cantu's mimetic activism

Following his early experiments in mimetic cuisine as a means of changing the world, Cantu developed a series of culinary projects aimed at educating the general public about the miracle berry's capability to make otherwise unpalatable foods taste good, reducing sugar consumption and transforming our food supply. These ventures included Cantu's *The Miracle Berry Diet Cookbook* (2013), a miracle berry-centered café called Berrista (2014–2015), a berry-infused brewery concept, and iNG (2011–2014), billed as a "flavor tripping restaurant" in which diners could experience the miracle berry's applications for fine dining. After a discussion of Cantu's early work in miracle berry-focused cuisine, I will focus my analysis on iNG, his most sustained engagement with miracle berry dining, demonstrating the high stakes of Cantu's grand mission to change the way we eat.

Cantu traced his work with miracle berries to 2005, when a friend asked for help finding solutions for a chemotherapy patient whose sense of taste had been degraded by treatment (Merwin 2013). His experiments led him to the miracle berry, which he continued to see in the context of social transformation for the rest of his life, even as he highlighted the berry's possibilities for culinary adventure and mimetic play. Having experienced homelessness and food insecurity as a young person, Cantu embraced the berry as a potential solution to world hunger as well as diseases like diabetes. Seeing much of the problem of hunger, food system instability, and environmental consequences of modern agricultural techniques as rooted in some plants seeming palatable while others are not, Cantu argued that the miracle berry would radically change how we eat by changing what we are willing to eat. Leaning in to the old adage that the difference between a flower and a weed lies in our aesthetic judgment, Cantu reasoned that if we could find weeds and undesirable plants appealing, we could eat well with what was already around us, suggesting agriculture itself might radically change in the face of a sensory revolution.

Though miracle berries have been part of the avant garde culinary scene since the mid-2000s, including occasional experimentation by boundary-pushing bartenders like Lance J. Mayhew, who explored miracle berry–infused cocktail recipes for *Imbibe* in 2009, Cantu was the first chef to center entire menus around the fruit. Before his experiments at Moto and iNG, most adventurous eaters had encountered the berry through internet sales or fringe "flavor-tripping parties," wild experimental eating events in which guests consumed miracle fruit before tasting their way through an array of assembled foodstuffs from aged cheese to lemon wedges. The social elements of these events share a kinship with Fluxus's event scores, such as Alison Knowles's *Make a Salad*, which offers a simple framework within which a commonplace experience opens up to aesthetic and social play. In the case of miracle berry parties, a table is set with ingredients, the participants follow basic instructions to consume the fruit, and the experimentation begins. We cannot predict exactly what will happen, but the event structure brings participants into a playfully concentrated focus on the aesthetic aspects of their immediate experience. As lawyer and flavor-tripping party planner Franz Aliquo explained to the *New York Times*, these events leveraged the social atmosphere of the party to help participants recognize the newness of the experience and allow themselves to explore with abandon, quickly tasting their way through the assembled foodstuffs available for the party before raiding the host's refrigerator for hot sauce and maple syrup, acting "like wild animals" (Farrell and Bracken 2008).

The wildly exploratory environment of these original flavor-tripping parties clearly inspired Cantu's early concepts for miracle berry cuisine. For instance, at a high-profile event at Moto, Cantu invited a group of wealthy regulars to sample an experimental menu, not telling them that their meal was prepared using ingredients he foraged from the restaurant's immediate surroundings, most of which would be considered inedible in an everyday context. Through the use of the miracle berry, Cantu made a palatable dinner out of these materials, revealing his subterfuge at the close of the meal to the delight of his patrons in order to record their responses and thus prove the successful application of miracle berries to haute cuisine. Not only did the berries allow mundane or unpleasant plants to take on a new context, becoming desirable rather than detestable, but they also created a shared social context for the surprised, delighted diners, adding value to the event and offering opportunity for shocking reversal of expectations, creating a dramaturgical context for the meal. Cantu describes the significance of this foraged meal in his TED talk, explaining that he sent his staff out to forage in Chicago's urban environment for everyday plants they could transform into fine food, eliminating the costs and waste of not only agricultural cultivation but also food transit in the process (Cantu and Roche 2011). Furthermore, in serving this foraged meal to wealthy patrons at his flagship restaurant, Cantu winkingly subverts the fine dining tendency toward serving fetishized and often costly ingredients from artisanal local farms, in their place offering transformed weeds gleaned from urban sidewalks. In this meal, the perennially ambitious chef maintains the notion of surprise and transformation that has remained central to the miracle berry as a culinary tool, but adds a new layer of both pleasure and significance by harnessing this transformation to a social good. Through the disruptive potential of the transformative fruit, the chef-artist mimetically creates a sense of limitless aesthetic production that is both outside the normal bounds of economic exchange and also economically significant. At the same time, Cantu exults in telling his audience that he charged wealthy patrons a "boatload of cash" for "free food," again offering a tantalizing additional mimetic layer (Cantu and Roche 2011). Free food dresses up as haute cuisine in a reversal of the fable of the emperor's new clothes. Expanding on the concept of this miracle berry dinner, Cantu soon opened iNG, a restaurant exploring the possibilities of the miracle berry for transforming not only cuisine, but the nature of eating.

Opening in 2011, iNG represented the next step in Cantu's project of bringing the miracle berry into the culinary mainstream through a combination of haute cuisine and popular culinary ventures. Originally billed as a venue for futuristic Asian-inspired cuisine, iNG soon shifted its focus more squarely to the miracle berry. ING extolled the transformative virtues of the miracle berry in several related ways, first with an exclusive kitchen table "flavor tripping" experience, then through the use of miracle berry to create flavor-changing cocktails, and finally through the restaurant's focus on full miracle berry–driven tasting menus. Recipes from iNG also appeared in Cantu's *Miracle Berry Diet Cookbook* (2013), which the chef promoted on national television programs such as *Good Morning America*. Just as Moto diners served as the original test audience for Cantu's early experiments in mimetic meat, faux fish, and foraged feasts, iNG diners were the primary audience for his later investigations into the possibilities of the miracle berry to mimetically reshape our foodways.

Expanding beyond Adrià, Blumenthal, and Achatz's application of mimetic techniques to transforming ingredients, concepts, or historic recipes, Cantu's miracle berry dishes focused primarily on the transformation of the diner. Neither exactly a scientific experiment, in which something previously undiscovered might be understood, nor a magic trick, in which the exact mechanisms that underpin the experience cannot be revealed without undermining the trick, these dishes function as a scientific demonstration, a theatricalized repetition of a chemical reaction calibrated to surprise and delight by combining multiple elements to produce a predicted, if counterintuitive, response. My partner and I dined at iNG several times during its short lifespan, each time experiencing the restaurant's theatricalized presentation of miracle berry. After a short primer on the berry's effects, the server presented a ceramic spoon containing about a tablespoon of fluffy pink powder. Alongside the spoon he placed a lemon wedge. The server instructed the diner to consume the powder, spreading the material around the palate in an attempt to coat all the surfaces of the mouth. This service instruction clearly distinguished the berry powder from a food, but also from a medicine; while the berries are commercially available both as whole fruit and as tablets, Cantu's restaurant was unique in offering a powdered version that evoked an illicit drug. The miracle berry did not become a course in the meal; rather, the consumption of the berry prepared the palate for the meal to come. After the powder dissolved, the server instructed each diner to taste the unaltered lemon wedge presented alongside the spoon. Once the lemon tasted like lemonade, the transformation was complete and the diner ready to begin the menu.

On our first visit, soon after the restaurant expanded its focus on the miracle berry beyond the kitchen table experience, miracle berry courses dominated the menu. Placing the diner in the role of experimental guinea pig and the server in the position of a magician's amanuensis, the event conveyed a Halloweenish delight characterized by gustatory risk-taking and a strong sense of anticipation of what was to come in each course. My partner and I were giggling from the first course, which arrived hidden within a menu folded into an origami cube. Two edible corn packing peanuts sprinkled with spices and dehydrated vegetables replicated the taste of a corn chip with salsa and guacamole. This use of an everyday household item (these same packing peanuts are used by many environmentally conscious online retailers) set a tone of irreverence and unpretentiousness that carried through the evening. This sense suffused the entire event, as we experienced a half-dozen courses of flavor-changing food and drink, from cocktails to desserts.

This transformation of the diner in order to transform the dining experience diverges from Achatz's manipulation of the scenographic elements of the meal or Heston Blumenthal's use of disorienting pleasure through contrast and imitation, or even from Cantu's own use of mimetic techniques at Moto. Much like Achatz's approach at Next, at iNG Cantu invited the diner on a journey. But while Next invites diners on a heterotopic journey to a culinary elsewhere connected to a tantalizingly unavailable historic or nostalgic referent, iNG promised a different trip, prominently referring to the tasting menu as an experience of flavor-tripping. The reference to both mind-altering drugs and travel situates the table as a launch-pad into a psychedelic alimentary elsewhere. Like cultic celebrants or astronauts, diners must prepare themselves for the journey ahead in order to properly experience it. Our servers on each visit highlighted the element of risk involved in the consumption of miracle berry, remarking that if, as it had been for some shocked guests, the change in our palates was too much for us we could reverse it with sips of hot water. In invoking this overwhelmed diner, the server invited us to compare our own reaction, perhaps favorably, to this prior experience. Our delight signified a kind of intrepid spirit versus that of the horrified guest who feared his palate had changed permanently. Unlike this apocryphal guest, we welcomed the dangers of the sensory journey; we came to flavor-trip.

Ultimately, the dishes on the flavor-tripping menu, much like the aforementioned experience of a miracle berry party, amused the diner through a demonstration of his own physiological response to the berry. As was common in my experiences at Alinea and elsewhere, I noticed iNG diners glancing in wonder at other tables throughout the meal. These glances were the sort we might make if we'd just fallen down a flight of stairs yet landed safely on our feet, a "did you see that" moment of checking in with those around you. The experience at iNG was one of the body being made to perform, in which the drama of the event played out within one's own brain, palate, and emotions rather than on the plate or table. Responding to Benjamin's discussions of technologies of representation, Michael Taussig imagines a mimetic "technology of embodied knowing" that generates an "unstoppable merging of the object of perception with the body of the perceiver" (Taussig 1993, 24–25). In imagining these transformative mimetic machines, Taussig conjures up something quite similar to Cantu's vision for the miracle berry, a culinary technology that reorients the subject's experience of his own body, awakening him to new possibilities and even disrupting existing economies, ways of knowing, and modes of living. Without manipulating food directly, the miracle berry serves as a technology for transforming the body's relationship to its own sensory stimuli and thus to food. Flavor-tripping constitutes a complex mimetic opportunity in which foods may be made to imitate others through the application of technology not to culinary tasks, but to the body. Instead of devising a mechanism to deliver one flavor after another through the use of fat-soluble compounds as Blumenthal did in his early experiment with flavor evolutions, Cantu simply had diners consume the miracle berry mid-course to change a savory pork dish that tasted like Hawaiian roast pig to the flavors of ambrosia salad. The mind-bending experience of sensing one material in two divergent ways, absent any transformation of the material itself, grounded the pleasure of the dish. Thus while Blumenthal's mimetic techniques highlight imitation and perception to trouble a Cartesian mind-body split, Cantu's celebrated that same perceived split in order to delight a diner by confronting him with his own complexity. My body provides me seemingly undeniable sensory information, and in the same moment I experience a pleasure of bewilderment as my brain both comprehends and denies it. I have not been tricked, but rather invited to trip, and the performance, the imitation, is both all in my head and quite real at the same time.

Later menus reflected iNG's evolving approach to its menu, which expanded the restaurant's miracle berry focus while also pursuing visual, alimentary, and physical approaches to culinary mimeticism. A 2013 iNG tasting menu focused on Salvador Dalí (a savvy reference to elBulli's location in the Spanish park that served as an inspiration for Dalí's work), which translated to the use of edible digitally printed gelatin transparencies overlaid onto sweet custards to give them the appearance of the artist's famous melting clocks. Two dishes, a play on tapas and a coffee-based dessert, were based on quotations from Dalí, with the remaining eight riffing on paintings. Mediterranean flavors dominated, from Spanish chorizo to olives and tuna, with notes of global trade and imperial cash crops contributing a sense of history and conflict (mezcal, rum, coffee, tonka bean). The miracle berry courses, once again prominently featured, included a beet-honey dish, a flavor-changing mezcal cocktail, and a mimetic low-sugar dessert. Deploying mimetic effects rooted in visual, dramaturgical, and taste-based evocations of resemblance as well as the chemical transformations of the miracle berry, this menu garnered critical praise for its complex, multisensory representation of the celebrated artist.

Despite its unique pleasures, iNG never truly found its footing, closing in 2014 to the disappointment of devoted fans. Undaunted, Cantu continued to explore new applications for the miracle berry, opening Berrista, a miracle berry–focused cafe offering sugarless mimetic "junk food," coffee, and pastry, in 2014. In 2015, Cantu used his signature theatrical approach to evangelize the miracle berry once more, setting up a table with free Berrista treats just outside a nearby Starbucks and vowing to give away his sugar-free donuts "however long it takes to make food better in the U.S." (Selvam 2015). This sense of himself as a lone activist advocating for better food reflects Cantu's belief that hunger was not only a matter of supply, but of perception. Convinced that "famine is not only a distribution issue, but what we think of as food" (Weiner 2011), Cantu ultimately moved from inventing new technologies for cooking to conceiving of a technology to change our perception of food's ontology.

A culinary visionary, Cantu seemed intent on pushing boundaries, especially those based in "common sense" thinking. During my brief stint in the kitchens at the twin restaurants, I sat in on a staff meeting between Cantu and the chefs, servers, and staff of the Moto and iNG, in which Cantu encouraged his team to innovate. When I visited, the annual staff party was coming up, and Cantu motivated his staff by discussing one of the distinctly Cantu culinary excesses they'd soon enjoy: bottles of Krug converted via rotory evaporator to cognac. His speech to his staff overflowed with ideas and with hints of secret initiatives bound to reinvigorate Chicago dining; even as an observer I felt caught up, brimming with the spirit of this potentially transformational enterprise. Sadly, two years after I marveled at his contagious enthusiasm in this staff meeting, Cantu took his own life (Gordinier 2015). Soon thereafter, his wife and business partner announced Moto's last dinner, held on Valentine's Day 2016. Achatz and Kokonas's Alinea group reached a deal to take over the space formerly occupied by Moto and opened a new casual concept, Roister, in the space where iNG briefly offered flavor-tripping menus to a few adventurous explorers.

In pushing against the boundaries of the restaurant's geography, economics, aesthetics, and relational practices, both Cantu and Achatz, in their own ways, aimed not only to remake fine dining, but to remake human experience. Achatz's efforts to remake the status of cooking and eating as meaningful endeavors capable of generating mimetic significance echo and extend Adrià's interest in moving beyond the context of nourishment and apply Blumenthal's culinary dramaturgy to entire restaurant spaces. Cantu took a different approach, aiming to remake the way we eat through a salutary mimesis that he hoped would rejuvenate our global food economy. Just as his expansive vision and passionate evangelism teased tantalizing new possibilities for culinary mimeticism as a tool for rethinking global food systems, Cantu's challenges and failures also demonstrate the difficulties of this transformation. A 2016 documentary on the chef's life captures both the frenetic energy and crushing disappointments that characterized Cantu's career, offering a tantalizing look at the chef's unrealized aspirations to open a culinary research center aimed at using food to "save the world" (Schwartz 2016). As this book goes to press, a cadre of six former Moto chefs, including *Top Chef* stars Chris Jones and Richie Farina, have joined San Francisco startup Hampton Creek to pursue Cantu's vision for sustainable substitute foods. Describing his motivation for developing mimetic alternative foods like eggless mayonnaise and substitute eggs composed of plant protein, Jones explains "All the dreams we had of making the world a better place at Moto, we have the opportunity to do that at Hampton Creek. I just wish Omar was around to see it" (Trotter 2016). Thus while Cantu's miracle berry revolution remains incomplete, his concept of mimetic cuisine that can transform food systems lives on.

The Next Chicago cuisine: Cantu and Achatz's culinary impact

In the decade after the founding of Achatz's Alinea (2005) and Cantu's Moto (2004), experiments in culinary representation have proliferated around the city. Graham Elliot redesigned his French bistro menu in 2011 to include mimetic twists like a savory apple pie amuse bouche: a cinnamon-infused cheese tuille filled with apple gelee (Bendersky 2011). Phillip Foss's El Ideas (2011–present), serves mimetic treats like a potato-leek soup and fried potato twist on the chef's daughter's favorite fast food snack of "frosty and fries," frozen with liquid nitrogen and presented in a diner-style milkshake glass. Jake Bickelhaupt and Alexa Welsh's 42 grams (2014–2017) explored the notion of cooking as performance, with the chef working in full view of diners. Meanwhile, celebrity chef Rick Bayless collaborated with Lookingglass Theatre, starring in and preparing the meal for a high-flying example of dinner theatre I discuss in the next chapter. These culinary ventures demonstrate the vitality and diversity of Chicago's culture of culinary mimeticism as a means of transforming experiences of dining. In the following chapter, I explore the work of chefs and artists who have approached similar aims from the opposite direction, rethinking the limits of human experience by bringing culinary mimeticism into new geographic and relational contexts.

Notes

1 The concept of offering guests access to a table in the restaurant's kitchen meant so much to Trotter, in fact, that he threatened to leave Chicago when the health department attempted to shut it down (Black 1997).
2 As of this writing, Achatz's approach changed once more, with Alinea offering different experiences and menu lengths depending on seating location in the restaurant. After focusing my analysis on Alinea's 2005–2016 menus, I briefly discuss this latest iteration, often referred to by Achatz and Kokonas as Alinea 2.0, below.

3 Like most of the serviceware in Achatz's restaurants, this sculpture is a creation of Martin Kastner, the artist and designer behind Crucial Detail. In later years, Alinea has explored other scenographic transformations of its entryway, such as the installation of live grass and wind chimes to evoke a summer lawn for a menu I experienced in 2012.
4 The 2018 season will feature four menus: two devoted to French cuisine and two to restaging different eras of Alinea's development.
5 The difficulty of acquiring tickets to Next changes from menu to menu, with popularity depending not only on the perceived quality of the particular menu, but also on the question of how available any particular experience might be in other contexts. For example, it was, at upwards of 900 dollars for a dinner for two with drinks, financially impractical for many to attend the 2012 blockbuster "Next: elBulli," but tickets to attend Achatz's restaging of thirty dishes from the recently shuttered Spanish icon were nearly impossible to acquire anyway. The restaurant subsequently developed a proprietary ticketing system, Tock, which Kokonas has licensed to other chefs. The use of tickets allows Next to compensate front of house and back of house laborers more fairly and also avoids the problem of costly no-shows. In addition to these financial benefits, ticketing neatly reinforces Next's mimetic approach to cuisine, casting diners as audience members who have scored seats to a limited run performance.
6 This trend continued in 2012's "El Bulli," 2016's "French Laundry," 2017's "Ancient Rome," and 2017's "World's Fifty Best."
7 I signed one of these nondisclosure forms, in accordance with which I omit discussion of any proprietary techniques I witnessed during my experiences of working in the iNG and Moto kitchens.
8 ING was a reboot of Cantu's prior casual concept, Otom.
9 This vision of mimetic meat has recently received renewed attention as Impossible Foods's mimetic "Impossible Burger" graces high-profile menus like New York's Momofuku, California's Umami Burger, and Chicago's M Burger.

References

Achatz, Grant. 2003. "Intellectualization of Food." EGullet Forum Post, March 7. forums.egullet.org/topic/17956-intellectualization-of-food.
Achatz, Grant. 2004. "Inside the Alinea Food Lab." EGullet Forum Post, November 2. forums.egullet.org/topic/53763-inside-the-alinea-food-lab/?page=2.
Achatz, Grant. 2010. "What Grant Achatz Saw at elBulli." *New York Times*, Feb 16. diners journal.blogs.nytimes.com/2010/02/16/what-grant-achatz-saw-at-el-bulli/.
Achatz, Grant. 2011. *Life, on the Line: A Chef's Story of Chasing Greatness, Facing Death, and Redefining the Way We Eat*. New York: Penguin.
Barthes, Roland. 2012 [1952]. "The Blue Guide." in *Mythologies*. Translated by Annette Lavers. New York: Hill and Wang. 134–137.
Battaglia, Andy. 2008. "Moto's Mr. Wizard Dreams Up Weird Science in the Kitchen." *Nation's Restaurant News*, April 14. 42(15): 36.
Bendersky, Ari. 2011. "Graham Elliot 3.0 Revealed: New Menu, New Chef, New Vibe." *Eater*, Feb 3. chicago.eater.com/2011/2/3/6698729/graham-elliot-3-0-revealed-new-menu-new-chef-new-vibe.
Bernstein, David. 2005. "When the Sous-chef is an Inkjet Printer." *New York Times*, February 3. www.nytimes.com/2005/02/03/technology/circuits/when-the-souschef-is-an-inkjet.
Black, Jonathan. 1997. "Charlie Trotter in His Prime." *Chicago Magazine*, September 1. www.chicagomag.com/Chicago-Magazine/September-1997/Charlie-Trotter.
Cantu, Homaro. 2006. "Systems and Methods for Preparing Substitute Food Items." April 20. U.S. Patent Number 7,307,249.
Cantu, Homaro. 2013. *The Miracle Berry Diet Cookbook*. New York: Gallery.

Cantu, Homaro and Ben Roche. 2011. "Cooking as alchemy" Video file. www.ted.com/talks/homaro_cantu_ben_roche_cooking_as_alchemy.
Caro, Mark. 2012. "What Other Chefs Say About Cantu." *Chicago Tribune*, April 5. articles.chicagotribune.com/2012-04-05/features/ct-dining-0405-homaro-cantu-bar-quotes-20120405_1_cantu-nuclear-power-plant-chefs.
Dudek, Nir. 2008. "Reading a Plate." *Gastronomica: The Journal of Critical Food Studies* 8(2): 51–54. doi:10.1525/gfc.2008.8.2.51.
Farrell, Patrick and Kassie Bracken. 2008. "A Tiny Fruit that Tricks the Tongue." *New York Times*, May 28. www.nytimes.com/2008/05/28/dining/28flavor.
Foucault, Michel. 1986. "Of Other Spaces." Trans. Jay Miskowiec. *Diacritics* 16(1): 22–27. www.jstor.org/stable/464648.
Freeman, Sarah. 2016. "Alinea 2.0: Reinventing the World's Best Restaurants." *Eater*, May 19. chicago.eater.com/2016/5/19/11695724/alinea-chicago-grant-achatz-nick-kokonas.
Gordinier, Jeff. 2015. "Puzzling Death of Chicago's Whirlwind Chef, Homaro Cantu." *New York Times*, April 17. www.nytimes.com/2015/04/18/dining/trying-to-make-sense-of-homaro-cantus-death.
Hemberger, Alan. 2014. *The Alinea Project*. Oakland: Small Batch Creative.
Iannolo, Jennifer. 2003. "An Interview with Charlie Trotter." *The Atlasphere*, December 15. www.theatlasphere.com/columns/031215_iannolo_trotter.php.
Jones, Robert Edmond. 1987 [1941]. *The Dramatic Imagination*. New York: Methuen.
Kamholz, Roger. 2013. "A Timeline of Charlie Trotter's Influence and Achievements." *Grub Street*, November 6. www.grubstreet.com/2013/11/charlie-trotter-timeline.
Kokonas, Nick. 2004. "Inside the Alinea Food Lab." EGullet Forum Post, October 28. forums.egullet.org/topic/53763-inside-the-alinea-food-lab/?page=2.
Lande, Samantha. 2012. "Next Season Tickets Sell Out Quick: Over 6600 Queue Up." *Eater*, Feb 13. chicago.eater.com/2012/2/13/6614241/next-season-tickets-sell-out-quick-over-6660-queue-up.
Lawler, Edmund. 2001. *Lessons in Service from Charlie Trotter*. Chicago: Ten Speed Press.
Martin, Adam. 2012. "The Food Trends Chef Charlie Trotter Started." *Atlantic*, January 2. www.theatlantic.com/entertainment/archive/2012/01/food-trends-chef-charlie-trotter-started/333639.
Mayhew, Lance J. 2009. "Miracle Fruit." *Imbibe*, January 18. imbibemagazine.com/miracle-fruit.
Merwin, Hugh. 2013. "Homaro Cantu on Miracle Berries, Chewing Tin Foil, and the Best Peanut-Butter Cookies Ever." *Grub Street*, January 22. www.grubstreet.com/2013/01/homaro-cantu-miracle-berry-diet.
Prentice, Jessica. 2007. "The Birth of Locavore." *OUPblog*, November 20. blog.oup.com/2007/11/prentice.
Reichl, Ruth. 2006. "America's Top 50 Restaurants." *Gourmet*, September 26: 131.
Reichl, Ruth. 2014. "My Dinner at Alinea." ruthreichl.com/2014/04/my-dinner-at-alinea.
Reingold, Jennifer. 2006. "Weird Science." *Fast Company*, May 1. www.fastcompany.com/56689/weird-science.
Rudoren, Jodi. 2012. "A Chef Whose Touch Will Last." *New York Times*, April 10. www.nytimes.com/2012/04/11/dining/charlie-trotter-a-chef-whose-touch-will-last.
Scheffler, Mark. 2006. "40 Under 40: Nick Kokonas." *Crain's Chicago Business*. www.chicagobusiness.com/article/20061019/PAGES/2075/40-under-40-2006.
Schwartz, Brett A. 2016. *Insatiable: The Homaro Cantu Story*. Chicago: Story Screen.
Selvam, Ashok. 2015. "Homaro Cantu and Berrista Sets Up Outside Nearby Starbucks, Offers Freebies." *Eater*, January 22. chicago.eater.com/2015/1/22/7874065/homaro-cantu-berrista-starbucks-free-coffee.

Taussig, Michael. 1993. *Mimesis and Alterity*. New York: Routledge.
Tep, Ratha, Rob Wiley and Kate Krader. 2004 "04 Tastemaker Awards." *Food and Wine*, November 1. www.foodandwine.com/articles/04-tastemaker-awards.
Trotter, Greg. 2016. "After Homaro Cantu's Death, Former Moto Chefs Seek to Carry on His Legacy – With Consumer Products." *Chicago Tribune*, March 4. www.chicagotribune.com/business/ct-moto-hampton-creek-0304-biz-20160303-story.
"Two Parties." *Parks and Recreation*. NBC. January 17, 2013. Television.
Verbeek, Alex. 2015. "Poetics of Taste – Understanding a Menu Design." *Bon Vivant*, June 24. www.bonvivant-mag.com/uncategorized/menu-design.
Vettel, Phil. 2011. "Next Review: Inaugural Menu Embraces Paris 1906 Cuisine." *Chicago Tribune*, April 25. www.chicagotribune.com/dining/restaurants/ct-live-0425-vettel-next-review-20110425-column.
Vettel, Phil. 2012. "Phil Vettel Reviews the Sicily Menu at Next." *Chicago Tribune*, June 28. articles.chicagotribune.com/2012-06-28/features/ct-di
ning-0628-vettel-next-sicily-20120628_1_dave-beran-grant-achatz-next-restaurant.
Vettel, Phil. 2016. "Alinea, Now As Much As $385 a Head, Puts on Quite a Show." *Chicago Tribune*, July 15. www.chicagotribune.com/dining/restaurants/ct-review-alinea-food-0720-20160715-column.
Weiner, Debra. 2011. "Chef Hopes Miracle Berry Becomes the Sweet Taste of the City and Worlds Beyond." *New York Times*, February 10. www.nytimes.com/2011/02/11/us/11cncberry.
Wells, Pete. 2005a. "Brain Food: Grant Achatz." *Food and Wine*, March 31. www.foodandwine.com/articles/brain-food-grant-achatz.
Wells, Pete. 2015b. "New Era of the Recipe Burglar." *Food and Wine*, March 31. www.foodandwine.com/articles/new-era-of-the-recipe-burglar.
Wells, Pete. 2015c. "Homaro Cantu, Science-Minded Chicago Chef, Dies at 38." *New York Times*, April 15. www.nytimes.com/2015/04/15/dining/homaro-cantu-science-minded-chicago-chef-dies-at-38.

4

EATING A WAY INTO HOUSE AND HOME

Alimentary performance as resistant strategy

Tacos

Pork tenderloin, salsa, tortilla (*La Pocha Nostra*, Phoenix, Arizona, 2015)

Saúl García-López attaches a raw pork tenderloin to his loincloth, rolling his hips to swing it in a provocative circle. After some playful interaction between the man and his meat, García-López positions himself behind a countertop and picks up a mallet. Swinging the wooden hammer in a descending arc, he repeatedly smashes it into his phallic tenderloin, flattening and tenderizing the meat, before slicing it into pieces and seasoning it with salt and spices. He fries these slices in a pan and offers them, accompanied by commercially produced tortillas and salsa, to members of the audience who have drawn close during his cooking. Far from disgust, many onlookers express desire, lining up for tacos and jockeying for the chance to taste the climax of the brief performance.

In the prior two chapters I have detailed several chef-driven evolutions in culinary mimeticism. I now turn to a coinciding trend in theatre and performance, in which artists incorporate food into performance events as not only an onstage prop or an audience engagement technique, but also as a performing object in and of itself, capable of producing as complex an array of alimentary representational effects as Adrià, Blumenthal, Achatz, Cantu, and others have created in their restaurant and research spaces. In the event described above, a part of a longer devised work entitled *Monstros in La Frontera,* La Pocha Nostra member Saúl García-López uses mimetic cookery as a means of negotiating space: the space between himself and his audience, between two sides of a border, between one identity and another, between the sensual and the emotional, between the familiar and the taboo. As he layers erotic meat-play with a performance of cooking and serving tacos, the distinction between cooking, eating, sex, violence, and consumption appears to dissolve. A mallet hitting meat, the sound of a knife slicing through muscle, the sizzle of flesh seizing as it hits a hot pan all evoke both the quotidian context of daily cooking and eating as well as erotic contexts of BDSM and violent contexts of the oppression that helps define the *fronteras* La Pocha Nostra explores in this performance. First investing the meat with an erotic aura through his mimetic use of it as a prosthetic organ, García-López then layers the familiar scene of street food atop this phallic foundation, leaving the audience to consider the issues of gender, sexuality, and identity bound up in the Old El Paso tortillas and salsa they jostle to consume along with his freshly cooked meat. García-López uses performance to invest simple edible elements, pork and tortillas, with a mimetic significance that evokes and exoticizes familiar foodways, bringing audience members into an immediate physical relationship with the performer's body while recalling their memories of classic dishes and the stories they evoke.

García-López's work is one example of the phenomenon I examine in this chapter, in which artists use culinary mimesis as a means of exposing, challenging, and reframing geographical, social, and cultural hierarchies. In a set of case studies ranging from the 1960s to today, I chronicle the intersection of food and performance in the work of Fluxus's Alison Knowles, feminist performance artists Carmelita Tropicana and Bobby Baker, and twenty-first-century chef-performers Michael Twitty and Rick Bayless. Just as the chefs I have discussed thus far have consistently pushed beyond the boundaries of the restaurant in exploring the vanguard of culinary mimeticism, the artists I examine here have used food as a means of reframing the significance of spaces such as the home, the kitchen, the gallery, and the historic plantation for activist purposes. Furthermore, these artists have used alimentary performances to redefine the imaginative terrain of ideology and identity, using food in queer, feminist, and anti-colonial contexts to challenge lines between the private and the public, between insider and outsider status, between masculinity and femininity. Finally, each of the artists I discuss below uses food to open a space in which the real, the imaginary, and the authentic collide and interpenetrate, allowing a mimetic reconfiguration of histories, memories, and geographies through mimetic cooking and eating.

Rather than suggest that they take their lead from Adrià or Achatz, I instead contend that these artists have responded to a similar impulse to reconfigure sensory and epistemological hierarchies through multisensory culinary mimeticism. Acknowledging that the work of creating alimentary performance has often paralleled or even anticipated rather than followed from the work of avant garde chefs, I make no attempt to prove definitive patterns of influence between these artists and the chefs I discuss in prior chapters. Instead, I draw resonances between these chefs and artists that help to clarify the significance of mimetic cuisine in not only culinary and performance contexts but also political and intellectual ones. Much like Achatz and Adrià have engaged with questions of originality and value in culinary discourse, these artists share an awareness of food's importance to the ongoing project of naturalizing or challenging boundaries between truth and falsehood or between the inauthentic and the authentic. Furthermore, as in Cantu's vision of culinary mimeticism as a means of saving the world, these artists deploy culinary representation as a tactic to resist ossified hierarchies against which oppressed peoples and new ideas must often struggle in order to carve out space. Finally, in a culinary field often dominated by white, straight, cisgendered male executive chefs, I highlight significant contributions to the advancement of culinary mimeticism made by women, people of color, and queer artists, among others, whose work sometimes escapes the attention of food writers when it occurs outside the context of fine dining. Working in performance and fine art contexts, the artists explored in this chapter bring food into performance and performance into food in order to disrupt hierarchies and transform professions, cultural contexts, and especially spaces by mimetically reframing the significance of the material substance of food, the physical act of cooking, and the embodied and social experiences of eating. These artists do so in disparate ways and spaces and to disparate ends, but each of these case studies sheds light on the shifting significance of food as a meaning-making medium and on the changing relationship between the senses, mimesis, and performance in the twentieth and early twenty-first centuries.

Before examining specific alimentary performances, I frame this chapter's intervention with a brief discussion of the relationship between mimesis, oppression, and resistance. Michael Taussig's famous treatment of mimesis and colonization in *Mimesis and Alterity* (1993) provides an essential framework for understanding culinary mimesis in the context of the works explored here. Recognizing the processes of mimicry and recognition at work not only in colonization but also in the resistant and adaptive strategies colonized and enslaved peoples used to survive attempts at domination and erasure, Taussig points out that, in practice, imitation and reality are not so easily separated. Taussig's epigraph for the book, drawn from Benjamin's "Work of Art in the Age of Mechanical Reproduction," reinforces his central claim that mimesis constitutes both imitation of reality and means of contacting reality simultaneously: "every day the urge grows stronger to get hold of an object at very close range by way of its likeness, its reproduction" (Benjamin 1969, 233). Insisting on a broad view of the mechanisms of mimesis, Taussig engages not only visual resemblance but also the evocation of similarities through sounds, smells, and tactile stimuli that interact with and conjure up memory, visual imagery, and sensory responses. This exploration of magic, colonization, and alterity reveals the ways in which representation and the thing represented cohere and impact one another reciprocally, "making us reconsider our very notion of what it is to be an image of some thing, most especially if we wish not only to express but to manipulate reality by means of its image" (Taussig 1993, 57). Taussig founds his study on a vision of mimetic excess which "provides access to understanding the unbearable truths of make-believe as foundation of an all-too-seriously serious reality, manipulated but also manipulable" (1993, 255). Closing his history of colonization, fetish, and mimesis, Taussig alludes to a world in which a contemporary subject uses the human mimetic faculty to seize "the freedom to live reality as really made-up," working with objects, bodies, and ideas to transform the world through mimetic means (1993, 255). This excessive mimeticism that transforms ideas and objects through a complex web of sensed and felt manipulations of the "real" matter they imitate helps frame the relationship between event, sensation, and meaning in the alimentary performances discussed below, each of which uses culinary mimesis to not only mirror but to manipulate and transform the material and social contexts in which they come into being.

Two elements of Taussig's work are critical for understanding mimetic cuisine in performance contexts. First, Taussig insists on a mimesis that both interacts with the senses and extends beyond them. Like Adrià, he refuses a hard line between sensation and intellect, instead recognizing the essential relation between mimesis and recognition, which can be brought on by the senses singly or in combination and constitutes a physical, affective, and intellectual response simultaneously. The artists discussed below rely not solely on visual, gustatory, or olfactory stimulus to create and manipulate resemblances, but instead craft mimetic assemblages of memory, history, sensation, emotion, and intelligence through multiple sensory stimuli, dramaturgical contexts, and performance acts. Second, Taussig highlights the way in which mimesis can erode the distinction between "real" and "imitation" or original material and its copy, especially in light of the colonial play of imitations his work describes. He describes this mimetic excess as "mimetic self-awareness, mimesis turned on itself, on its colonial endowment, such that now, in our time, mimesis as a natural faculty and mimesis as a historical product turn in on each other as never before" (Taussig 1993, 252). Through this process, "selves dissolve into senses and the senses show signs of becoming their own theoreticians as world histories regroup" (Taussig 1993, 253). The artists discussed here work in just this way, erasing and reforming lines between selves and senses as they cook food that regroups world histories, reframes ideologies, and carves out new spaces in which the senses and knowledge cohere rather than diverge. They do so through the use of "real" materials imbued, through mimetic contexts and performance frameworks, with the ability to represent forgotten histories as well as imagined futures through alimentary performance.

With these framing concepts in mind, my main examples flow chronologically, beginning with Alison Knowles's use of food as a means of rupturing gendered boundaries between the domestic and the public spheres in the 1960s and onward. Next, I examine feminist culinary performances by Carmelita Tropicana before turning to Bobby Baker's sustained engagements with food and performance from the 1970s to the turn of the twenty-first century. Finally, I close with the notion of edible geographies, discussing issues of colonization and authenticity in two antithetical yet related culinary performances: Michael Twitty's mimetic reenactments of slave cookery and Rick Bayless's *Cascabel*, which uses culinary mimeticism to assert a magical preeminence within Mexican cuisine. Through this series of case studies, I trace multiple ways in which artists have used culinary mimeticism to reconsider the relationship between sensation and meaning, constructing performances through which cooking and eating can change relations between people, alter the meaning of everyday actions, and intervene in situations of injustice.

Art imitates life imitates art: food and the representation of "real life"

An international movement that exposed the fragility of perceived divisions between art and everyday life, Fluxus emerged in part from John Cage's late 1950s experimental composition course at New York's New School for Social Research, where artists like George Brecht and Dick Higgins experimented with strategies for composing from everyday life. Within the larger context of Fluxus's dismantling of sensory and representational hierarchies, Alison Knowles's work in food-based art and edible event scores stands out as one of the most significant examples of the 1960s turn toward edible art. The concept of the event score, developed by Brecht as part of his work in the course, became a common element in a diverse set of artistic experiments and practices that often focused on texts, objects, and performances rather than on the creation of static images. Perhaps due to their origins in musical composition, in addition to their typical basis in physical action, the scores created by Fluxus artists like Brecht and Alison Knowles have generally been considered unconcerned with representation. Yet viewed through the lens of excessive mimesis, Fluxus's taste-oriented work, from event scores to Fluxbanquets and especially Knowles's food projects, retains particular relevance for this study.

While Fluxus historian Hannah Higgins refers to these olfactory and gustatory works as "relegated to the margins" of the movement, the mimetic aspects of Fluxbanquets were substantial. Meals featuring clear foods, for instance, distillates of coffee, tea, tomato and juice, or George Maciunas's unrealized concept of monomeals, with a single flavor explored through a series of common textures and preparations (Higgins's example includes fish candy, fish ice cream, fish salad, and fish tea) use mimetic techniques to rupture the relationship between taste and the other sensory elements of alimentary experience, rendering the objects eaten a spur to contemplation and conversation (Higgins 2002, 46). Other mimetic Fluxus food performances, like Knowles's 1969 "Shit Porridge," made of one of her favorite materials, beans, but mimetically resembling the eponymous excrement, anticipate work like Homaro Cantu's famed roadkill, garbage, and toilet bowl dishes or Heston Blumenthal's vomit soup and snot smoothies. In considering these rare moments of mimetic play in a movement that was largely anti-representational, Higgins importantly observes that artists like Knowles and Maciunas undercut the dominant sensory hierarchy that places taste at the far end of the continuum of ability to communicate meaning. Instead, these mimetic meals pushed "representation itself toward the primary mode of experience" (Higgins 2002, 49). By uniting rather than separating representation and proximal sensory experience, artists like Maciunas and Knowles opened an important breach in established assumptions about the relationship between the two, paving the way for contemporary culinary mimeticism.

While food was treated as both art and craft for millenia before the 1960s, Knowles's work helped bring cooking and eating into the gallery spaces, public fora, and publications that characterize the world of "serious" art. In taking food seriously as an artistic medium, Knowles helped put the everyday on display for contemplation and attention. While much of her work is, if not anti-mimetic, disinterested in representation per se, in this section I examine a handful of projects of relevance for contemporary culinary mimeticism. Recalling Taussig's point about the inextricable binding of material reality and illusion through which mimesis constitutes "the nature that produces second nature," Knowles uses real labor, real foodstuffs, and real actions of cooking and eating to produce a representation of cooking. Or, as an observer of her 2012 enactment of *Make a Salad* on New York's High Line walkway explained, indicating the mutual influence of materiality and imitation in the re-performance of the now-classic work, "it's art imitating life imitating art" (Morais 2012). In particular, Knowles's food work lays important ground for contemporary struggles over the art-ness of cuisine, in which chefs like Achatz and Adrià have turned to mimeticism to distinguish themselves from the entanglement with the everyday established in Knowles's food-based art.

First performed in 1962, *Make a Salad* has become one of Knowles's best-known event scores in part due to prominent performances of the eponymous instruction since the turn of the twenty-first century. While its original incarnation involved Knowles creating and serving the salad herself to an audience of a few dozen people as part of an evening of Fluxus works from multiple artists, subsequent versions, including the 2008 Tate Gallery performance I discuss below, have served much larger audiences, including more than one performance for an audience in excess of one thousand people. The full text of the work, as later published in collections of Knowles's event scores, is as follows:

> Proposition
> Make a salad.
>
> *(Knowles 1992, 1)*

Knowles diverges from Brecht's score format, posing the work as a "proposition." The seductive undertones of the word connect intriguingly with its central action, the provocative merging of domestic labor with the male-dominated space of the professional art world where the piece has been subsequently performed and re-performed for decades. As one of the only female members of the US wing of Fluxus, Knowles's choice to make a salad may stand out as a particularly feminine offering subtly slipped into a masculine event context. But at the same time, through the use of the term proposition, Knowles positions her work as reframing others' activities, claiming actions of others under the rubric of her work. The capacious quality of the proposition extends to cover quite prominent events, as Knowles remarked to a reporter covering the High Line *Make a Salad*: "'You know, I was sitting in the Presidential dining room a while ago, and they served a salad.' She didn't mention this at the time to President Obama. 'They didn't realize they were doing my piece.'" (Morais 2012). This anecdote drives home the proposition's creative scope: everyone everywhere who makes a salad participates in Knowles's work, whether they know it or not.

While relational artists have since produced pieces that treat feeding audiences as their main action, like Rirkrit Tiravanija's now-classic *Untitled (free)* (1992), Knowles's treatment of cooking itself as performance distinguishes her work from this tradition. Observers have rightly identified Knowles's performances of *Make a Salad* as "labor-oriented" in that they display the artist and her collaborators at work, their labor the primary source of auditory and visual interest during the score's performance (Robinson 2004). Thus it's worth noting how carefully Knowles distinguishes her own labor from that of the collaborating chefs with whom she often works. A 2008 performance of *Make a Salad* at London's Tate Gallery featured the artist and a group of professional chefs collaborating to prep salad ingredients and drop them twenty-five feet from a bridge onto a tarp held by college student volunteers. As the artist and chefs worked, the assembled audience of 2,500 people listened to the amplified sounds of chopping and tearing vegetables accompanied by a small string orchestra. After tossing the salad with the tarp and stirring with a sterilized garden rake, Knowles personally served over two hundred pounds of salad to the audience. While famous for her work with food, in this performance Knowles visually and performatively identifies herself as distinctly not-chef, her female body clad in everyday clothes next to largely male chefs in uniforms. She confirms this division by referring to her culinary collaborators as the Tate's "professional chefs" (Knowles 2009, 140). However, this distinction is not about modesty or an erasure of the artist's presence in the event. On the contrary, Knowles retains ownership over the event as the only person to speak during its execution, announcing the next set of ingredients to be tossed from the bridge: "And then I would announce that the carrots were coming over. ... and every time that I poured something, I announced it and everyone would cheer. Beets. Yay!" (Knowles 2010). By acting as emcee, Knowles retains the power to direct the audience's intellectual, sensory, and affective responses to the event, positioning herself in the domain of the artist.

Knowles's record of the event demonstrates the critical distinction she draws between herself, the artist, and chefs who assisted her. Her drawing of the event features two large figures, one labeled ALISON drawn with straight lines of stress and energy radiating from its head (Knowles 2009, 142). This figure reaches energetically toward the left of the image, emptying a bowl of vegetables. The contents of this bowl sprawl across the page, some seemingly on a trajectory to land wide of the tarp, on the venue floor. Next to this figure, one labeled CHEF carefully upends a platter, its contents streaming straight down at the tarp. This figure wastes no energy and features no indication of emotion. At the event, this distinction between artist and chef became apparent not only through action, with Knowles raking and serving, but also through costume choices. The bodies of the chefs, clad in matching white shirts and black and white striped aprons, contrasted sharply with the artist's loose salmon-colored blouse and pendant necklace. Here Knowles's costumed body serves an essential function within the work, creating a space in which the amateur and the everyday literally interconnect with the professional and the special occasion. This complex set of qualities exist simultaneously in

Knowles as the artist, allowing the performance to represent life to itself through the framework of art. In imitating life imitating art, *Make a Salad* transforms both at the same time, inviting attention to the places where distinctions between the two blur.

Knowles carefully merges elements of the everyday and of art in another of her famous food works, *Identical Lunch*. Embarked upon by Knowles in 1969 when her colleague Philip Corner noted that she ate the same meal for lunch each day, *Identical Lunch* became one of Knowles's longest-running and most complex event scores. At first the artist resolved to formalize the practice of her unchanging mid-day meal, dining at the same restaurant on the same food and documenting the experience in writing and photos. Eventually others took up the event score, introducing new variations as they did. For instance, Corner, whose experiments with the lunch were published in a volume by Knowles in 1973, ate his way through the entire menu at the restaurant where Knowles's score first took place. While colleagues often pushed *Identical Lunch* into the realm of the abject or defamiliarized, as in Maciunas's choice to pulverize the constituent elements into a blender, Knowles remained committed to repeating the original identical meal, a tuna sandwich on buttered wheat toast with buttermilk or soup. Instead of abandoning this everyday meal, Knowles allowed her score to accumulate variations as Corner, Maciunas, and others took up her project, allowing the iterative performances of dining to rub against one another and create opportunities not only for performances of the everyday, but re-stagings of the event that form a funhouse mirror to the mundane. For instance, in a 2011 staging of *Identical Lunch* at New York's Museum of Modern Art, Knowles first performed her own version of the meal, lunching on sandwiches with museum guests, before executing Maciunas's version, offering everyone sips of the resulting tuna milkshake (Nathan 2011). This process of accumulation has transformed *Identical Lunch* from an anti-mimetic practice of art in the everyday to a mimetic recreation of a prior instance of the artist's work, which itself constitutes a new intervention, a retrospective of the passage of Knowles's lunch from life into art and back again. Randy Kennedy's description of the MOMA *Identical Lunch* details its mimetic elements, noting both the use of a specially designed table fashioned to evoke mid-century Formica and the oddity of the repetition of identical lunches alongside the anachronistic accompaniment of glasses of buttermilk (2011). In this restaged *Identical Lunch*, enacted in the MOMA cafeteria, eleven diners joined the artist for a meal that was simultaneously an enactment of the score and a journey through its own history, complete with period scenic elements and surprise twists like the aforementioned tuna shake. Kennedy notes the liquid lunch gains new significance in its contemporary context: "In a world where molecular gastronomy, with its edible emulsions and foams, has become part of 'nonart reality,' it actually tasted like something one might pay $30 for somewhere outside Barcelona" (Kennedy 2011). Kennedy's evocation of Spanish avant garde cuisine such as Adrià's highlights the way in which Knowles's food experiments have completed a mimetic circuit, beginning in a state of non-art reality, transitioning through the rarefied spaces of the museum and the fine art journal, and returning to the in-between space of the

MOMA cafeteria. Along the way Knowles's sandwich score gained both visual representational strategies, such as the Formica table, and culinary representational weight, Maciunas's tuna shake anachronistically aligning with mimetic techniques such as culinary deconstruction. In its early incarnations, Natasha Lusetich has observed that the lunch performed time itself, "involving the percipient/performer in listening deeply to the dialectical, ordinary-musical, actual-virtual, lived-phenomenal production of existence, the only difference being that of scale" (Lusetich 2011, 86). In its more recent history, the lunch has come to perform not only the immediate moment of existence, but also a mimetic reproduction of history and memory. Yet in contrast with Kennedy's recognition of the meal's affiliation with culinary avant garde practices, Knowles continues to highlight the critical dividing line between herself and chef-professional: "She pronounced her sandwich, made by the cafeteria's executive chef, Lynn Bound, to be 'state of the art,' among the best she had had in four decades of tuna-sandwich connoisseurship" (Kennedy 2011). In this statement of sandwich connoisseurship, Knowles yet again carves out space for alimentary artistry. The tuna sandwich occupies multiple artistic registers for different practitioners, simultaneously serving as the material of an event score constructed by the non-chef, Knowles, and as an artform in itself under the expert manipulation of chef Bound.

Knowles's studied cultivation of culinary amateurism extends as well to her iconic use of beans. In a typically matter-of-fact explanation, the artist recalls that she first began working with dried legumes because they were affordable and she knew how to cook them (Nathan 2011). This pragmatism belies her work's deep, exhaustive, even playfully obsessive exploration of all things bean, as seen in her 1963 *Bean Rolls*, which collects an idiosyncratic abundance of information on beans of all sorts. The "canned book" consists of a tin containing dried beans along with scrolls inscribed with bean recipes, fables about beans, ads, and other material produced in Knowles's search on the topic at the New York Public Library. Anticipating the contemporary information age, when the gathering of esoterica would become a popular pastime, this work focuses audiences on both the immediate materiality of a foodstuff (the dried bean) and its cultural significance (the scrolls) simultaneously. While it never constructs a mimetic representation of a bean, *Bean Rolls* offers its reader a chance to reconfigure her internal image of the bean, to attach new meaning to the everyday by working with material and context together in a performance event.

Redefining the spaces in which she cooks, Knowles points to her work as shifting the focus of the institutional space of the museum. Discussing MOMA's *Identical Lunch*, for instance, she reflects on the piece's influence on curatorial process: "now instead of what color is the wall, they're talking about how many seats should be at the table, and how many strangers should be there, and how many guests would Alison invite, and what time of the day should it be. These are very different questions, daily questions" (Knowles 2010). This substitution of one question for another extends into not only museum spaces and theatrical spaces that Fluxus artists challenged with their work, but also in the other direction, into the everyday. While Knowles steadfastly insists her own art is not feminist, she acknowledges the fact that her work brought what was then "women's work" into the public sphere and has the power to inspire new attentiveness to the meanings of domestic labor. Knowles suggests, for instance, that an audience member might decide to go home and make a salad, treating domestic labor as art rather than "wishing they could go to the movies" (2015, 46). By reframing the significance of culinary labor, Knowles thus aims to reframe the significance of the acts of eating and cooking, empowering the unnamed cook in her example to see her work as significant in itself, worth attending to for both its immediate sensory qualities as well as the meanings one might apprehend within it. In replacing movies with salad, Knowles intervenes in the hierarchical relationship between art and the everyday, proving through culinary representation that such meaning is real and reproducible.

Chicken sushi to cannibalistic cake: feminist mimetic foodplays

While Knowles, one of the only US women affiliated with Fluxus, has consistently disavowed any specific feminist impulse in her work, feminist artists of the late 1960s and 1970s followed her lead in making food a central material, subject, and theme in their work. 1970s and 1980s feminist work with food often treated it as a material imbued with literal and figurative slipperiness that provided unique representational and performative possibilities. Judy Chicago, Miriam Schapiro, and their collaborating students built sculptural mimetic still lives out of bread dough and installed mimetic foam breasts and eggs dripping down the walls of the iconic installation kitchen in their collaboratively built *Womanhouse* (1972). Chicago, Suzanne Lacy, Sandra Orgel, and Aviva Rahmani employed foods like uncooked animal kidneys and chicken eggs as scenic elements and props representing physical and psychological trauma in *Ablutions*, their 1972 performance piece exploring rape. In her 1980s performance art monologues like "Yams Up My Granny's Ass" and "I'm an Ass Man" US artist Karen Finley alternately captivated and horrified audiences by massaging canned yams, smearing ice cream, and spreading canned beans and liverwurst on her performing body. In what Christine Simonian Bean calls a "material strategy," Finley's 1980s work often combined food, text, costume, and her own body to create grotesque, provocative, humorous and often combative feminist performance art (Bean 2016, 89). While the food engagements of US performance artists in the critical period of the 1970s and 1980s often consisted of small bites like these and usually avoided feeding audiences, artists like Carmelita Tropicana, on whom I focus in this section, recognized the critical role food could play in staging uncomfortable aspects of real life while imagining new ways of living.

Milk, chicken, chocolate: Carmelita Tropicana's queer culinary mimesis

Paralleling but diverging from the trend of slippery abjection in Chicago and Finley's work, Carmelita Tropicana's alimentary performances from the early 1980s to the 1990s include both the visceral disgust of slippery raw chicken carcasses and the appealing familiarity of comfort foods like chocolate, flan, and *arroz con pollo*. In each of her food projects, Tropicana, an alter ego of writer and performance artist Alina Troyano, is specifically interested in food as a representational medium. Reminiscing about her early performance work, Tropicana conceives of the project of the Women's One World Cafe, which nurtured a groundswell of lesbian theatre and performance art in New York in the 1980s, as a play of representations: "The idea of a lesbian stereotype is a paradox given that lesbians have been historically invisible. If lesbians were imagined at all it was mainly as butch. One of the things I loved most about these early years at WOW is that we, that is lesbians, were able to come up with our own representations" (Román and Tropicana 1995, 87). Grappling with the challenging simultaneous reality of mainstream heteronormativity and the impossibility of a single truthful representation of queer female existence, the artists of WOW created a kaleidoscopic array of characters and performance strategies, both drawing on and subverting the paradoxical stereotypes Tropicana mentions. Along with Tropicana, who first performed at WOW Cafe's 11th St. location in 1983, artists like Split Britches, Holly Hughes, and the members of the Five Lesbian Brothers repurposed, celebrated, satirized, and transformed the materials of popular culture, high art, and everyday life into a new set of fantastical, mimetically excessive, and campy representations of queer lives and stories.

While each of the queer performers of WOW and related spaces used the raw materials of culture to imagine a new reality into being, Carmelita Tropicana took the notion one step further, frequently using raw ingredients in a subversive performance of queer identity manifested through food. Tropicana's early work typically featured the artist in a costume adorned with faux fruit, an ironic variety of the excessive mimesis that characterizes much of her performance. Tropicana's plays and performance pieces often involve food as a metaphor and prop, marking differences in taste, memory, and foodways as a way of highlighting and deconstructing stereotypical notions of identity. For instance, *Milk of Amnesia/Leche de Amnesia* (1994) tells the story of Alina/Carmelita's return to Cuba and resulting negotiation of multiple tastes and identities. The play's central metaphor juxtaposes the thick, sweet condensed milk of Cuba, where Alina was born, with the thin skimmed milk of the United States where she was raised and where Carmelita first came into being. Tropicana would later return to milk in a New Year's Eve celebration at New York's P.S. 122 in which she prepared flan for the audience in a gesture inviting a sweet new year. In this and all her performances, Tropicana layers multiple and multivalent flavors and identities in order to conjure a way forward built from the flavors, histories, and representations inherent in the colonial, patriarchal, racist, and heteronormative systems she both draws upon and lampoons. As Chon Noriega argues, Tropicana constructs this path forward "on the basis of a unity rooted in colonialism – which is to say, othering – rather than humanism" (2000, xii). Much of her food work thus highlights the violent forgetting of food histories involved in colonization, re-membering a new culinary reality through performance.

Tropicana pushed further toward the use of food as a representational medium in her performances involving one of the most famously malleable ingredients in contemporary cuisine: chicken. Two contrasting uses of chicken arise in Tropicana's early work: a paradoxical instance of anti-cooking in her famous chicken sushi (1984, 1987) and a fetishistic transubstantiation of her own sexual identity into a dish of *arroz con pollo* in the performative essay "Food for Thought" (1987a). Perhaps Tropicana's best-known use of poultry occurs in the camp Japanese–Cuban fusion "chicken sushi," prepared as a cooking segment of the satirical talk show *Carmelita Chats* (Dolan 1985, 30). In this parody of one of the most prominent platforms for women on television, the cooking show, Tropicana begins with a stereotypical tale of cultural encounter through food, explaining that after a cooking class with "master chef Japanese honorable Benihana-san" she took "the mystery of the Orient, the flavor of the Spanish, I put together to create the Japanese-Cuban cooking" (1987b). Introducing the three ingredients of the dish (canned black beans, a whole raw chicken carcass, and paprika), Tropicana anthropomorphizes the chicken carcass by offering several strategies to "make friends with the chicken," including dancing with it, singing to it, and slapping it around. The artist then invites an audience member to bang a wooden spoon on a pot as she conducts a "Japanese ritual," reciting a nonsense combination of Japanese brand names and words commonly heard in US contexts: "Toshiba, Mitsubishi, origami, arigato, Nagasaki, ah-so pollo" (1987b). Smacking the chicken with a sword, Tropicana declares she is ready to cook. She pours the can of beans over the chicken, sprinkles paprika over it, and finally adorns it with paper cocktail umbrellas, declaring "oh how beautiful! I can't believe my eyes, can you?" (1987b). In this moment, the camp chef ironically exposes the mimetic process of culinary encounter through which hybridizing appropriation masquerades as knowledge and even love. In this case the process is deliberately incomplete and undercut: we imagine the cold canned beans and uncooked chicken slipping sluglike down our throats, we smell the combination of viscous elements, canned bean juice and raw chicken slime, mingling on the plate, and our throats tighten as we laugh.

While Tropicana did not serve her dish of raw chicken with black beans to her audience in 1984, she revisits chicken sushi and pairs it with a cooked alter ego in "Food for Thought," an essay that appeared the same year as she performed a standalone version of "Chicken Sushi" in Germany. Combining a satiric history of the invention of chicken sushi with the preparation of *arroz con pollo*, Tropicana mimetically superimposes pleasure and abjection in an exploration of the relationship between food and identity. Tropicana's friend and queer performance scholar Jose Muñoz identified Tropicana's use of individual and collective remembering as a crucial response to the "devastating force of cultural and political amnesia" that confront exilic identity (Muñoz 1995, 82). In "Food for Thought," Tropicana uses food to enact a similar strategy of creative remembering. By layering the memory of chicken sushi atop the preparation of *arroz con pollo*, she makes a politically radical call for honest histories of foodways. Simultaneously, Tropicana invests this dish with mimetic resemblance to herself and her history, laying claim to the power of a classic Cuban dish to represent memory.

After beginning the essay with a brief discussion of the role of food in art and culture, with references to Pablo Neruda's food poems and Dan White's infamous "twinkie defense" in his trial for the murder of Harvey Milk, Tropicana explains she was led to a philosophical investigation of her relationship to food when her girlfriend called her a "food slut" (1987a, 187). Embarking on a mental journey through a culinary geography, Tropicana first discusses the interrelationship of food and identity in Cuban culture before turning to culinary transculturalism. She begins with a memory of chicken sushi: "I combined the mystery of the Orient with the flavor of the Spanish and created my masterpiece, the chicken sushi. Why had I combined these two cuisines? Was this a precursor to the multiculti revolution?" (1987a, 188). In this reference to chicken sushi, Tropicana recalls, repeats verbatim, and mimetically enlivens her prior parody, casting it as a symptom of her diseased relationship with food before immediately broadening the diagnosis to include world history and geography on a sweeping scale. From Columbus to British colonizers, Tropicana recounts a culinary geography of theft and violence and then ties that geography to foundational notions of cultural identity. Driving her point home, Tropicana paints a picture of US patriotism as founded on erasure of culinary history of indigenous peoples: "I cannot leave out the Yankee doodle dandies on the 4th of July grilling their hamburgers, hot dogs, and portabello mushrooms. They gotta thank the Arawaks of the Caribbean who invented the barbacoa they call BBQ" (1987a, 188). Returning to the present, Tropicana invokes the mimetic process of culinary appropriation, pushing it to an absurd mimetic excess. A bagel with lox and cream cheese gives her "an immediate admiration of the Jewish people" at first bite. The artist narrates eating her way through cultures, from India to Japan and China, and imagines a world brought together through food in a metaphorical bed of rice, "individual glutinous grains sticking to one another until a bed is created, a bed we can all lie in peacefully, the lion with the lamb, the chicken with the shrimp" (1987a, 189). Having laid down this metaphorical bed of rice, Tropicana closes her story by describing the seduction of her partner with a masterful rendition of *arroz con pollo* in which the rice becomes a mimetic double for Tropicana. Without touching her partner physically, Tropicana reveals that she "fell into *la petite morte*" (1987a, 189). Treating the food as a phallus, Tropicana casts herself as Cupid, her partner "pierced…with my arrow, an arrow of arroz con pollo" (1987a, 189).

"Food for Thought" involves a mimetic conjuring of magical food which the reader, depending on her familiarity with the referenced dish, may indeed imagine herself consuming. But, like Finley, much of Tropicana's food work did not cross the boundary of the stage until later in her career, when she began feeding the audience delicious morsels that contrast with or connect to the food elements on the stage. For instance, her 2011 performance lecture at the Brooklyn Museum included a chocolate prize for both winners and losers of a game in which Tropicana quizzed participants about the true origins of common foods such as chicle, a major ingredient in early twentieth-century forms of commercial chewing gum. This product of the sapodilla tree, which was popular with Mayans from at least 200 BCE, made US entrepreneurs like Thomas Adams and William Wrigley rich even as consequent overharvesting devastated forests in Mexico, Guatemala, and Belize and wreaked economic devastation in Mayan communities (Matthews 2009). While quizzing her players about the fraught and often unknown histories of common foodstuffs, Tropicana includes chocolate as a sweet treat for winners and losers. However, the artist does not allow participants an easy, saccharine closure. Instead, in offering an ingredient with its own complex colonial history, Tropicana insists on taking the bitter with the sweet.

As these examples demonstrate, Tropicana's work treats ingredients and dishes as mimetic doubles for bodies and histories. As her work evolves, she moves from food as a thematic element to food as a material strategy and finally to sharing food with her audience as a means of creating intimate contact with colonial histories. This movement from food as subject to food as performer to food as a primary element of audience experience constitutes an eruption of substance as food evolves from apprehensible subject matter into sensed presence. In moving from mimetic representation of food to mimetic representation through food, Tropicana also moves from the abject, in chicken sushi, to the seductive, in *arroz con pollo*, before merging the two in an uncanny blend in chocolate, an iconic foodstuff of empire served as a prize for both winners and losers in a game of reconstructed culinary memory.[1]

Consuming bodies: Bobby Baker's feminist mimetic cannibalism

While for Knowles and Tropicana food is a prominent recurring theme and material, for British multimedia artist Bobby Baker it is a constant. From her first major work, the food-based installation *An Edible Family in a Mobile Home* (1976) to her use of tea as a gesture of disturbing hospitality in *Kitchen Show* (1991), Baker's art consistently incorporates food as a material, a context, and a subject of her events and performances. While a few of Baker's works include food as a material without offering audiences alimentary stimulation, all involve food in some fashion, often exploring the unstable terrain between the consuming body and the body to be consumed. For instance, in *Drawing on a Mother's Experience* (1988), Baker draws equivalence between her maternal experience, her experience of food and eating, and her own physical body. The artist creates and ultimately wraps herself, "like a swiss roll," in a food painting made of ingredients like beef, beer, currants, treacle, biscuit crumbs, and flour, offering the audience a visual and olfactory stimulus as she crushes, stomps, and tosses foods onto a plastic canvas. Even *How to Live* (2004), in which Baker abandons the terrain of domesticity and takes up the clinical space of the psychologist's office, features a frozen pea as the artist's primary psychoanalytic subject. I focus on 1976's *An Edible Family in a Mobile Home* and the 1990s *Daily Life Series*, major works produced on either side of Baker's long hiatus from performance art between the birth of her first child in

1980 and her return to the stage with *Drawing on a Mother's Experience* in 1988. In the interim, Baker turns from an overtly mimetic approach to cooking and eating in her dark and playfully cannibalistic edible family to a more subtly representational use of cooking and eating to produce threateningly parodic versions of domesticity in *Daily Life*. Again and again, Baker's experiments in culinary mimeticism expose the porous boundary between the female body as consuming body and the female body consumed by domestic labor, by hungry children, by the weight of her own existence, and in some cases, by her audiences. Ultimately, her multiple approaches to culinary mimeticism cohere into an expansive representation of the consumable and consuming performance of mainstream femininity that uses food to rupture expectations and make space for a new attentiveness to its sensory and affective demands.

As with Knowles, one of Baker's most critical interventions lies in her intuition that the domains of the domestic and of everyday life are neither meaningless nor incapable of being represented in ways that captivate and consume us. Rather, as Griselda Pollock points out, Baker's work takes up material which "falls below the threshold of recognition" due to its association with domesticity and with women's lives (Pollock 2007, 178). In response to this problem of recognition, Baker's edible work constitutes a mimetic recuperation, provoking audiences to deploy their mimetic capacity to recognize significance as a cure for the representational invisibility of women's experience. In the face of the assumed insignificance of the domestic lives of women, Baker does not so much mount a counter argument as reveal a world of obvious significance that has hitherto been hidden by the inability of conventional artistic forms to express the complexity of women's daily lives.

In her first major work of edible art, *An Edible Family in a Mobile Home* (1976), Baker turned to food not only to satisfy a longstanding urge to create "a whole family out of cake," but because food provided a medium capacious enough to communicate in ways other media could not. Frustrated with conventional artistic practice, Baker speaks of *Edible Family in a Mobile Home* as a "turning point," explaining "I couldn't fit my ideas into traditional art forms and then I discovered my own language" (Baker 1994, 28). In contrast to Hegel's view of food's capacity for meaning as limited by the problem of consumption, *Edible Family in a Mobile Home* demonstrates that ephemeral acts of cooking and eating can produce an abundance of representations. Contextualizing her cakes physically, in a domestic space, and linguistically, through the act of naming the figures and the installation, Baker invests these foodstuffs with representational weight. But through the use of materials such as store-bought biscuits, tea, and home baked traditional cakes, Baker also capitalizes on a wealth of meanings already present in the materials with which she works. Atop this mountain of meanings sits the significance of acts of cooking and eating themselves, each of which contrasts, complements, or complicates the significance of the mimetic elements of the installation.

Like Knowles, Baker also worked in non-traditional spaces, installing *Edible Family* in her own mobile home in a bid to attract a wide audience. Installing each member of the family in their own room, she created a garibaldi biscuit and chocolate cake son, coconut cake baby, meringue daughter, fruitcake father, and mobile tea service mother complete with cakes, sandwiches, and fruit. The entire space was wallpapered in newsprint and magazine clippings and then iced. Baker greeted visitors with tea served from the mobile mother's body, and guests were invited to eat their way through the installation. As the week-long installation progressed, the process of eating morphed from art patrons consuming polite slices of cake offered by the artist to local children grabbing fistfuls of the coconut baby and stuffing them into their mouths, until all that remained of the youngest family member, with whom Baker identified most as the baby of her own family, were crumbs (Baker 2007, 38). Baker's discussion of *Edible Family in a Mobile Home* makes clear that, by eating it, participants contributed to, rather than destroying, an accumulation of representation in the piece:

> With that specific piece I was thrilled at the prospect of the family disappearing; that the work would be lost and that it would be absorbed into other people's bodies. I am fascinated with the object becoming part of the body and then being shat out, the whole material cycle; so that you make a work of art which represents something and then it is physically transformed.
>
> (Baker 1999)

Satisfied with the ability of food to draw a wide audience, Baker nevertheless lamented that few participants were able to experience the transformation from "a representation of perfect, spotless, sugary-sweet family life" to a stinking, decayed set of plundered sweets and stripped armature "more like *The Texas Chainsaw Massacre*" (2007, 39). The importance of transformation as an aspect of her culinary language ultimately led the artist to explore theatrical work in which audiences could experience a range of sensations and transformations in one sitting.

In conceiving *The Kitchen Show* (1991), the first of her five *Daily Life* performances, Baker began with an interest in highlighting virtuosic domestic labor before arriving at a performance of hospitality. While peeling carrots in her kitchen, the artist "decided that an international satellite link should be set up where my live actions would be beamed around the world to crowds of cheering spectators. The next best thing was to open my kitchen to the public and display a set of live actions" (Baker 2008). In calling her performance's home kitchen setting "the next best thing," Baker highlights an essential quality of *Kitchen Show*, which positions the revealing display of the artist's kitchen as a kind of making do. In a gesture of mimetic excess, Baker reaches for what's to hand, namely the familiar tropes of domesticity, in order to remake them into a simultaneously sardonic and celebratory examination of women's work and its confounding virtues. As Lucy Baldwyn argues, Baker's work both celebrates and undermines stereotypes of domestic femininity, often by deploying "the visceral qualities of food: its proximity to the body and to emotions, and its ability to represent what we would rather forget" (1996, 37). This reference to proximity highlights the way in which Baker exploits the materiality of food to undertake a mimetic intervention into the immaterial yet materially significant ideologies of gender. By using food as a performance material, Baker invests a familiar substance with mimetic weight, transforming, à la Taussig's theory of mimetic excess, it into a representation made of the same stuff as the real thing. Then Baker feeds this transformed material, invested with new significance, to her audience. In doing so she invites her audience to attend to the often invisibilized aspects of women's labor in daily life, taking these edible representations of womanhood into themselves.

In response to the overwhelming social force pushing her to perform an idealized domestic femininity, Baker responds with mimetic excess, explaining that "I can turn the tables quite successfully [...] making use of the image of myself as a middle aged woman and subverting that, constantly shocking and breaking down those expectations" (Oddey 1999, 276). By simultaneously playing herself alongside an ironic representation of an ideal woman in a process Jenny Lawson calls "self-conscious citationality" (2011, 358), Baker leans into this notion of female mimeticism in order to expose invisibilized truths about women's lives, casting the audience in the double role of spectators and personal guests. Futhermore, by enacting this mimetic excess through food, Baker ruptures the delicate boundary between guest and host, actor and audience, bodily sensation and intelligent interpretation, instead creating a risky interpenetration of categories of experience which must be carefully held separate for these divisions to hold.

Tellingly, *The Kitchen Show*'s first moment consists of Baker serving tea or coffee to her guests. As a contemporary ritual of hospitality, the offer of a beverage reads as mundane. Yet as the artist makes, pours, adds sugar and milk, and stirs her audience member's drinks for them one at a time, all while describing the process in detail, she initiates a complex sensory contact between herself, the audience member, and the context of domestic hospitality, one that lasts the duration of the performance as the drink is consumed and the cup is held in a hand or lap. As Baker explains, her initial interest in food sprang from an urge to create a kind of contemplative disorientation that recalls Benjaminian incorporation: "It came together with the idea I had very early on of wanting to make work that related to those moments in time where just for a split second you experience an extraordinary complex set of realities, associations" (Baker 1994, 31). In narrating the ritual of tea service as she enacts it, Baker invites just this sort of incorporative play of associations, focusing the audience on her physical action as a way of unlocking memories and associations that will reverberate through the rest of their experience of the performance.

In narrating this gesture of hospitality, Baker also highlights the way that gestures of welcome bind the guest and the host in a relation of uneasy power, echoing Derrida's insights into the hostility of hospitality (2000). As Baker pours tea and coffee, she explores the burden of welcoming people into one's home, explaining that when guests arrive in her kitchen "I don't like them to sit there with nothing. It makes me feel anxious" (1991, 165). The gesture of tea service thus becomes a partial means of resolving anxiety, a reassertion of control over the interloper in one's home through the offer of a gift that puts the guest in one's debt. Baker emphasizes the anxiety of this risky togetherness in her discussion of performing in her own home: "There's a great risk in opening my kitchen to the public: to be in such an intimate environment where you can't avoid seeing what's actually happening. I've become so bound up with the people during the performances, that I actually think I know them" (Baker 2007, 155). *The Kitchen Show*'s mimetic production of hospitality so closely resembles the real thing that it fools even the artist herself. But Baker's performance disrupts this resemblance almost as soon as it creates it, using a literal gesture of binding to layer new representational offers atop the accumulating set of meanings haunting her tea service.

The making of tea is the first of thirteen gestures comprising *The Kitchen Show*, each of which Baker memorializes in a physical adjustment to her costume (other culinary gestures include hurling a ripe pear against the kitchen cabinet with all her strength). For this first gesture, she binds her hand in the perfect position for politely holding a teaspoon, freezing the action of stirring and keeping the memory of her hospitality fresh in the visual field of the performance as the audience drinks and watches the remaining acts. This literal binding parallels the other senses in which Baker's use of tea binds her audiences to her and her to them. Through her tantalizing mimesis of domesticity, Baker presents a housewife slightly askew, and through the sensory contact of tea and drinker, she binds herself and her audience to that off-kilter representation. This off-kilter quality is driven home by the binding tape itself, which Baker chose because "it's sort of flesh-coloured, but it's not. I find it very interesting looking at those bandages, their notion of what colour your skin is" (Baker 1994, 35). Baker's choice of a tape that is not quite skin but means to approximate it helps drive home her mimetic engagement with domesticity as performance. Just as her performance of domesticity is both true and also feels not-quite-right, the uncanny but not-quite resemblance between hand and bandage reminds us that performing woman's work is an act of impossible representation.

Baker compounds this sense of risk in the next installment of the *Daily Life* series, *How to Shop* (1993). Through a series of actions, video clips, and lecture segments in the tone of an academic talk, Baker first theorizes shopping and then takes the audience on a field trip through a supermarket. Presented as a quest in the mode of Bunyan's *Pilgrim's Progress*, Baker's supermarket journey features seven objects corresponding to the seven virtues. Parsley stands for Humility, sardines for Obedience, shaving cream for Patience, an apple for Joy, oil for Courage, wine for Compassion, and, finally, bread for Love. As in *Kitchen Show*, Baker's interactions with these everyday objects demonstrate that, far from meaninglessness, the actions of everyday domesticity are fraught with often terrible meanings and consequences, especially for the lives and bodies of women like Baker. Her interactions with her edible materials again surface a lurking hostility beneath everyday life. For instance, staging obedience, Baker crams a can of sardines lengthwise into her mouth, producing a tinny forced grin that evocatively highlights the discomforts associated with women's affective labor. At the close of the event, Baker enacts her final virtue, Love. Hearkening back to the mimetic cannibalism of *An Edible Family in a Mobile Home*, the artist prepares a version of communion for her guests, serving them garlic croutons cooked *a la minute* onstage. In this moment of onstage cooking, Baker exposes the uneasy combination of love and destruction at the heart of the impossible domestic virtue she lampoons.

Connecting domestic virtue with the religious ritual through which bread and wine mimetically substitute for the broken body of a martyred savior, Baker adds the action of cooking, usually omitted from the communion ritual. As she prepares her croutons, Baker demonstrates her culinary prowess, continuing the theme introduced in *Kitchen Show*. She invests the material substance of the bread with her labor, sacrificing it in a gesture of love that overlays the context of communion, referred to in some Christian traditions as a "love feast." Furthermore, as she toasts the croutons in fried garlic, Baker highlights the sensory pleasures of a ritual usually treated as only symbolic rather than constituent of a meal in itself. The smell of frying garlic and warm bread fills the lecture hall as she fries "Mother's Pride" brand bread in small pieces and carefully deposits the resulting croutons into baskets to be distributed, ala the Christian parable of the loaves and fishes, to the audience. The moment may be taken as either (or both) appealing and terrifying, capable of evoking cannibalism or comfort. Again, just as Baker performs multiple characters, presenting a self bounded by and struggling against convention alongside a historically situated and socially constructed category of womanhood, so does her bread, opening an invitation to incorporative reverie that might, however briefly, reframe relationships between self and other, male and female, human and divine, real and imagined.

Where artists from Judy Chicago to Carmelita Tropicana staged acts of cooking and eating as a means of bringing women's experiences to light, Baker intensifies and extends this feminist fascination with food into a fully embodied set of culinary representations, from cannibalistic cake to torturous tins of sardines. Like Shakespeare's Mistress Quickly, Baker's work proclaims the way in which performing domesticity eats one out of house and home but manages, through mimetic reconfiguration of these same materials, to "have some of it out again" (*Henry IV Part 2*, II.i 61–63). While their methods and aims diverge, each of these artists use food to draw formerly hidden realms to the surface of their performances, revealing the complex play of representations lurking behind quotidian spaces of kitchen sinks and dining tables. Furthermore, both Baker and Tropicana use the materiality of food as a means of exposing and disrupting quotidian systems of oppression, from the hidden hostility of domestic hospitality to the erased imperial histories of everyday foodstuffs. Through excessive mimesis, Tropicana and Baker construct a representation of reality from the everyday materials and acts that constitute it, offering their audiences a space for incorporative reverie that, however briefly, allows them to imagine worlds that work otherwise.

Staging culinary geographies: issues of justice and authenticity in alimentary performance

While the feminist artists above laid the foundation for culinary mimeticism as a contemporary activist strategy, I turn now to two recent examples of performance that expose the challenges and possibilities of culinary mimesis as a means of claiming places, stories, and histories. First, I consider Rick Bayless's *Cascabel*, a performance event in which the Oklahoman celebrity chef constructs an imaginative culinary geography that buttresses his claims to authentic connection with the Mexican culinary traditions that have made him a star. Alongside this mimetic strategy for claiming culinary space, I consider Michael W. Twitty's reenactments of historical African-American cookery, which recreate the past in the present in order to trace accurate African-American culinary histories. Using representation as an activist tool in support of culinary justice, Twitty cooks in the style of historical reenactment, using period costumes, tools, and methods to performatively reintroduce lost, or purposefully hidden, culinary knowledge into the public sphere. Advocating a version of terroir based in blood memory, Twitty re-uses and transforms the same mimetic tactics through which enslaved cooks managed to preserve their traditions and with which white culinary writers and chefs have appropriated and claimed these traditions as their own. Meanwhile, Chicago celebrity chef Rick Bayless uses an imaginative, world-reconfiguring mimesis to construct a theatrical representation of a culinary origin-story that undergirds a claim to authenticity essential to his haute-Mexican cuisine empire. For both performers, mimesis plays a central role in situating the chef's body and history within a critical culinary geography and genealogy. Furthermore, through the staging of food and cooking, each chef constructs an edible claim to the culinary traditions in which he works, implicating the audience who eats in the staging and realization of that claim as he brings it into being and invests it with an excess of representational weight. By examining Twitty's historical mimesis alongside Bayless's imaginative representation, I clarify the stakes of culinary mimeticism in enacting and framing issues of culinary justice and demonstrate the significant power of mimetic excess in the staging of culinary claims to authenticity, ownership, and ethical cookery.

Mimetic terroir: staging artifice and authenticity in the theatrical restaurant

Rick Bayless's career in many ways exemplifies the thorny relationship between culinary mimeticism, culinary appropriation, and culinary injustice. Critics, including Twitty, highlight Bayless as an exemplar of culinary injustice due to his position as a white Chicago chef treated as the US standard-bearer for Mexican cuisine (Arellano 2016, Saini 2016, Twitty 2017b). This critique hinges on a concern over the way in which Bayless mimetically stands in for "real" Mexican cuisine in the US, obscuring Mexican chefs in the process. On the other hand, Bayless specifically positions his culinary work as engaged with justice through his focus on generating celebrated representations of Mexican foodways. The tension between these two views of Bayless's work, each of which hinge on issues of representation, creates a powerful disjunction between the chef's image of himself and his representation in critical culinary discourse. In *Cascabel*, Bayless's 2012 theatrical collaboration with Chicago's Lookingglass Theatre, the chef deploys culinary mimeticism to resolve this tension, if only temporarily.

Before discussing *Cascabel*'s staging of an alternative culinary origin story, I first explore the tensions between representation, appropriation, and culinary justice in Bayless's career as a whole. Both the critics and Bayless himself often position his work as about representation. Bayless casts himself as an advocate for Mexican cuisine in the US, helping to nurture US appreciation of traditional Mexican cooking and its history. Indeed, the chef achieved such incredible prominence as an expert in Mexican cuisine that the Obama administration hired him to prepare the state dinner served to Mexican President Felipe Calderón in 2010. Treating the honor as political rather than personal, Bayless argued that the inclusion of traditional Mexican dishes in a state dinner represented a step forward for both the nation and his adopted cuisine: "when we are doing something very special it no longer has to be European or gussied-up American but from the heritage of a whole bunch of people in our country who have never been in the spotlight" (Burros 2010). Here Bayless argues for the representational impact of the event, suggesting that this highly theatrical event has the power to make visible the large number of Mexican-American citizens by treating Mexican cuisine as worthy of a US state dinner. At the same time, Bayless both acknowledges the typical conflation of European and US culinary traditions and, a moment later, distinguishes "American" cuisine from Mexican. Thus, while his sense of culinary justice is rooted in geography, that geography is shifting and contingent: "American" cuisine is that which has been in the spotlight, while Mexican cuisine, though "American" both in its geography and its connection with a prominent US constituency, remains distinct and separate from the mainstream, deserving to be brought to public prominence.

Bayless's sense of himself as a culinary advocate extends to his discourse of Mexican food as pure and authentic yet underrated by US chefs. In discussing the impact of bringing Mexican food to the White House, Bayless explains "French chefs come to the kitchen and are amazed at how complex Mexican food is, the layering of flavors. The food speaks for itself. It's not being whipped into submission like a French chef would do" (Burros 2010). The chef's praise of Mexican cuisine evokes the language of colonization, treating the French tradition as a tortured affair of bringing ingredients into submission. Mexican foodways, on the other hand, "speak for themselves," possessed of an authenticity that recalls unspoiled territory, ancient wisdom, and a space into which the white culinary anthropologist can invite fellow chefs on a voyage of discovery.

This tendency for Bayless to present himself as an advocate of a set of foodways he loves while speaking largely to an assumed audience of white people has led to pushback not only from Twitty, but from Mexican and Mexican-American culinary writers in particular. Dan Pashman of *The Sporkful* addressed these critiques with Bayless in a 2016 series of podcasts called "Other People's Food" (Saini 2016), and Bayless subsequently defended his position in a comment thread on NPR's story about the debate, arguing that his outsider status ought not be considered a negative aspect of his culinary work. In fact, Bayless has suggested the opposite. In comparison to native-born chefs, Bayless argues that an outsider has the benefit of objectivity rather than relational affiliations to specific dishes that might prevent the chef from reaching culinary perfection, famously arguing that his "greatest gift" as a chef is that he lacks a Mexican grandmother, leaving him free to view Mexican culinary traditions from an objective distance rather than through the lens of childhood experience and family traditions (Lam 2012). This claim to authenticity through outsider status resurfaces often in Bayless's career and in media discourse around his work. For example, Bayless ignited a firestorm of critique when he commented, in a Zagat interview, that San Francisco "doesn't really have much of a Mexican food tradition" (Alvarez 2013). Los Angeles restaurant reviewer Jonathan Gold earlier took Bayless to task for aiming to "introduce" Mexican cuisine to California through his consulting work for LA restaurant Red O (William-Ross 2010). When Bayless denied ever making such claims, *O.C. Weekly*'s Gustavo Arellano reprinted Bayless's original assertion that he opened Red O to explore "how the true flavors of Mexico, from central and southern Mexico, would play in Southern California" (Arellano 2016). Calling Red O "LA's ultimate palace of pretense," food blogger Bill Esparza painted the restaurant not as "authentic Mexican cuisine" but rather an authentic Los Angeles food venue, using an anti-mimetic critique to condemn the restaurant's attempts to convey authenticity through artifice and celebrity (2010). Describing the Bayless controversy in 2016, Arellano cast the problem as one of representation rather than appropriation. Rather than simply cooking the food of another culture, Arellano argues that Bayless's cuisine repackages it as his own in a process of mimetic colonization: "he really, truly believes he's the modern-day incarnation of Quetzalcoatl, the Mesoamerican deity that Spanish chroniclers claimed was the light-skinned, bearded savior of the Aztecs" (Arellano 2016). Arellano provocatively indicates the critical mimetic facets of Bayless's work through which the chef/anthropologist lays claim to an authentic Mexican-ness out of reach to Mexican chefs themselves. In Arellano's formulation, Bayless accomplishes a colonizing mimetic substitution, first asserting the need for a mimetic representation of Mexican foodways and then filling that need with his own culinary labor.

Viewed within the context of this critical debate over Bayless's work, *Cascabel* constitutes a mimetic claim to culinary authenticity. A co-creation with Heidi Stillman and Tony Hernandez, *Cascabel* indulges Bayless's love of theatre. The performance, accompanied by a multi-course meal, casts the chef as an outsider whose command of a traditional dish transfixes Mexican locals, bringing them back into a magical harmony with their heritage, their bodies, and one another. While the show commanded enough strong reviews and receipts to earn a revival in 2014, food and performance scholar Joshua Abrams noted the production's lack of culinary and theatrical sophistication, arguing it "fell prey to a flattening of both theatrical and culinary promise" (2013, 287). As Abrams points out, the production is light on geographical detail, evoking a generic outdoor space in its scenic design. It is spotty in its culinary execution, serving up an intriguing mimetic first course of "crab on the beach" featuring avocado-tortilla sand but also a bland chocolate cake whose spun sugar "shards of festivity" Abrams calls a "theatrical disappointment" (2013, 287). Yet *Cascabel* also constitutes something more complicated: a mimetic intervention into Bayless's own culinary history and geography, using culinary performance to create an alimentary argument for Bayless's right to this tradition and his importance within it.

Cascabel's narrative, centering on the cooking of a transcendent *mole*, treats Bayless as a soulful chef who regains the heart of the woman he loves, an innkeeper, and saves her from marriage to a boring businessman. As he cooks for the workers at the inn, each is inspired to perform outlandish circus acts in response to the gustatory rapture of Bayless's dishes. While Bayless's speaking part is relatively small, he cooks onstage throughout most of the evening, dances with the innkeeper, and interacts with the audience as the evening makes its way to a convivial concluding scene of drinking and dancing in celebration of the successful meal. Set in the Goodman Theatre's Owen performance space, the environment for the remounted *Cascabel* I saw in 2014 evoked not so much a restaurant in Mexico as a massive US-American backyard dinner party. Patrons could choose pricier floor seats at larger communal tables (with opportunity to meet the chef/star at the conclusion of the show) or less expensive seats in the narrow balcony with smaller tables allowing greater intimacy. We chose the latter due mostly to the price differential, but also to the improved sight lines for the show, which allowed us to witness Bayless's cooking. Upon arrival, we made our way to a table on the house left side of the balcony, which would prove a perfect vantage point for a high-wire act that took place just above our heads and a vertical balletic duet performed on the pole extending floor-to-ceiling just to our right. Our server provided us with menus and the event commenced. The actual meal, eaten by the audience, occurs roughly at the same pace as the dining experience onstage, though the onstage meal is like a restaurant's family meal, created by and eaten among fellow laborers, while the show's audience experiences a restaurant-style meal with servers delivering plates in a predictable rhythm of *amuse*, appetizer, main course, and dessert.

At *Cascabel*, audience members experienced opulence in the midst of a performance of the homespun, the economics being performed and the material conditions of the event itself standing in uneasy tension with one another. We traversed the theatre's marble architecture, tucked into an appetizer of caviar canapes, filled our cups from a supply of unlimited alcoholic beverages, and witnessed highly polished circus acts alongside trappings of the everyday (or performances of everydayness that we may or may not have recognized from our own lives), such as disposable plates (bamboo) or self-service beverages from an ice bucket left in reach beside the table. Most characters onstage were laborers. The only main character who appeared to have access to wealth was the production's antagonist, a businessman able to afford an ostentatious ring for the innkeeper, the chef's love interest. He later gives this ring to the chef to use in his own proposal to the innkeeper, suggesting a rightful awarding of the prize of a woman's love and fidelity to the man who inspired such heights of poetry and fancy from the everyday people depicted in the story. The chef's food inspires the workaday characters to new heights, in many cases literally, as in the aforementioned high wire act and a trapeze routine performed on the inn's chandelier. By the conclusion of the event, the inn and its inhabitants are transformed, the inn and innkeeper are saved, and the characters celebrate, singing and dancing together in exuberant recognition of the power of Bayless's transcendent meal to reconnect them with what truly matters.

Alongside its plot of culinary transformation, *Cascabel* simultaneously stages a mimetic defense of Bayless's claim to authenticity. The performance inherently relies on a complex artifice, the mimetic doubling of the audience's meal with those of the characters, to create opportunities for both the extension of the audience's perception through the drama and the projection of audience experience onto the characters. *Cascabel* invites us to fall in love with Bayless along with the innkeeper. This double-facing mimetic routine, with the plate connecting the diner to character while also extending her proximal senses into the dramatic world, becomes triply mimetic when one considers the aforementioned controversy over Bayless's status as a white Mexican restaurateur. An anthropologist by training prior to his turn to cooking, Bayless tells the story of his development as a chef through the lens of cultural knowledge, arguing that his love for Mexico ultimately created his love for Mexican cuisine. It's this claim to authenticity which suffuses *Cascabel* with an air of idiosyncratic travel. *Cascabel*'s theatrical meal, an extension, intensification, and reverberation of Bayless's culinary empire, transports us to Bayless's Mexico, one in which a humble (white) chef has the power to reignite the passions of a lovelorn Mexican woman with his *mole*.

The performance of authenticity that pervades the event, despite the clear disjunction between Bayless's performing body and the dramatic context of the story, leads reviewer Chris Jones to suggest that the true subject of the play is Bayless himself: "You feel like you are watching a culinary artist exploring his roots. It's fictional but also weirdly sans artifice" (2014). To unpack Jones's notion of fiction without artifice, I return to the concept of mimetic excess once more. The play accomplishes two overlapping representational strategies through the device of the shared and simultaneous actor/audience meal. First, we experience a mimetic doubling of character and audience member. Second, by watching Bayless prepare the dishes served to the characters, the audience mimetically experiences Bayless cooking for them. Bayless really cooks; we really eat. Watching the cooking, hearing the knives hitting the cutting board, or even smelling the cilantro as Bayless picks leaves from stems, we simultaneously rely on our proximal senses of taste and touch to encounter the cuisine as it is made. The fictional context of the performance links the two events, and the commensal element of our dining suffuses the experience with a sense of reality and tangibility. The Bayless onstage retains a close representational allegiance to the Bayless of *Top Chef*, Chicago television, local events, and James Beard awards. Indeed, many members of the audience have come to see Bayless more so than we have come to experience this production. Yet Bayless's character differs from the real chef in critical ways. He is poor; he is possessed of no celebrity; he is welcomed without question or critique by each of the play's Mexican characters; he is a humble cook serving Mexicans in Mexico rather than a chef/anthropologist helming a US restaurant empire. He is there for love; he is a chef returning to his emotional and culinary home. Thus the fictional world of *Cascabel* reinforces and enlivens a context the chef feels to be emotionally authentic if not literally true. Just as the "real" Bayless claims a deep ownership of his adopted cuisine that enriches the cuisine itself, this fictionalized Bayless returns to the mythic locale represented in *Cascabel* to revitalize the spirits of those who labor there. Even as we consume the literal foodstuffs Bayless prepares, the chef invites us to consume an alternative culinary origin story as well.

Food that tells the truth: Michael Twitty's plantation cookery

Having explored the use of culinary mimesis to stage imaginative claims to culinary authenticity in *Cascabel*, I turn now to an alternative use of culinary representation to stage erased histories. In an act of rebellion against a systematic erasure of enslaved cooks from the histories of foodways they inaugurated, culinary historian, activist, and performer Michael W. Twitty mimetically restages dishes devised by African-American slaves. Working in period costume and using historically specific tools, techniques, and ingredients, Twitty cooks recipes created by enslaved African-Americans on the grounds of historic plantations. In this section I present Twitty's culinary activism as an inversion of Bayless's *Cascabel*, which stages a claim to culinary authenticity through an imaginative externalization of the chef's emotional and intellectual connection to Mexican foodways. In contrast to this assertion of culinary ownership through mimetic substitution, Twitty's activist cooking demonstrations combat culinary injustice by enlivening history, staging an argument for culinary mimeticism as a means of telling the truth.

Highlighting representation as critical to culinary injustice, Twitty conceives of his project as an antidote to the process through which black culinary contributions vanish or are supplanted by whitewashed histories. As an undergraduate, Twitty published an article arguing against the amnesiac "lost heritage" fallacy that often haunts white histories of the African diaspora, arguing that enslaved African-Americans resisted this erasure by preserving their history through social ritual, foodways, crafts, and music, among other tactics (Twitty 2000). In his work as a food historian and performer, he interprets the significance of these methods of preserving culture, revealing what he calls the "persistence of memory" through which, "despite the possibility of being sold twice in a lifetime, enslaved Africans found ways to preserve their unique global civilization" (Twitty 2000). His interest in the ingenuity through which enslaved peoples preserved their culinary history through creativity, innovation, and mimetic subterfuge led Twitty to reenact these culinary histories in the present through performance. Referring to his period garb as "transformative historical drag," Twitty mimetically calls centuries-gone cooks into being by performing traditional songs, cooking techniques, and above all the labor that has been erased as slave stories have been romanticized, whitewashed, and ignored (Twitty 2017a, 1). Twitty's plantation performances serve as a forceful counter to this erasure, a performed activism he describes as mimetic combat: "When I put on the clothes that transform me into a representative of my ancestors, when I pick up the cooking pot and change heirlooms and heritage breeds and wild foods into delicacies, I am doing it as an act of war" (Twitty 2015). Because the injustice Twitty attacks is rooted in stories, this act of culinary war invokes mimesis to combat pernicious representations of Africa, and of blackness, that helped justify mass enslavement and continue to reinforce systematic oppression of black people in the United States today. These acts of erasure exemplify Twitty's definition of culinary injustice: "what you get where you go to plantation museums and enslaved blacks are not even talked about, but called servants. We are invisible" (Twitty 2013). That culinary media, especially television, has been instrumental to this erasure explains the necessity of live performance as a means of claiming space for Black culinary expertise in our popular culinary histories.

Twitty's recreation of the foods of slavery constitutes more than historic reenactment; it serves as a mimetic penetration of the facade of whitewashed history by Twitty's performing body. Twitty first met with pop culture stardom in his famous 2013 open letter to Paula Deen, who at the time was subject to public shame due to revelations that she had used racial slurs earlier in her career (Twitty 2013). Dispensing quickly with the false dichotomy of "is she or isn't she a racist," Twitty instead offers a critique of Deen's career as founded on representational injustice. Like the fictional Colonel Sanders, Deen built an empire by mimetically appropriating black foodways under the guise of a folksy, whitewashed Southernness, the Central and West African influences on this cuisine ignored and erased in lucrative televised performances of working class white Southern authenticity. A complement to his culinary discourse, Twitty's plantation performances serve as a mimetic rebuttal to claims like Deen's. For instance, performing in period costume at Monticello, Twitty prepared a recreated slave meal of grilled rabbit, okra soup, and hominy in 2016, explaining to journalist Erika Beras that events like these constitute a radical reinsertion of black bodies and stories into historic sites of enslavement: "It's like the equivalent, you know – I'm Jewish, so I guess I can say this – the equivalent of having a bar mitzvah at Auschwitz. You know, why not?" (Beras 2016). As Twitty performs historic culinary reenactment, his gay, black, Jewish body physically refutes the invisibility he means to undo, boldly reinserting black bodies where they have been incompletely erased.

Extending the notion of culinary mimesis as a means of embodying truth, Twitty draws an equivalence between himself, his food, and his ancestors through his restaging of historic cooking practices. In *The Cooking Gene*, his 2017 account of his culinary journey through the US and beyond, the chef describes a complex set of resemblances that occur between himself, his ancestors, and the food with which he stages history in the present. As Twitty narrates his cooking, he describes a process through which the scent of burning wood, blood from animal carcasses, herbs, and roots suffuses his skin with new aromas, blurring the lines between the objects with which he works and his laboring body (2017a, 2–3). In this moment Twitty's body, in addition to the material of wood, tools, animals, plants, and spices with which he cooks the meals he serves, transforms, infusing the meal with a mimetic resemblance to other times and people but also to himself, and himself to it.

Constructing a version of historical terroir, Twitty offers an embodied enactment of culinary labor as an alternative to the disembodied functions of capital on which other notions of culinary history have depended. Disembodied notions of terroir have often privileged landowners and slave owners as the central characters in culinary narrative based on their ownership of lands and people. For instance, Thomas Jefferson's ownership of slave James Hemings enabled him to accumulate culinary accolades while obscuring Hemings's substantial contributions to international cuisine.[2] As a solution to this ahistorical appropriation of culinary narrative, Twitty calls for a terroir of the diasporic body itself, rooted not in locations but in the moving body and individual, ingenious adaptations to new contexts, ingredients, and culinary traditions which were then passed down to new generations of cooks (Eaton 2017). While this concept of terroir in the blood recenters the bodies of enslaved African-Americans in traditions from which they have been incompletely erased, Twitty draws careful distinctions between culinary appropriation and culinary collaboration. For instance, Twitty refers to white Baltimore chef Spike Gjerde's collaboration with African-American farmer Denzel Mitchell to create Snake Oil hot sauce as an example of culinary justice (2017b). But like many others, he holds up Bayless as an example of unjust culinary appropriation in which white chefs gain fame and wealth through "mastery" of culinary traditions while chefs native to those traditions work in relative obscurity. Twitty points out the disjunction of elevating a white chef to national prominence while ignoring the countless Mexican and Mexican-American chefs working throughout the country: "When was the last time you saw a Mexican American with heart, who can cook, have his own gourmet multimillion-dollar restaurant that he can bring people to and charge them all that money? That's culinary injustice" (2017b). Twitty's critique, and his career, exemplifies the complex politics of culinary mimeticism. Even as culinary re-enactment mimetically brings purposefully erased histories back into public spaces that shape the US's cultural memory, mimesis plays a major role in culinary injustice through techniques of appropriation, substitution, and the ludic and lucrative re-enactment of native cuisines in colonial spaces. As Taussig insists, this mimetic practice is neither one-directional nor simple. It is, however, powerful and captivating. Thus the movement for culinary justice of necessity engages with mimesis. First, culinary critics expose and critique the mimetic process by which foodways associated with marginalized and oppressed peoples are detached from their history and geography and claimed by others for their economic and cultural benefit. Second, culinary mimesis itself works as an intervention, a means of restaging and reclaiming foodways.

While issues of economics, sustainability, and access are all critical to culinary justice, Twitty's project insists that representation, and stories themselves, play an equally crucial role in creating just food cultures. Furthermore, Twitty argues that culinary mimesis is not only possible, but essential to the pursuit of culinary justice: "So, farmers, cooks, eaters, growers, producers: With your seeds, tell stories; with your meals, communicate your message; with your tables, tell the truth" (2015). As Twitty's body of work demonstrates, the history of US culinary injustice has been bound up with mimesis as white chefs and culinary writers perform ownership of appropriated traditions. His plantation performances reverse that mimetic flow, using culinary mimeticism to tell stories and reveal truths through food. Rejecting the misconception that food is a silent, inert, ahistorical material, incapable of telling its own stories, Twitty demonstrates the power of culinary mimesis as a mode of activism centered on representing the truth.

Mimesis and culinary resistance: implications for alimentary performance

Each of the performances surveyed above advance the development of food, cooking, and eating as elements of theatre and performance art and help to frame the unique dramaturgical and design considerations inherent to alimentary performance. For instance, as Bobby Baker's work demonstrates, surrounding the common contexts of cooking and dining with a performance framework immediately opens food's representational horizons by priming audience members to experience food and cooking in terms of mimetic resemblances. Where an everyday demonstration of a garlic crouton recipe or a moment of serving tea may function largely outside the context of mimesis, Baker's *How to Shop* and *Kitchen Show* take these same culinary events and wrap them in layers of representational weight through the use of dramaturgical material, the playwright/performer's language and action, and the social convention of performance, reframing the association between a quotidian culinary action and its meaning just enough to allow a play of culinary representations to emerge. Works such as *Edible Family in a Mobile Home* demonstrate the temporal dimensions of food design and dramaturgy. Food functions as a means of attending to the passage of time (hot to cold, fresh to decayed, solid to melted). Cooking and eating also serve, as in Twitty's plantation performances, to evoke times and places through memory and association (childhood foods, historical dishes and ingredients, first drinks, last meals). Finally, Carmelita Tropicana's food work reminds us that attention to food as a design and thematic element necessitates not only awareness of its alimentary, visual, textural, auditory, odiferous, and other sensory qualities, but also a food's social, economic, political, and cultural history.

Furthermore, these alimentary artists each employ food as a means of resisting hierarchies, either ideological, geographical, historical, social, or temporal. Knowles uses food as a relational strategy, mimetically reconfiguring the relationship between domestic and professional spaces, challenging the boundary between insignificant everyday and exceptional event. Tropicana uses faux fruit, chicken, and chocolate to craft a queer accumulation of ideas and sensations that creatively remembers exilic experience while summoning a queer future into being. Baker deploys food's sensory and contextual meanings simultaneously, creating representations that exceed interpretation and meanings beyond language. Twitty, like Knowles, positions cooking as performance, reenacting labor in order to rearticulate erased histories so audiences can eat their way into authentic and just understandings of cuisine. Finally, Bayless's *Cascabel* provides an example of the ways in which mimetic cuisine may function to articulate claims of belonging, with their own implications for culinary justice and injustice. Using divergent approaches and with disparate political and social aims, each demonstrates the possibility of culinary representation to enact Taussig's excessive mimesis, providing incorporative opportunities to simultaneously sense and imagine new worlds, new histories, and new ways of living.

Notes

1 Finley's later work has moved in a similar direction, with the artist setting aside canned yams in favor of "pleasurable" substances like chocolate sauce and honey, each of which she offers audiences to taste as part of her recent performances (Bean 2016).
2 Founded by US chef Ashbell McElveen in 2014, the James Hemings Foundation aims to educate the public about the contributions of Hemings, who McElveen calls "a ghost in America's kitchen, overshadowed and still enslaved to the narrative that gives Thomas Jefferson credit for introducing gourmet cuisine to the nation" (McElveen 2016).

References

Abrams, Joshua. 2013. Review of Cascabel. *Theatre Journal* 65(2): 284–287.
Alvarez, Alex. 2013. "Chef Rick Bayless Prompts Question: What Makes Mexican Food Mexican?" ABC News, April 17. abcnews.go.com/ABC_Univision/Entertainment/chef-rick-bayless-prompts-question-makes-mexican-food/story?id=18969623.
Arellano, Gustavo. 2016. "The Problem isn't Rick Bayless Cooking Mexican Food – It's That He's a Thin-Skinned Diva." *OC Weekly*, March 28. www.ocweekly.com/restaurants/the-problem-isnt-rick-bayless-cooking-mexican-food-its-that-hes-a-thin-skinned-diva-7075113.
Baker, Bobby. 1991. "Kitchen Show: One Dozen Kitchen Actions Made Public." London: Artsadmin. Reprinted in *Bobby Baker: Redeeming Features of Everyday Life*. edited by Michèle Barrett and Bobby Baker. 2007, 164–170. New York: Routledge.
Baker, Bobby. 1994. "Food is My Own Language." Interview by David Tushingham. In *Food for the Soul: A New Generation of British Theatremakers*, 25–41. London: Metheun.
Baker, Bobby. 1999. "Risk in Intimacy." Interview by Adrian Heathfield. *Performance Research* 4(1): 97.
Baker, Bobby. 2007. "A Historical Artist." In *Bobby Baker: Redeeming Features of Everyday Life*, edited by Michèle Barrett and Bobby Baker, 23–78. New York: Routledge.
Baker, Bobby. 2008. Kitchen Show. DVD Jacket Text. Live Art Development Agency.
Baldwyn, Lucy. 1996. "Blending in: The Immaterial Art of Bobby Baker's Culinary Events" *TDR* 40(4) (Winter, 1996): 37–55. hwww.jstor.org/stable/1146589.
Bean, Christine Simonian. 2016. "Sticky Performances: Affective Circulation and Material Strategy in the (Chocolate) Smearing of Karen Finley" *Theatre Survey* 57(1) (January). 88–108. doi:10.1017/S0040557415000575.
Benjamin, Walter. 1969 [1936]. "The Work of Art in the Age of Mechanical Reproduction." in *Illuminations*, edited by Hannah Arendt, translated by Harry Zohn, 217–251. New York: Schocken Books.
Beras, Erika. 2016. "This Historian Wants You to Know the Real Story of Southern Food." NPR: Weekend Edition Saturday, October 1. www.npr.org/sections/thesalt/2016/10/01/496104487/this-historian-wants-you-to-know-the-real-story-of-southern-food.

Burros, Marian. 2010. "Rick Bayless, the Chicago Chef, to Prepare a State Dinner." *New York Times*, May 11. www.nytimes.com/2010/05/12/dining/12dinner.

Derrida, Jacques. 2000 [1997]. Of Hospitality. Response by Anne Dufourmantelle. Translated by Rachel Bowlby. Stanford: Stanford University Press.

Dolan, Jill. 1985. "'Carmelita Tropicana Chats' at the Club Chandalier." *The Drama Review: TDR* 29(1) (Spring1985): 26–32. www.jstor.org/stable/1145595.

Eaton, Hillary. 2017. "Michael Twitty, the African American Jewish writer, is poised to give us a new way to think about Passover." *Los Angeles Times*, April 10. www.latimes.com/food/dailydish/la-dd-michael-twitty-20170410-story.

Esparza, Bill. 2010. "Red-O: Tinga tu Madre and Guacaviche at LA's Ultimate Palace of Pretense, Cuisine by Rick Bayless?" *Street Gourmet LA*, August 2. www.streetgourmetla.com/2010/08/red-o-tinga-tu-madre-and-guacaviche-at.

Higgins, Hannah. 2002. *Fluxus Experience*. Berkeley: University of California Press.

Jones, Chris. 2014. "Review: Cascabel by Lookingglass Theatre Co." *Chicago Tribune*, August 5. www.chicagotribune.com/entertainment/theater/reviews/chi-review-cascabel-lookingglass-theatre-column.

Kennedy, Randy. 2011. "Tuna on Wheat (Hold the Mayo)." *New York Times*, February 3, C1.

Knowles, Alison. 1992. *Event Scores*. New York: Left Hand Books.

Knowles, Alison. 2007. *Artforum International* 46(1): 143–144.

Knowles, Alison. 2009. "Fluxus Long Weekend." *PAJ: A Journal of Performance and Art* 31(1): 139–148.

Knowles, Alison. 2010. Interview by Judith Richards. Archives of American Art Oral History Program. Smithsonian Museum. www.aaa.si.edu/collections/interviews/oral-history-interview-alison-knowles-15822.

Knowles, Alison. 2015. "Make A Salad." Interview by Julia Sherman. *Lucky Peach* Summer (The Plant Kingdom): 43–46.

Lam, Francis. 2012. "Cuisines Mastered as Acquired Tastes." *New York Times*, May 30, D1. www.nytimes.com/2012/05/30/dining/masters-of-a-cuisine-by-calling-not-roots.

Lawson, Jenny. 2011. "Food Legacies: Playing the Culinary Feminine." *Women and Performance: A Journal of Feminist Theory* 21(3): 337–366.

Lushetich, Natasha. 2011. "The Performance of Time in Fluxus Intermedia." *TDR: The Drama Review* 55(4): 75–87.

Matthews, Jennifer. 2009. *Chicle: The Chewing Gum of the Americas, from the Ancient Maya to William Wrigley*. Tucson: University of Arizona Press.

McElveen, Ashbell. 2016. "Our Mission." James Hemings Foundation Website. www.jameshemingsfoundation.org/ashbell-mcelveen.

Morais, Betsy. 2012. "Salad as Performance Art." *New Yorker*, April 26. www.newyorker.com/culture/culture-desk/salad-as-performance-art.

Muñoz, José Esteban. 1995. "No es fácil: Notes on the Negotiation of Cubanidad and Exilic Memory in Carmelita Tropicana's 'Milk of Amnesia.'" *TDR* 39 (3) (Autumn): 76–82. www.jstor.org/stable/1146465.

Nathan, Emily. 2011. "Noshing with Knowles." *Artnet*, January 20. www.artnet.com/magazineus/news/nathan/alison-knowles-identical-lunch1-21-11.asp.

Noriega, Chon A. 2000. "Introduction." In *I, Carmelita Tropicana: Performing Between Cultures*, Alina Troyano with Ela Troyano and Uzi Parnes, edited by Chon A. Noriega, ix–xii. Boston: Beacon Press.

Oddey, Alison. 1999. *Performing Women: Stand-Ups, Strumpets and Itinerants*. London: Routledge.

Pollock, Griselda. 2007. "Daily Life 1: Kitchen Show." In *Bobby Baker: Redeeming Features of Everyday Life*, edited by Michèle Barrett and Bobby Baker, 178–183. New York: Routledge.

Robinson, Julia. 2004. "The Sculpture of Indeterminacy: Alison Knowles's Beans and Variations." *Art Journal* 63(4): 96–115.
Román, David and Carmelita Tropicana. 1995. "Carmelita Tropicana Unplugged: An Interview." *TDR* 39(3) (Autumn, 1995): 83–93. www.jstor.org/stable/1146466.
Saini, Anne Noyes. 2016. "Other People's Food Pt. 1: White Chef, Mexican Food." *The Sporkful*, March 21. www.sporkful.com/other-peoples-food-part-1-rick-bayless-white-chef-mexican-food.
Shakespeare, William. 2006. *Henry IV Part 2*. Edited by Barbara A. Mowat and Paul Werstine. New York: Washington Square Press.
Taussig, Michael. 1993. *Mimesis and Alterity*. New York: Routledge.
Tropicana, Carmelita. 1987a. "Food for Thought." in *I, Carmelita Tropicana: Performing Between Cultures*, Alina Troyano with Ela Troyano and Uzi Parnes, edited by Chon A. Noriega. 2000, 187–190. Boston: Beacon Press.
Tropicana, Carmelita. 1987b. "Chicken Sushi." Performance documentation, 18:11. Hemispheric Institute Digital Video Library. hdl.handle.net/2333.1/nvx0k8r2.
Tropicana, Carmelita. 1995 [1994]. "Milk of Amnesia/Leche de Amnesia ." *TDR* 39(3): 94–111.
Twitty, Michael W. 2000. "The Persistence of Memory." *The Journal of Negro History* 85(3): 176–182. www.jstor.org/stable/2649074.
Twitty, Michael W. 2013. "An Open Letter to Paula Deen." *Afroculinaria*. afroculinaria.com/2013/06/25/an-open-letter-to-paula-deen.
Twitty, Michael W. 2015. "With Your Tables, Tell the Truth." Sustainable Agriculture Conference Keynote, Carolina Farm Stewardship Association.
Twitty, Michael W. 2017a. *The Cooking Gene*. New York: HarperCollins.
Twitty, Michael W. 2017b. "Culinary Justice: Defining a Theory of Gastronomic Sovereignty." Lecture. 1:22:34. University of Michigan Sustainable Food Program. youtu.be/7DL7yY3r-ig.
William-Ross, Lindsay. 2010. "What's the Beef? Rick Bayless and Jonathan Gold's Online War of Words." *LAist*, August 31. laist.com/2010/08/31/red_o_drama.php.

5

THE PROOF IS IN THE EATING

Mimesis, participation, and embodied knowledge

Pea soda

(Woyzeck, Madison, Wisconsin, 2013)

Daniel Millhouse, playing the Canary Bird, tiptoes across the performance space. Dressed in feathers, a top hat, a three-piece suit, and a pair of horn-rimmed glasses, he carries a silver tray laden with small plastic cups of the sort used to dispense liquid medications. "Pea soda?" He offers a cup to each audience member in the risers before him. As a woman in the front row hesitates, uncertain, he proposes a toast. She demurs, but her companion plays along, clinking their plastic cups together and drinking. Seated next to these two, a woman avoids Millhouse's gaze, crossing her arms defensively. He nods his understanding and moves along to a group of teenagers already reaching for their glasses, giggling to one another. At the end of the row, a pair of audience members crane their necks to watch as the first few guests react to the soda. Some smile in surprised enjoyment. Others grimace and shake their heads. Meanwhile, Alec Phan, playing Woyzeck, watches as Niccole Carner and Kailen Fleck, playing Marie and the Drum Major, share a drink and dance an elaborate tango.

This chapter's reference to the British proverb, "The proof of the pudding is in the eating," signals my study's shift from historical and theoretical perspectives to one based primarily in reflections on the doing of cooking and eating. While culinary mimeticism may be productively observed and theorized from the outside, the processes of cooking and eating vary so significantly with each instance that in order to understand them one must also experience them directly. Indeed it is the multisensory, intimate, embodied nature of culinary mimeticism, which insistently combines processes of mimetic recognition with critical reflection on the nature of representation itself, that animates this study. The concluding section of this project thus draws on my own work in alimentary performance in order to develop both practical and theoretical knowledge of the ways in which food and the participatory act of eating function mimetically in theatre and performance. The above account narrates one such performance, a 2013 production of Buchner's *Woyzeck*, in order to demonstrate the inherent interrelation of foodstuffs themselves, the social contexts they create, and the experiential aspects of their consumption in the overall experience of alimentary representation. First, the design of the edible element, in this case a beverage, constitutes a representational offer made by the creative team. Its material composition communicates information to the audience: the effervescent green liquid served in a sterile medicine cup references the medical scenario in which the play's main character finds himself. Contextualized within a full menu of pea-flavored edible elements, this ounce of pea soda represents another evolution in a strange progression of alimentary experiences. Second, the Canary Bird's offer of soda during the performance activates a social circumstance which informs each audience member's interpretation of the unfolding moment. The audience, already socialized into the conventions of witnessing performance, must now also decide how to interact with the actor as server and with one another as fellow diners. Third, through the act of consumption, the pea soda offers additional layers of embodied experience for those audience members who choose to smell, touch, and taste the beverage. Moreover, the soda's taste and texture evoke two conflicting reference points. The cool, carbonated sweetness of soda exists alongside the vegetal flavor of English peas, which happen to be the only food the play's main character, Woyzeck, is allowed to consume. Confronted with these multiple layers of significance and opportunities for choice, audiences actively make meaning of the creative team's representational offer. In this moment, audience members not only consume but participate in culinary mimeticism: embodied, subjective meaning-making at close range.

The intimacy of this meaning-making signals a radical shift from experiences of mimetic recognition rooted in the presumed equivalence of knowledge, distance, objectivity, and visuality. While I have already explored several ways in which mimetic menus and individual dishes stimulate recognition in diners and audience members, theatrical events which treat eating as a primary mode of mimetic experience offer opportunities to think through the ways that mimetic eating might resonate with and diverge from mimetic experiences such as the viewing of a painting or a film. Positioning culinary mimeticism as a form of embodied mimesis that actively engages audiences in critical and experiential meaning-making, I contrast this mimetic recognition that is felt, sensed, and thought with the illusionistic mimesis, meant to be seen at a distance, that Brecht and Boal affiliate with "culinary theatre." Contrary to criticism of mimetic cuisine as insubstantial or dangerous, I argue that in fact culinary mimeticism, which blurs experiences of recognition with critical examination of the mechanisms of mimesis itself, constitutes a new variation on the radical, critical, participatory exploration of truth, knowledge, and representation that Boal and Brecht both envision. In the remainder of this chapter, I thus attend both to tactics for crafting alimentary performances and, equally importantly, to the ways in which audiences and diners recognize and interpret experiences of eating in the context of alimentary performances. I discuss a series of interrelated alimentary performance experiments: Georg Buchner's *Woyzeck* (Madison, 2013), featuring a menu of pea transformations; August Strindberg's *Miss Julie* (Chicago, 2014), featuring a menu of aphrodisiac candies; a food-based performance mashup under the auspices of the PQ Makers event (Prague, 2015); Shakespeare's *Titus Andronicus* (Phoenix, 2017), accompanied by a menu of ancient Roman mignardises; and four American Society for Theatre Research working groups on food and performance (2014–2017). In each case, I outline the means through which food works as a vehicle for performance and meaning, as a catalyst for performances of cooking and eating, and as a performing object in itself. Returning to my prior analysis of developments in culinary mimeticism from the 1960s to today, I discuss the ways in which these practices make new experiences of representation possible in contemporary theatre and performance, establishing an active and multisensory model of mimetic participation founded not in looking but in eating. Combining written accounts of alimentary performances with recipes and development processes, I invite readers to not only think through, but also to cook and eat through these case studies in an experiment in culinary mimeticism at a distance.

Thoughts on eating and meaning in performance

As the examples I cite throughout this volume demonstrate, the mechanisms through which culinary representation may unfold are diverse and vary according to the unique circumstances of each instance of the phenomenon. Acknowledging this variability, I nevertheless identify four fundamental means through which cuisine functions mimetically in theatrical and performance contexts, each of which may occur alone or in combination with the other three. I do not propose these four contexts either as mutually exclusive or as a comprehensive framework for culinary mimeticism. Rather, these four contexts helpfully demonstrate the range of means through which culinary representation may occur. First, the act of cooking itself may function mimetically, as it does in Bayless, Twitty, and Baker's culinary performances. In mimetic cooking, the chef's labor itself constructs a representation of another time, place, or action, such as an alternative reality as in Bayless's *Cascabel* or an historical reenactment as in Twitty's plantation cookery. Second, mimetic eating may occur in tandem with mimetic cooking when diner/participants implicitly or explicitly take on the position of a performer, completing the representational circuit of an edible performance. For example, in licking Achatz and Beran's mimetic "foie-sting" from metal beaters, diners at "Next: Childhood" completed the illusion of the menu by adding the essential element of their participation, allowing other diners to witness them nostalgically restaging an iconic childhood food memory. Third, edible elements themselves may amplify or complicate the representational contexts of mimetic cooking and eating through representational aspects of their visual, olfactory, auditory, textural, or alimentary qualities, as Adrià's spherified olives or Cantu's Cuban cigar sandwich demonstrate.

Finally, culinary mimesis may also depend upon dramaturgical context. This mimetic context may spring individually or collectively from the memory of audience members, as in the play of associations inspired by Baker's use of familiar foodstuffs in new contexts in *Edible Family in a Mobile Home*. Or, as in "Sound of the Sea," additional sensory input (a recording of ocean sounds) as well as contextual information (the dish's title and the server's explanation of how to consume it) can prime a diner, participant, or audience member to bring their mimetic faculty to bear on the experience of eating, changing both the potential meaning of a dish and its sensory impact as it does so.

Moreover, the means by which audiences attend to and recognize culinary mimeticism vary widely along with artists' use of the above four frameworks. Audiences may experience culinary representation dramaturgically within performance contexts, primed by the recognition of framing, sequencing, and contextualization of otherwise "ordinary" edible experience to interpret a production's alimentary experiences mimetically, as in Baker's transformation of a quotidian crouton into a ritual of communion in *How to Shop*. Once primed to interpret their eating in this fashion, eaters may also make meaning from personal culinary reference points, as artists employ a cooking technique or category of foodstuff to connect an audience's edible experience to other contexts, memories, or places. In these modes of mimetic eating, dramaturgical frameworks prime the eater to make meaning of eating by connecting their immediate sensory experience with a wider context of memory or cultural knowledge. Second, an alimentary performance may interact with culinary discourse to present an audience with the tantalizing challenge of tasting the past, using historical ingredients, techniques, and preparations to mimetically evoke a prior moment in a contemporary bite of food, as in Twitty's plantation performances. Third, an audience member's process of recognition may spring from an extraordinary moment of eating, unfolding in the model of Benjamin's definition of mimeticism, in which alimentary experiences evoke nonsensuous resemblances by stimulating our mimetic capacity to recognize surprising similarities. For example, *Woyzeck*'s menu of pea transformations mimetically reproduces the main character's growing sense of detachment from reality in its increasingly strange variations on a common foodstuff. Finally, performances may rely on a sensory variety of remix, mimetically reproducing sensory elements common to the thing represented but transposing them between senses and experiences. For instance, in several of the examples I explore below, artists translate language, typically experienced visually and auditorily, into alimentary formats. In each case, alimentary performances work within discursive, intelligible, and social contexts and sensory, apprehensible, and material ones simultaneously. Recalling Adrià's insistence on treating intelligence as a sixth sense, I suggest that establishing a strict separation of these terms would mean disentangling of elements that are always already intertwined. Critically, each of these forms of mimetic eating function not through visual or auditory illusionism alone, but multi-sensorially, as audiences sort through both illusionistic and non-illusionistic sensory and intellectual stimuli in a process of meaning-making that varies from eater to eater and from moment to moment.

Before continuing with a discussion of several examples that illustrate these multiple facets of culinary representation and recognition, I first attend to the social context of these performances. In particular, two issues of participation arise as cruxes for alimentary performance: individual negotiations of choice and consent and social relations of hospitality. Since these issues haunt nearly every alimentary performance, I address them generally here before tracking their influence on the specific performance examples I discuss below. The need to negotiate relational issues of choice, consent, and resistance in the design of alimentary performance elements emerges in part due to the inherent intimacy of tasting. Of all the senses, the act of tasting requires the most interaction with the object being sensed; taste at a distance is impossible. Audiences experience the visual and auditory elements of design through what we may construe as passive means: we open our eyes and see; we offer our attention and hear. To avoid seeing or hearing would require acts of refusal for hearing and sighted individuals: closing or covering the eyes, removing glasses, blocking ear canals, turning off hearing aids. Alternatively, when artists offer audiences food as an element of theatrical design, we of necessity ask audiences to commit to an affirmative act of consumption. They must open their mouths and take in the edible element in order to fully experience it. Along with this necessary physical contact comes a greater degree of required risk and participation on the part of the audience member experiencing an alimentary performance rather than a performance that communicates largely through visual and auditory stimuli.

Furthermore, alimentary performances offer audience members a choice of degrees of participation, each of which may impact not only an audience member's potential recognition of mimetic resemblance but also the representational significance of the experience of eating and watching others eat. One may gaze upon, touch, or smell an object to gain a partial understanding of its qualities and still refuse the final action of eating. Audience members may refuse to eat entirely, they may taste briefly without completing the act of eating, or they may eat and through digestion make the food design a part of their own body (at least temporarily). Each of these possible choices impacts the ecological relationship between audience, performer, food, and performance. As audience members embark on individual sensory experiences, the act of eating transforms the object eaten, the body of the eater, and the experiences of those around the eater. Therefore, in addition to what we might consider the immediate aesthetic considerations for food, from color to texture to aroma and flavor, creators of alimentary performance elements must take into account how they ask audiences to interact with food. What choices will audiences perceive upon encountering edible elements? What are the ramifications of those choices within the larger framework of commensality that alimentary performances of necessity inhabit? To explore these questions further, I turn to a brief discussion of hospitality and its role in the design, execution, and interpretation of alimentary performance elements.

The social conventions of food service often occur within the context of hospitality. A concept essential to survival in the ancient world, hospitality has since become a term implying welcome and sharing of resources between the owners of a space and their guests. Restaurants regularly invoke hospitality as a framework, referring to diners as guests and offering complimentary refreshments to start and end the meal, nurturing a sense of social relationship between diner and restaurateur. We refer to those in food service as working in the hospitality industry. When introducing performance experiences that involve eating, we often invoke hospitality as a matter of course, usually in the contemporary context of generosity and welcome. Still, the ancient concept of hospitality, which rests on the management of tenuous relationships between insiders and outsiders, remains key to structuring the meaning of convivial exchange, as food and hospitality inform and create social context for one another. In this ancient context, hospitality meant protection for the guest welcomed within a stranger's home (as in the Greek term *xenia*, province of Zeus) and captured within it not only the traveler's need for sanctuary but also the hostility from which hospitality protected him. While the term hospitality today connotes ease, comfort, and a species of kindness, Jacques Derrida's philosophical examination of the social and cultural mechanisms of hospitality helpfully reminds us of its basis in unequal power relations between the insider who offers hospitality and the outsider who receives it:

> No hospitality, in the classic sense, without sovereignty of oneself over one's home, but since there is also no hospitality without finitude, sovereignty can only be exercised by filtering, choosing, and thus by excluding and doing violence. Injustice, a certain injustice, and even a certain perjury, begins right away, from the very threshold of the right to hospitality.
>
> *(2000, 55)*

Derrida's acknowledgment of hospitality's dependence on exclusion and control mirrors the ways that participation transforms artist/patron relationships. Understanding that hospitality involves both ritualized kindness and a fundamental inequality and exclusion helps to explain the fear that participants so often experience in the face of immersive or participatory theatre and in particular alimentary performances. For Derrida, this ritualized kindness based on exclusion constitutes an artificial performance of social relations, a tenuous peace founded on inequality. Thus the fraught relationship between mimesis and authenticity again comes to the fore, haunting the social context of hospitality that underpins many alimentary performances. This imbrication of hospitality and hostility helps foreground the interpenetration of thought, sensed, and felt experience in meaning-making for the participant/audience/eater in alimentary performances. As eaters actively make meaning from multisensory mimetic experience, they work not only with the material elements of the foodstuffs offered, but the social elements of the multifaceted performance environment in which they eat. Situating participants as both audience members and guests, mimetic eating inherently ruptures both of these contexts, foregrounding the artifice of hospitality as well as that of the performance event and inviting audiences to actively make meaning of the relationship between the two.

Since the social frameworks in which an audience eats are often as significant as the foodstuffs themselves, I propose viewing alimentary performances as tripartite phenomena consisting of mimetic edible elements, the social framework of dining, and the experience of mimetic eating. Before discussing several theoretical experiments in alimentary performance, I offer an example of the practical influence of this tripartite view of culinary mimesis in the development process for one recent production. Staging two intertwined classic texts, Arizona State University's 2017 "edible *Titus Andronicus*" juxtaposed Shakespeare's early modern adaptation of Roman history and myth with an edible interpretation of four dishes from Apicius's *Art of Cooking*. Both texts present a tantalizingly incomplete and fanciful rendering of the past, a quality emphasized in the production to encourage audience members to use their mimetic faculties to fill in the aporia generated by inevitable gaps in our knowledge of the places and times represented. Offering visual, auditory, and alimentary representations of a largely inaccessible Roman past, the production asked audiences to imaginatively conjure a Rome that was both familiar and strange, a provocative mashup of their expectations and associations along with elements that challenged or deepened these associations. Working in candy, I designed a menu featuring common ancient Roman flavor combinations in formats drawn from contemporary avant garde cuisine. Offered by the corrupt emperor Saturninus as a means of appeasing the audience, which the performance mimetically positioned as the crowd of Roman citizens, each element functioned in counterpoint to the scene in which it was served. In a brief snapshot of a performance development process, I demonstrate the means by which my collaborators and I explored a tripartite model of culinary mimeticism in an edible performance.

Rehearsal tasting

Carbonated grape, Apician honey glass, bay leaf pâte de fruit, olive marshmallow, spiced wine crisp (*Phoenix, AZ, February 2017*)

In a rehearsal room in Phoenix, Arizona, a group of college students taste a series of ancient Roman mignardises as part of an early rehearsal for a production of Titus Andronicus. *The first element, a mimetic play on champagne in the form of individual carbonated grapes offered exclusively to the first row of audience members, aims to establish a relationship between social class and the consumption of fanciful mimetic dishes. Next comes a cumin, pepper, and fennel-spiced honey glass adapted from Myrhvold's Modernist Cuisine, distributed in celebration of Saturninus's wedding to Tamora, queen of the Goths. A bay leaf pâte de fruit coated in juniper sugar serves as a picnic treat for the royal court's hunting trip to the forests outside Rome. An olive marshmallow accompanies Saturninus's airing of grievances against Titus to his assembled courtiers. Finally, Saturninus offers the guests at Titus's bloody final dinner a welcome gift of a crispy puff of methylcellulose-thickened grape juice spiced with saffron and clove, a meringue-like variation on the sweetened spiced wine Conditum Paradoxum. As performers taste their way through these elements, we discuss our immediate physical, emotional, and intellectual responses to each item. The bay leaf candy reminds one actor of the forest, while the crunch of the wine puff evokes breaking bones for another. The honey glass tastes and looks like another world to a young performer who contrasts the futuristic visual presentation of the clear isomalt candy with the earthy flavor of cumin, which stirs memories of the past. Each of these responses intensify or transform again when we contemplate the interplay between text and alimentary experience by situating these elements in their intended location in the performance's timeline. Finally, we explore the social context of the service event. The sixteen performers take turns posing as audience and server, improvising their exchanges. Some refuse the food offerings, while others ask questions or request seconds. Performers improvise as many variations on audience response as possible. Actor/servers take notes as each responds in turn to these performances of dining, attempting to incorporate them all into the context of the production. The reluctant diner gets a nod of encouragement or a wink. The eater who refuses gets a smile and a nod of the head or a small bow. The enthusiast questioner is quietly answered with either a point to the menu or a question in turn. The playful participant is offered an eating contest as performer and diner each stuff as many marshmallows into their mouth as they can at one time. An audience member who attempts to photograph her carbonated grape is offered a selfie with the performer/server. When two participants are caught up in conversation with one another about their impressions of the food, the server joins in with his opinion. In preparing for these varied responses, the cast aims to create a context of exploration and interpretation for the audience, attending to the issues of hospitality and participation inherent in culinary mimeticism and encouraging the audience to treat their edible experience as an opportunity for both pleasure and meaning-making.*

This account of a rehearsal demonstrates one process for generating embodied mimetic experiences that invite the audience member into active alimentary meaning-making. Of course, the practical tactics for incorporating culinary mimeticism into performance contexts are as diverse as foodways themselves. As Adrià establishes, culinary representation captures within itself the possibility of visual, olfactory, alimentary, haptic, auditory, and intellectual stimulation, among others. Furthermore, each aspect of culinary representation may work dynamically within the context of the others even as some elements may come to the fore and others recede in any particular performance. Similarly, a multitude of possible stimuli, from the dramaturgical to the sensory, may prompt moments of mimetic recognition on the part of a diner even as other aspects of a diner's experience reframe or contrast with these moments of recognition. Finally, since alimentary performances position individuals as both audience members and diners, culinary representation in this context also depends upon the social frameworks of hospitality and participation. In the alimentary performances discussed below, I thus explore multiple variations on the mimetic frameworks I have established above in order to demonstrate the diversity of possible approaches to, and implications for, treating culinary mimeticism as a basis for alimentary performance.

Edible scholarship: experiments in discourse, cuisine, and performance

In this section, I ground my theoretical overview of mimetic eating in the context of a long-term collaborative scholarly engagement with the possibilities of food as a performing object and means of scholarly and creative inquiry. Beginning in 2014, the American Society for Theatre Research's food and performance working group has queried the relationship between these two vast fields of human activity and inquiry, exploring the possibilities of food as a medium of intellectual and creative exchange.[1] Driven by an initial commitment to "digesting the relationship between the acts of art-making, cooking, and labor through the process of breaking bread together," the group incorporated the everyday acts of cooking, serving, and eating into each session, positioning these activities as both objects of and methods for scholarly and creative inquiry. Each year, participants undertook both traditional scholarship and inquiry-driven performances of cooking, serving, and eating food together. This playful disruption of the standard format of academic conference sessions offered us a chance to rethink the nature of knowledge and the ways in which ideas might be communicated, understood, shared, experienced, and consumed. Following Paul Carter's notion of "material thinking" and Barbara Bolt's concept of "materializing practices" (Carter 2004, Bolt 2004), working group participants used food-based inquiry as a method for these sessions, moving between linguistic and intelligible discourses and material, sensible, and edible contexts as a means of productively relocating a sometimes universalizing academic discourse into multiple moments of alimentary experience. As Michel de Certeau's collaborator and co-author Luce Giard notes in *Living and Cooking*, the practice of cooking itself "rests atop a complex montage of circumstances and objective data, where necessities and liberties overlap, a confused and constantly changing mixture through which tactics are invented, trajectories are carved out, and ways of operating are individualized" (1998, 201). In describing the "secret, tenacious pleasure of doing-cooking," Giard articulates an embodied intelligence, a set of practices through which "with moving hands, careful fingers, the whole body inhabited with the rhythm of working, and the mind awakening, freed from its own ponderousness, flitting from idea to memory" in a "writing of gestures" (1998, 153). Similarly, Nicola Perullo insists that "Taste is the paradigm of embodied knowledge, which originates and develops in and through the body, and which is not conceivable otherwise" (2016, 25). Throughout four years of work, working sessions explored similar notions of embodied knowledge by treating the experience of cooking, eating, drinking, and talking together as an endeavor of similar significance to the writing of scholarly texts. The group repeatedly confronted questions central to culinary mimesis: how does food mean, and how might one deploy food's ways of meaning to communicate not only about but through cooking and eating? In the next section, I briefly describe a few critical moments from these working sessions as a means of positing a few possible answers to this question and framing the performance experiments I discuss for the remainder of this chapter.

Milk and cookies

(Megan Marsh-McGlone, "How Breastmilk Performs," 2014, Baltimore, Maryland)

Scholar and performance artist Megan Marsh-McGlone begins her edible presentation by sharing documentation of her recent blood work. She is free of communicable diseases, as demonstrated by a printout of test results that she places on a table at the front of the room. She opens a small cooler, removing a set of lactation syringes designed for feeding infants small amounts of human milk. Each syringe is filled with a quantity of her breast milk. Participants are offered this milk as an accompaniment to cookies infused with herbs and other ingredients thought to induce lactation. Before partaking, each participant must sign a legal waiver acknowledging they are consuming the milk at their own risk.

The above account narrates one of the most provocative edible elements shared in four years of the working group's sessions. In this edible performance event, Marsh-McGlone designed a hybrid environment that transplanted the real objects, actions, and substances essential to the medicalization of breastfeeding into the space of the academic conference, offering a mimetic reproduction of and reflection upon this context's registers of power and meaning. Marsh-McGlone's breast milk syringes demonstrated some of the concerns evident in her writing, specifically the overlapping statuses of mother's milk as a valuable commodity, regulated foodstuff, and medically controlled body fluid. As participants made individual decisions about whether or not to consume Marsh-McGlone's "milk and cookies," this triply marked food also performed as an object of scholarly attention. Central to these decisions was the mingled risk, thrill, and discomfort conveyed by the mimetic context of Marsh-McGlone's presentation. The breast milk offered was "real," and so were the medical syringes and medical information provided by the artist. Yet by juxtaposing the material trappings of breast milk's status as a medically managed foodstuff with the context of the academic conference performance event, Marsh-McGlone successfully enfolded these real elements within a mimetic frame of medicine and maternity. Breastmilk, syringes, and medical waivers, taken out of the context of doctor's offices and the expected spaces of child-rearing and placed on the stage of an academic presentation, took on additional representational weight, inviting audience members to question the operations of power, hospitality, obligation, risk, consumption, and titillation underscoring their decision to either eat and drink Marsh-McGlone's "milk and cookies" or abstain. On one hand, this event exemplifies mimetic eating, in which a diner/participant places himself in a performance context by choosing to consume a foodstuff within a representational framework. The consumer enters a theatricalized relationship with the artist, partially and playfully occupying both the space of the offspring and also, through the consumption of the lactation cookies, the maternal figure desirous of feeding someone with one's own body. On the other hand, Marsh-McGlone's milk and cookies demonstrate the representational power of dramaturgical framing of foodstuffs. As in "Sound of the Sea," the discursive framing, serviceware, and attendant actions required as part of the ritual of consumption each play a critical role in establishing the dish's representational offers, which the diner may accept or reject in choosing to eat, not eat, or consume the dish resistantly or critically. Furthermore, Marsh-McGlone's alimentary performance highlights this interrelation of hospitality, mimesis, and risk by juxtaposing a seemingly benign offer of hospitality, the "milk and cookies" with which guests might be welcomed, with signifiers of bodily threat necessitating a literal requirement of consent.

Vanilla wafers

(Ann Folino White, "Tasting the Past: Transhistorical Experiences with Food and Celebrity," Minneapolis, Minnesota, 2016)

Before distributing her cookies, Ann Folino White passes out sheets of tasting notes. As each of us receives a small handful of vanilla wafers, Folino White invites tasters to contemplate resemblances between the wafers' flavor, aroma, appearance, and evocative associations and those of the recipe's celebrity author, Ethel Barrymore. Juxtaposed on the sheet are the recipe (a simple combination of eggs, shortening, sugar, salt, baking powder, flour, and vanilla) and a photograph of Barrymore. Alongside each category of tasting notes, Folino White has gathered contextual information for both the wafers and the celebrity. For instance, under appearance: "Wafers should range in color from a light vanilla to a pale golden hue. Miss Barrymore limited her palette to white, black, and/or gray." Participants regard, sniff, and finally taste the wafers, making notes about both the cookies and the impression of the actress they evoke as they go.

Folino White's vanilla wafers, an element designed to accompany a paper on the role of celebrity cookbooks as historical artifacts, offered an experiential proof of the complex relationship between culinary discourse and culinary representation. In this case, Folino White deployed multiple strands of culinary mimeticism as a means of enabling participants to "taste the past." This experience of eating responds to Korsmeyer's argument that those aspiring to taste the past must do so with the knowledge that such an act is inherently bound in a temporal geography (2015). In endeavoring to recreate an historic dish, the cook and the diner must recognize their specific location in the present, turn their attention backward to the past, and attend to the divergences between the two as they cast their alimentary attention toward another time. Thus tasting the past involves addressing oneself to the material circumstances of history. If possessed of the appropriate information and resources, a cook may account for differences in historical and contemporary ingredients, cooking methods, customs, and palates in order to effectively evoke the past in the present, as in the case of Twitty's plantation performances. In order to comprehend the resulting dish as "historic," the diners who consume it must also attend to the divergence between contemporary and historical flavor combinations, culinary techniques, and conventions of eating presented in the experience of the dish. Alternately, as in Tomaska and Achatz's menu for "Next: Ancient Rome," a dish that represents the past might foreground the gulf between available knowledge and a complete recipe, inviting a diner into an imaginative journey defined as much by what we cannot know as what we can.

Folino White's performance of tasting the past combined these two methods, hewing faithfully to its historical recipe but also exposing the tantalizing distance between our desire to know Barrymore and our ability to fully reckon her sensory aspects through the wafer's mimetic relation to her body. In their visual aspects, Folino White's notes make clear, the wafer and the woman share provocative alignments. Meanwhile, while the earthy yet floral scent of vanilla clearly identifies the wafer as a faithful version of its class of baked goods, Folino White notes that nothing is known of Barrymore's preferred perfume; we cannot be sure if we are smelling the star or not. Yet this incomplete knowledge does not preclude an experience of tasting the past. Instead it in some ways intensifies the experience. Participants embark upon an imaginative performance of tasting that reproduces, with a difference, the ways in which Barrymore's fans might have simultaneously felt closer to and farther from the star as they read her recipe, reproduced her culinary labor step by step, served the cookies to friends, and tasted her "favorite" treats together while imagining the star doing so in her own home with her own friends. Folino White's wafers thus offered participants a triple mimesis in which we explored a cookie's ability to stand in for a historical figure and also repeated and substituted ourselves for historic Barrymore fans who may have in turn imaginatively projected themselves onto the star. Furthermore, Folino White's demonstration of the possibilities and limitations of tasting the past suggests the boundary between sensible and intelligible knowledge may be rendered permeable during acts of incorporation. These reenacted vanilla wafers reinforce the notion that food's special significance as a threshold between the sensible and intelligible lies partly in its very ubiquity, its everydayness. We encounter food repeatedly through the quotidian act of eating, but only sometimes do so in such a way as to cross or look through this threshold. These moments of experiencing eating differently thus offer a strange deepening of the everyday, creating an awareness of the significance of the ordinary while at the same time marking a particular moment of eating as extraordinary in its capacity to generate new insights.

Crab salad soda

("Mimetic crab: An amuse bouche," Kristin Hunt, "How to Do Things with Food(s)," 2014, Baltimore, Maryland)

28 ml vodka; one can lump crabmeat; one stalk celery; juice of one lemon; 225 g sugar; 340 ml water

Puree all ingredients and allow to infuse, refrigerated, for three days before triple-straining. Add one tablespoon of resulting syrup to carbonated water over ice to form crab salad soda. Garnish with celery stick.

Crab Cotton Candy

("Mimetic crab: An amuse bouche," Kristin Hunt, "How to Do Things with Food(s)," 2014, Baltimore, Maryland)

113 g sugar; 75 g corn syrup; 75 g water; 3 g Old Bay seasoning

Combine all ingredients in a saucepan and heat on medium until sugar boils. When candy reaches 300 degrees Fahrenheit, remove from heat and spread on a silicone mat. Break cooled candy into small pieces. Spin in a cotton candy machine designed for hard candy. Divide resulting crab boil cotton candy into bite-sized portions and sprinkle with additional Old Bay seasoning. Serve with crab salad soda.

I developed the above recipes as the first tasting element for the inaugural working group, "How to Do Things with Food(s)," co-convened in Baltimore, Maryland in 2014. The design of "mimetic crab" stands in for one of the discoveries of this working session: the multiplicity of food's ways of meaning must be confronted by those interested in "doing things" with it. Since food functions simultaneously as, among other possible options, a representative medium, a practical material, an invitation to action, an object of exchange, and an experiential threshold, scholar-artists must take these disparate functions into account in order to conduct edible inquiry. "Mimetic crab" purposely evoked each of these aspects of culinary mimeticism in order to prime participants to experience the edible elements offered later in the session as openings to the threshold I discuss above, rather than either quotidian experiences of dining or culinary explications of theoretical principles. Prominently signaling its ingredients, this *amuse* juxtaposed a "real" crab element, soda made with canned crab, with a "faux" crab treat, cotton candy made with a popular seafood seasoning blend. In placing crab and not-crab side by side, the dish provoked diners to consider what the significance of "real" ingredients might be within the context of mimetic cuisine. Then, at the close of the session, co-convener Joshua Abrams's edible element, an "authentic" Maryland crab boil delivered from a local restaurant, offered participants a chance to compare the experience of eating a disjunctive mimetic riff on crab elements with that of traditional crab eating, with all the theatrical residues of plastic bibs, brown paper napkins, and wooden mallets, in the professional space of a scholarly event. Together the *amuse* and the crab dinner evoked a thematic, material, alimentary, and economic connection to the conference's host location, the port of Baltimore, Maryland. Through the surprising and, for some participants, revolting offer of crab soda, the *amuse* also constituted an invitation to action, dividing the group into those who chose to drink and asked for seconds, those who sipped and dumped, and those who refused the dish altogether. For each diner, the dish offered a chance for an incorporative reverie or a moment of introspection about one's own tolerance for gustatory risk.

In 2016, when I revisited this dish as one element of an essay delivered in the form of a box of candy, the resulting white chocolate truffle with crab salad spices and candied celery offered an opportunity to taste the past with a difference, allowing those who tasted the dish in 2014 to recall their original reaction and compare this new bite to their memory of the prior experience. In this case, by omitting crab itself and producing a candy flavored with elements associated with the seafood salad soda, this mimetic reproduction evoked revulsion through its naming convention and the memory of the prior foodstuff while providing the diner a pleasant alimentary experience in the here and now. Meanwhile, through the inclusion of written citations in the packaging of the edible essay, the crab salad candy offered those who had not attended the 2014 session a means of casting their attention backward, imaginatively reenacting an event they had not witnessed by combining a description of the original dish along with its mimetically transformed reproduction. In its gesture toward the past, this box of candy demonstrated food's capacity to contain and comment upon history through, rather than in spite of, its unique capacity to focus one's attention in the present.

While these three examples represent just a taste of the edible inquiry conducted by dozens of artists and scholars in these sessions, they indicate as well the multiplicity of possible approaches to culinary representation in short, focused formats. Each experiment simultaneously explores the representational possibilities of food, the experiential aspects of meaning-making that attend mimetic eating, and the mimetic significance of the social frameworks in which one eats. Responding to and extending the concerns of these brief experiments, I have also undertaken multiple full-length performance events focused on culinary representation. In the following discussion, I detail three related experiments in culinary mimeticism that explore some of the aforementioned strategies for incorporating culinary representation as a theatrical element: evocation of culinary resemblance, invocation of culinary reference, and representation through sensory remix.

Woyzeck: an experiment in culinary resemblance

Pea soda (*Woyzeck, Madison WI, 2013*)

150 g juiced frozen peas; 50 ml canned pea juice; 1 l water; 100 ml simple syrup; juice of 1/2 lemon: Combine, strain, carbonate.

In March 2013, I directed, adapted, and designed the menu for a production of Büchner's *Woyzeck* at the University of Wisconsin-Madison. The title character, a soldier, endures humiliating physical tests, cruel superior officers, and the dehumanizing treatment of a maniacal doctor fascinated with his urine. He also, in the name of science, subsists on a diet consisting only of peas. Unfinished upon the author's death, *Woyzeck* is traditionally reinvented in each new production. Scenes are rearranged or removed, language is adapted, and characters are added and subtracted. Taking the expected creative license, our production team set out to give audiences an intimate sensual experience of Woyzeck's descent into madness through an experiment in alimentary dramaturgy. As opposed to a program or other contextualizing material meant to connect the audience to the production, the play's main dramaturgical element would be a set of edible elements distributed periodically during the main action of the performance. Rather than mimetically represent Woyzeck himself through either visual, thematic, or other modes of resemblance between the edible material and the character, this menu aimed to evoke resemblances between audience and character experience by allowing the audience to taste what the character tastes. Accordingly, our menu for the show, a progression of six small pea-based dishes served to audience members by the actors during the action of the play, attended to the uniquely monotone quality of Woyzeck's meals. By serving the audience dishes that explored multiple variations within the miniscule boundaries of Woyeck's alimentary reality, the performance used taste as a threshold between the sensible and the intelligible, inviting the audience to periodically enter into an alimentary affiliation with the character in order to understand his experience through embodied mimetic recognition.

Each made largely of peas, the performance's edible offerings also visually mimicked the form of peas while transforming them through the use of new textures, temperatures, and culinary contexts, playing on the familiarity of a common foodstuff to provide a moment of surprise, reflection, or shock as the element is consumed. The menu treated the pea similarly to Achatz's "Rhubarb: Seven Different Textures," which explores multiple surprising preparations of a familiar ingredient, including gently cooked fruit, spherified liquid, and crisp translucent film. The experience began with a familiar touchstone before progressing through pea transformations that mirrored the increasingly hallucinogenic state of the main character by refracting the everyday vegetable through the lenses of other familiar dishes. As they entered the playing space, each participant received a single pea on a toothpick. For the remaining five dishes, the audience received strange versions of familiar childhood foods, evolving from mundane to surprising textures, flavors, and temperatures in the course of the seventy-minute performance. During the show, audience members ate their way through pea-flavored chewing gum, pea gummy candy, pea soda, pea popsicles, and a final pea cake ball coated in a smooth green candy shell.[2] Audience members, seated in three sets of risers arranged in a triangle around the main performance space, had the option to take or refuse each offering and were free to ask questions of the chorus members, who described each element briefly as they distributed them. At the play's climax, in which Woyzeck murders his lover, a chorus member ladled the final pea cake balls from the chest cavity of a life-size cake and fondant replica of her corpse, suspended over the audience throughout the show and lowered to the stage floor for service. The chorus distributed this final element to audience members before ushering them out of the space, offering interested parties the chance to take a closer look at Marie's corpse cake on the way.

Mimetic priming played an important role in preparing the audience to accept and participate in this alimentary dramaturgical experience. Production dramaturg Laura Farrell-Wortman and production gardener Adam Farrell-Wortman collaborated to create a lobby display of growing organic pea vines planted in the dozens of now-empty cans of peas used in the preparation of the show's edible elements.

A one-page paper menu, provided in lieu of a traditional descriptive program,[3] gave audiences the full list of ingredients for each pea transformation, and a series of cans marked "refuse" allowed audiences to discard unwanted food. The printed menu also reinforced the mimetic context in which the creators invited the audience to experience the play's edible elements. By asking them to identify carbonated pea juice as "pea soda" or chicle gum base infused with powdered dehydrated peas as "pea gum," the menu primed audience members to test these edible experiences against their expectations, contemplating whether or not a popsicle indeed captured the flavor of peas but also whether such a dish still constituted a popsicle per se. By constructing this collision of conflicting recognitions we aimed to intertwine the audience's sensory experience with the character's, mirroring some of Woyzeck's alimentary experience. Along with this sensory affiliation with the character, audience members might also experience memories of their own prior consumption of peas. By evoking these memories, the dishes opened a vista to what Giard refers to as "a miniscule crossroads of histories" evoked by individual culinary customs (1998, 171). The familiar flavor of peas might spark a memory of childhood dinners, while the texture and temperature of popsicles might evoke summer afternoons. As they consumed each dish, we hoped that audience members would experience incorporative moments in which their present experience intertwined, even briefly, with the recollection of prior sensations. In doing so we offered those who chose to eat a chance to approach Woyzeck's own increasingly disjunct sense of time and place in fleeting, repeated moments of alimentary mimetic recognition.

While the menu aimed to create a partial experiential allegiance between the main character and the audience, its mimetic elements also asked audience members to choose exactly how far their participation would go. Though Woyzeck's eating occurs under duress, audience members ate by choice, free to reject or accept, swallow or spit out each pea-flavored morsel. For instance, an audience member might nibble at a pea gummy candy, pausing occasionally to reflect on its flavor and texture, while watching Woyzeck shove peas into his mouth as fast as he could as the doctor timed him with a stopwatch. In addition to this differentiation of consent, the menu also created a differentiation of experience through the mechanism of mimetic recognition. Much as "Rhubarb: Seven Different Textures" evokes thoughtful consideration of the original ingredient, the menu of pea transformations elicited a critical engagement with the qualities of peas and their influence on Woyzeck's experience. Meanwhile, Woyzeck himself demonstrates little evidence of similar reflection on the meaning of his alimentary experience. Throughout the show, Alec Phan, the performer playing Woyzeck, unreflectively consumed the same untransformed green peas that the audience had received as their first element. In contrast, the audience received increasingly surprising pea transformations, differentiating their literal alimentary experience from that of the actor performing in the center of the space and inviting them to consider the significance of each transformation as to what it revealed about the character's mental and emotional state, the significance of the scene unfolding, or the relationship between Woyzeck's experience and their own.

Furthermore, while Woyzeck's social world is characterized by disconnection and violence, the acts of serving and eating food created an array of possible social exchanges, many of them pleasant, each contributing to the potential meaning of the pea elements in relation to the performance as a whole. As audience members ate, many compared their responses with their companions and strangers, looking about the space to see who refused, who ate, what techniques they used to consume the offered dishes, what faces they made, and whether they finished every morsel. As the chorus members conversed briefly with audience members during each exchange of food, patrons learned that the performers anticipated and allowed for them to ask questions and compare notes with neighbors. Each actor prepared an expansive individual repertoire of responses to nervous, eager, disinterested, delighted, and revolted patrons, and many audience members treated the interaction between patrons and actors as part of the performance experience, watching one another negotiate each offer of food. Some audience members took the edible elements as a playful respite from the drama's main action. For instance, upon distribution of the pea soda during the barroom scene, two gentlemen gamely clinked their cups together in a toast before downing the liquid as a shot. Another patron, who arrived alone, produced a flask of liquor and spiked the pea sodas of those nearby when the drinks were passed around, creating an impromptu pea cocktail. On many nights during the three-week run of the show, audiences talked quietly with one another about each tasting element during and after eating, discussing whether or not a particular dish tasted like peas, how the food might have been prepared, and what associations a particular element evoked for them.

Perhaps because peas are not often treated as a delicacy in US food culture, on the whole, audience members readily recognized their eating as functioning mimetically, focusing largely on issues of recognition, representation, and resemblance rather than solely on the pleasures of a particular dish. Many audience members discussed the meaning of the sequence of peas with one another during and after the show, interpreting the edible elements as conveying representational significance. Audiences also contextualized the edible aspects of the event and the performance as a whole within their own taste for risk or experimentation. For the enthusiastic, taste evoked play and exploration and provoked participation and discussion. For reluctant or resistant participants, taste was an intrusion or an unwelcome reminder of childhood constraints. Many patrons commented that peas reminded them of a fraught childhood relationship with green vegetables. Still, some elements seemed to invite misinterpretation due to their visual similarity to the original untransformed pea. For instance, one woman consumed the pea gum in one bite, confusing it for another real pea and expressing incredulity while her companion insisted, pointing to her mouth and to the menu, that she'd just swallowed her gum. Other guests expressed disgust at the menu or declined to accept any of the offerings. Some ignored the food offerings entirely, one patron determinedly crossing her arms over her chest and gazing off toward the main action in a gesture of refusal each time a chorus member approached with a pea element.

Such acts of refusal, which the performers accepted without any attempt to cajole the audience member into eating, reinforced the divergence between Woyzeck's servitude and the audience's freedom to control their alimentary experience. As these examples demonstrate, tasting food in a mimetic context catalyzed both enthusiastic and repulsed participants' reactions. In both cases, sensory experience also formed a temporal threshold, a vista onto memory that both highlighted and contrasted immediate experience. Taste layered prior experience onto immediate sensation, bringing audience members' histories and memories alongside Woyzeck's in ways that seemed either delightful or horrifying, depending on one's point of view.

Miss Julie: *discourse, memory, and culinary reference*

Garlic marshmallow (*Miss Julie*, Chicago, IL, 2014)

284 g sugar; 200 ml corn syrup; 1 head roasted garlic; 6 sheets gelatin; 145 ml vegetable broth. Heat syrup, sugar, and garlic to 300 degrees Fahrenheit. Combine with bloomed gelatin and broth. Whip in stand mixer until fluffy before pouring into silicone-lined pans to set. Slice into small cubes and dust with powdered sugar.

In February 2014 candy designer (and *Woyzeck* scenographer and cake designer) Leigh Henderson and I collaborated on alimentary design for an adaptation of Strindberg's *Miss Julie* I directed at Chicago's Northeastern Illinois University. While Woyzeck's menu explored the potential for creating mimetic resemblance between character and audience, this menu used culinary reference points within popular culture as its primary mimetic framework. Combining familiar culinary discourse, recipes, and contexts for eating, the creative team composed a menu of aphrodisiac candy that highlighted the relationship between desire and consumption in the story of a young aristocrat, Julie, seduced and ultimately destroyed by an ambitious valet, Jean. Each candy element combined familiar foods, such as marshmallows and conversation hearts, with ingredients reputed to 'stimulate libido, such as garlic and oyster. The seventy-minute performance included six edible elements served during added monologues by Kristin, the play's third character and a chef, who recited musings on the relationship between taste and desire from Brillat-Savarin's *Physiology of Taste*. After a lengthy development process that explored ideas such as avocado and asparagus marshmallows and liquorice-filled candy bones, we settled on six final recipes: capsaicin cotton candy, black truffle caramels, garlic marshmallows drizzled with honey, red wine gummy candies, black pepper conversation hearts, and a chocolate-covered oyster truffle. A chorus of musicians served each element, which was passed from patron to patron along the rows of the theatre in traditional white paper cups nestled in rectangular white candy boxes. As with *Woyzeck*, patrons learned when and how to consume their edible offerings through their interactions with the chorus, who encouraged them to eat while acknowledging their freedom to decline each offering.

Rather than the relationship between audience and character, this experiment focused on the potential connection between taste and text. Each edible element offered the audience a moment of alimentary experience that reflected the performance's exploration of desire, power, and consumption, offering a chance for mimetic recognition of the ways in which similar patterns of power and dominance occur in everyday life. As in René Girard's mimetic theory of desire and violence, the central conflict of *Miss Julie* proceeds through mimetic reproduction of desiring patterns as Jean and Julie come to desire one another through a process of triangulation that leads to a brief union, an inevitable conflict of interest, and a final instance of sacrificial violence (1966). Both Jean and Miss Julie desire qualities of one another they feel are viewed as worthwhile by others. Jean envies Julie's access to her father's qualities of capital and class, while Julie envies Jean's freedom and connection to the vitality of the common people celebrating just outside. Each mimetically appropriates these qualities as the play proceeds, and each mimetically projects utopian futures in which their desires are fulfilled and they have successfully established new identities which integrate these desired features of one another. For each character, the mediating source of their desires also stands as an obstacle to their fulfillment. Jean expects Julie's father to refuse him as a suitable match for his daughter, while the townspeople outside openly mock Julie for her indiscretion with her valet. In the play's final moment, Jean and Julie enact Girard's notion of mimetic scapegoating, with Julie killing her pet canary to prove her love for Jean before ultimately killing herself when faced with Jean's rejection. All the while the two main characters pursue their game of cat and mouse in the confines of Kristin's kitchen, eating, drinking, and discussing themselves in terms of the foodstuffs they consume. Jean compares Julie to a fine wine and asserts dominance over his mistress by showing off his knowledge of French viticulture. Julie establishes her independence and connection to the common people by insisting she prefers beer, yet succumbs to Jean's offer of wine and becomes intoxicated as the show continues.

In keeping with the text's themes of mimesis and desire, the menu reinforced the relationship between imitation and sexual dominance through its focus on aphrodisiacs, many of which draw their reputed power from mimetic resemblance to sex organs, sex acts, or the evocation of states of arousal. For example, the aphrodisiac component of the menu's first element, capsaicin cotton candy, is thought to stimulate sexual arousal by creating a feeling of warmth and a flush in the cheeks that mimics common physical indications of sexual arousal. While capcaicin creates mimetic resemblance by inducing a bodily response to its consumption, oysters, the aphrodisiac element of our final offering, are traditionally thought of as evoking visual, textural, and olfactory resemblances to female sex organs. Finally, through visual, textural, and contextual means, the menu mimetically represented the commodified relationship between money, food, and romantic love through its winking variation on popular Valentine's Day gifts like truffles, caramels, and candy hearts.

The production dramaturgically supported the audience's recognition of the text's themes of desire and power through a few related discursive strategies.

Audience members received a paper menu that included quotes from Brillat-Savarin and listed each candy's aphrodisiac elements. As the chorus served each element, Kristin spoke directly to the audience to deliver monologues explicitly referencing the aphrodisiac quality of relevant ingredients. Both the paper menu and monologues focused on French gourmet, culinary writer, and lawyer Jean Anthelme Brillat Savarin, who famously espoused a mimetic theory of food and identity in his oft-quoted line, "tell me what kind of food you eat, and I'll tell you what kind of man you are" (1854, 25). Since the drama unfolds in a kitchen and features repeated reference to the relationship between distinction, cultural capital, and one's taste in food and drink, the inclusion of the iconic gastronome's musings on food, culture, and pleasure helped further connect each menu item with the themes of power and dominance unfolding in the main action. Furthermore, the use of a commonplace candy delivery mechanism of individual items nestled in paper cups inside a white paper box evoked the traditional Valentine's Day gesture of a box of candy used to communicate affection or stimulate romantic interest. By hewing to typical candy formats such as conversation hearts, caramels, and chocolate truffles, the production highlighted the complex relationship between this ritualized exchange of goods, seduction, and sexual dominance. Through the use of aphrodisiacs, identified as such by the text of the menu and discussed in detail in terms of their ability to inspire sexual arousal in Kristin's monologues, the menu again foregrounded relationships between desire, compulsion, and consumption both within the world of the play and in the wider social context of contemporary foodways and social conventions. These dramaturgical elements combined to render the candy legible in relation to the text, encouraging audience members to connect and contrast the alimentary and social experience of eating the menu of candy with the visual and auditory experience of observing the onstage action.

While *Woyzeck*'s menu intensified the text's fixation on peas, inviting audiences into a sensory affiliation with Woyzeck, *Miss Julie*'s menu amplified the play's themes of consumption and desire, positioning the audience outside of either Jean's or Julie's personal experience. Instead, the edible elements connected thematically with the text and with its cultural context. The aphrodisiac candy called upon the eater to recognize multiple layers of signification even as they transformed in the process of degustation. First, the production's alimentary elements intensified the experience of presence for audiences and actors as they discussed the candy, compared their interpretations of each element, and even fed one another during the play. Second, the menu relied on several connections to the past and, notably, to audience members' experiences of both elite and popular culture to make the menu both palatable and intelligible to participants. References to Brillat-Savarin and elite gastronomic delights such as black truffles and oysters abounded, but occurred alongside evocations of penny candy like conversation hearts and carnival food such as cotton candy. As with *Woyzeck*, audience reactions depended on multiple dimensions of taste, both in terms of literal sensation and in terms of preference. One couple left the show intensely engaged in a discussion of the familiar and strange aspects of each candy, demonstrating the tension that occurred when a candy's texture or shape conformed to memory while its flavor did not. For these patrons, this tension felt provocative and engaging, creating an intensification of the risque context of the events that unfolded onstage. A solo audience member commented that consuming the candy heightened her understanding of themes of power and dominance in the play. Several patrons asked if they could purchase additional candy, imagining it as a gift that could encapsulate the experience of the performance for friends unable to attend. Others used the candy as a metaphor for the production as a whole, describing it as familiar and strange, like the performance's interpretation of the classic work. A few audience members walked out or protested, not necessarily over the play's overt sexuality, but over the production's use of taste as a mode of experiencing the themes of the show. One particularly displeased audience member wrote to the theatre's artistic director, complaining that the use of food created a distraction from a classic text in "abysmally poor taste." While this dissatisfied audience member did not express gustatory displeasure, the concept of using one's sense of taste, of eating during a production of a classic work, became in itself distasteful. Specifically, this audience member viewed alimentary elements as a distraction, calling his attention away from the visual and auditory elements of the production and instead focusing him on the play of associations bound in touching, tasting, and interpreting the experience of eating aphrodisiac candies.

Eating *Miss Julie*: sensory remix at PQ Makers 2015

In an exploration of cooking and eating as performance itself rather than an element of a larger *mise-en-scène*, in June 2015, Henderson and I presented *Edible Dramaturgy: Exploring Death and Fetish Through Candy*, a mashup of the two menus discussed above in a four-hour durational performance of cooking and eating at the Prague Quadrennial Makers exhibition. In keeping with the Prague Quadrennial's tradition of including exhibits of design, seminars from major theatre artists, performance events, and curated projects, PQ 2015 featured three curated projects in addition to its main theme. "Tribes" featured a series of events centering on masked performers in public spaces. "Objects" combined theatrical props and objects with their stories and histories in a museum installation. The third curated project, the "Makers" exhibition (hereafter referred to as PQ Makers), explored food, cooking, and theatre through a series of durational performance events. Curated by Icelandic designer Rebekka A. Ingimundardóttir, PQ Makers featured a small kitchen and a long dining table used by twenty-four teams to create and share a series of edible events within the historic Galley at Bethlehem Chapel. Ingimundardóttir, an installation artist, created the kitchen, filled floor-to-ceiling with tools and ingredients, and selected the performances. The call for submissions asked makers to recycle a prior work, putting "theatre design and food design together at the same table and us[ing] food as their theatrical material" (Ingimundardóttir 2015, 320). In light of the event's focus on the process of making, organizers asked artists to complete all food preparation during the

Mimesis, participation, and embodied knowledge   149

four-hour event, rather than preparing in advance. Priming the audience to explore each event actively, organizers posted placards in the space proclaiming "this is not a theatre this is not a gallery so talk eat drink whistle touch feel smile and enjoy." These events featured no recognizable backstage; the making of the performance constituted the entirety of the action, with participants free to experience all aspects of the event.

This insistence on rethinking the assumed conventions of its associated spaces ("this is not a theatre this is not a gallery") signalled the organizers' interest in an experience that reconsidered taste's position in the sensory hierarchy. Inverting Aristotle's famous organization of the senses, this event established taste as the primary means through which the assembled artists would create theatrical representations, with visual and auditory elements playing a supporting role. By proclaiming the space was neither a theatre nor a gallery, the organizers effectively destabilized any expectation that audiences came primarily to see and hear. Instead, placards reminded visitors to "talk eat drink whistle touch feel smile," an exhortation that proved effective as visitors ate, drank, and chatted throughout most of the performances. The exhibition also made taste a tactic for interruption of the everyday, rethinking temporal linearity and interpenetrating apprehensible and intelligible experience. Given the significance of this international collection of taste-based performances, I briefly trace the range of responses to this provocative frame before drawing out a few implications about the relationship between representation and sensation and between apprehensible and intelligible experience in the event as a whole.

Among the twenty-four artists and groups participating in PQ Makers, approaches to using food as a theatrical medium were quite diverse. *Tasting Notes*, by the US collective A Change of Harp, translated composer Luciano Berio's "Sequenze" into four dishes, each composed of raw vegetables. Here, as the title of the event indicates, creators used dramaturgical framing and mimetic priming to represent a classic work of music through a set of acts of food preparation and consumption. Throughout the performance's four hours, artists chopped and served raw vegetables while describing their relationship to each section of Berio's composition, which played in the background. Only through the intervention and guidance of the performers could visitors understand the relationship between individual tastes and textures and the musical original being transformed and performed during the event. Taste functioned as a doubling of sound, mimetically reproducing aspects of the work through a palate of flavors defined by raw vegetables and reinforced through shapes and textures created through the artists' performed labor.

Fatt, a free-form creation of a version of the traditional Levantine salad fattoush, took a different approach to the notion of culinary representation. In this large-format salad, Lebanese artist Miriane Zgheib treated her edible components as visual and social raw material, creating an installation of vegetables and pita bread fragments reminiscent of Knowles' *Make a Salad*. Again, flavor and texture worked as anchors, using the sense of taste to create contrast between the remembered sensation of a traditional dish and an innovative presentation and consumption format. In contrast, the Danish performance art group Sisters Academy, in *Sisters Academy * Sisters Eat*, used costume to evoke the social atmosphere of a convent, enlisting visitors in a performance of labor preparing beets and other foodstuffs as a way of providing an embodied experience of an all-female environment with attendant foodways. For *Sisters Eat*, mimetic cooking, in the form of culinary labor, formed the initial representational intervention that primed the audience to later attach representational significance to the consumption of the foods they had prepared.

A Tragedy in Four Acts, a response to Euripides's tragedy *Iphigenia at Aulis* by Rudolf Skopec and Ladislav Vondrák of the Czech Republic, was the final and perhaps most controversial PQ Makers offering. Rejecting the event's focus on taste in favor of a sacrificial destruction of food, the artists gathered together a massive amount of raw vegetables onto the space's central table, which groaned under the weight. Setting a pot of water to boil in the corner, the performers dropped unpeeled raw onions into the seething liquid, flooding the room with an acrid aroma. Smashing, chopping, tossing and stomping on the vegetables, the artists rearranged the environment multiple times, carrying a prep table laden with more vegetables into the main gallery and enlisting visitors to help them set this centerpiece atop the table where guests had consumed many previous theatrical meals. Later the audience gathered around the main table again, frantically clearing it off at the artists' urging before the two men leapt atop it, struggled together and then dragged one another across its length. Upon the completion of this ritual, the artists swept aside the destroyed vegetables, hastily cleared the now-chaotic installation space, and offered the assembled group glasses of plain tap water. While audience members smelled, touched, heard, and saw massive amounts of food during the performance, the artists created tension between these senses and taste itself, making the tantalizing choice not to serve any of this food to the audience.

I linger on this performance due to the debate about taste that it inspired. At the performance's conclusion, Ingimundardóttir initiated a discussion with the assembled artists and guests, arguing that the work failed to offer the audience an engagement with taste. When Skopec and Vondrák countered with the question: "Can you not taste emotions?", Ingimundardóttir responded with a firm "No." Interestingly, this dispute inverted the typical critique of alimentary representation as unreal or insubstantial. On the contrary, for Ingimundardóttir, the reality of eating was essential to a valid experience of alimentary performance. One can not taste emotions figuratively, Ingimundardóttir asserted. Still, one might indeed taste an alimentary artwork capable of representing emotional states such as Iphigenia's. As the assembled artists and participants, several of whom were themselves presenters at PQ Makers, debated both aesthetic quality and the physical and metaphorical parameters of taste, the concept of taste as distinction amongst competing aesthetic options dominated. For the organizers, the performance sidestepped the representational agenda of the event and its own title's promise to offer audiences a taste of *Iphigenia at Aulis*. For the artists, the organizers failed in their refusal to understand the artists' taste in performance. The event's video artist accused the performers of working in bad faith and poor taste, destroying a sacred space for collaborative creation through an attitude of confrontation and rejection. The artists responded with annoyance and incredulity at the perceived provincialism of the critique. Fittingly, the assembled artists and audience members ended the exhibition with a conversation about pushing the bounds of taste, some debating the nature of taste outside of a sensory context while others longed for a literal taste of the tantalizingly inaccessible vegetables.

Before discussing *Edible Dramaturgy*, our alimentary performance at PQ Makers, I pause to share a few observations about the exhibition as a whole. Led by the call to recycle a performance, many of the events used taste as a means of moving a text or experience from an intelligible, logical concept into a sensible, apprehensible experience and, in some cases, back again. Due perhaps to a drive to clarify the relationship between sensible and intelligible content in each piece and prime audience members to make mimetic connections between the two, many of the performances sprang from classic texts. Of the twenty-four performances, the majority worked with texts deemed canonical and signalled these texts in their titles: *King Lear, The Cherry Orchard, No Exit*, the *Iliad*, and many more. *Edible Dramaturgy* was one of two pieces drawn in part from *Miss Julie*, and though, unlike many of the other performances, it did not signal this relationship in its title, it did so through other textual means. As artists negotiated taste as a primary sensory mode of experiencing performance, the social and aesthetic power of taste as distinction manifested itself in our choices of source material. In addition to classic texts, many artists chose classic contexts, from the literal (*Tasting Notes*'s classical music) to the historical (*Sisters Academy*'s evocation of an ancient convent) to the culinary (classic or familiar dishes from fattoush to gazpacho). Even the most oppositional of the offerings, *A Tragedy in Four Acts*, grounded itself in a classic tragedy.

As these twenty-four artists and groups grappled with the idea of food as a theatrical medium, the stakes of taste intersected with and struggled within the bounds of Cartesian logic. Even as artists attempted to interpenetrate the sensible and intelligible, the performances of PQ Makers suggested we often rethink lines between thought and experience by first drawing those lines again, evoking a common background of thought and memory before piercing, reinforcing, or attempting to wipe away that framework through sensory experience. When performing artists translated text or context into food, they demonstrated sophisticated knowledge of the originals even as they purposefully left space for the alimentary stimulation of mimetic recognition. Each performance encouraged guests to discover for themselves the associations made between edible performance and classic text or context, asking them to taste the work, sense the connections. But these attempts to trouble the relationship between thought and sensation, between intelligible and sensible, often hinged upon an initial legibility that depended on taste as distinction.

Through these movements back and forth from text to taste, the PQ Makers performances asked audiences to exercise multiple senses of taste, alone or in combination, depending on each performance's approach. The exhibition as a whole relied upon taste as a cultivated ability to discriminate between aesthetic elements, enabling the guest to distinguish the relationship between the flavor, color, and texture of a bite of food and a few bits of text from a classic work. In the use of classic texts and recipes, taste worked as cultural capital, represented by the knowledge of that original text or simply by the awareness that the work itself had been deemed significant. The event also deployed taste as action, a mode of engagement that represents a decision to interact with a performance while also changing it, reducing the available material for consumption by others and initiating labor as performers refilled cups and made new cakes, switched on blenders, and whisked spun sugar. I turn now to a discussion of these competing and interconnected aspects of taste within the PQ Makers performance of *Edible Dramaturgy*.

Habanero cotton candy (Edible Dramaturgy, Prague, Czech Republic, 2015)

1 quartered habanero pepper, 113 g sugar, 75 ml corn syrup, 75 ml water. Combine, heat to 300 degrees F, adding habanero at 150 degrees and removing as soon as desired level of spice is achieved. Cool, break into pieces, melt, and drizzle over dowels to create thin strands of candy floss.

Edible Dramaturgy combined the two prior menus for *Woyzeck* and *Miss Julie* and remixed them for the PQ Makers context, transforming them from edible dramaturgy and design meant to function as one element of a larger performance event into edible performance in their own right. The event's design drew heavily upon the model of Benjaminian incorporation, which construes both eating and reading as potential thresholds capable of disrupting the relationship between subject and object. Inspired by a playful combination of eating and reading, a lingering in text and taste at the same time, we laid each edible element on the dining table over a coating of plastic wrap that covered large printed selections of the text that originally accompanied each bite of food. The first element, a fresh snap pea, appeared atop Woyzeck's introduction of himself as a "soldier, rifleman in the second regiment, second battalion, fourth company, born on the Feast of the Annunciation." The second, a pea gummy candy, sat above a line from Woyzeck's doctor, asking "Did you eat your peas already, Woyzeck?" Pea soda, the third element, accompanied another quote from the doctor, explaining to passersby that the title character had, for months, eaten nothing but peas and asking them to "Notice the result. Feel how uneven his pulse is." The fourth item, habanero candy floss, was hand-spun with the help of several audience members into a large pile and placed atop a line from *Miss Julie*'s Kristin: "I'll be frank, I'm not sure it's wise for Miss Julie to dance twice with the same man." Wine gummies, set with agar agar and sliced by an audience member, were lined in tidy rows above Jean's line to Julie, "I could love you, yes, no doubt. You are beautiful. Yes, you are refined. Nice when you want to be." The penultimate dish, black pepper conversation hearts, appeared alongside edible ink pens with which we invited guests to write their own messages on the candy hearts. Accompanying this sixth element were Julie's lines to Jean wondering whether she was drawn to him through weakness or love, ending with the desperate question, "Do you know what love is?" The seventh element, a garlic marshmallow-filled pea cake ball cooked to order in small batches and filled on-site with the help of the audience, accompanied the final lines of our original production of *Woyzeck*: "A good murder. A real murder. A beautiful murder. As good a murder as you'd ever want to see."

In addition to remixing the performances themselves, combining previously distinct menus into a new experience, *Edible Dramaturgy* also recombined and reframed the relationship between creator and audience in terms of their participation in cooking and eating, their ability to choose when and in what context to experience each edible element, and their access to sensory and intelligible material connected with the performance as a whole. Guests could assist in cooking, wander through the space, taste raw ingredients, sample final dishes, and ask questions. The performers focused on the labor of creating and serving food, providing unrehearsed, conversational answers to participant questions and engaging in discussion with guests while frantically preparing enough food to keep the table filled throughout the event. Using a set of microphones distributed throughout the space, the event's media artist mixed recordings of songs from each show with live sounds, including bits of conversation happening in the gallery and the sounds of food preparation in the adjacent kitchen. At the same time, he intercut still images from the original performances with live video feed from the food prep and presentation areas onto screens positioned throughout the space. PQ participants, Prague residents, and even area dogs wandered through the gallery. Some stayed for hours helping spin sugar, slice wine gummies, or inject garlic marshmallow centers into pea cake balls. Some tasted a few elements. Others ate their way through the menu in order, from start to finish.

Ultimately, *Edible Dramaturgy* invited audience members to experience incorporative eating by engaging in sensory remix, reframing the relationship between tasting, seeing, hearing, touching, smelling, and thinking as ways of experiencing performance. In this taste-based mashup of two earlier performances, text existed in context of taste and taste in context of text, each extending in different directions for the eater depending on her prior experience of flavor, story, texture, food preparation, and performance. This playful tasting-as-incorporation positioned the participant's sensory experience as a means of stimulating mimetic recognition of surprising resemblances. For instance, the menu's final element, a pea cake with a garlic marshmallow center, united the two prior menus and offered guests a chance to experience the shocking recognition of familiar flavors in new contexts so critical to the sensory and temporal disruption of incorporation. It also layered past and present multiple times, in the texts and traces that accompanied the eating and in the recollection of these flavors and textures in other contexts. The richness of one's experience of this food, the complexity of the relationship between play and knowledge in one's eating, depended on one's prior experience. It also depended on taste as distinction: the ability to recognize a classic, to appreciate the labor of artists even as one consumes that labor, to contextualize the relationship between original and adaptation, to linger over a text, and to recognize a mind–body split even as one plays at undoing it.

As I have discussed earlier in this volume, the relationship between taste and text can also constitute a threshold between present and past. To open this threshold, participants must recognize the multiple traces in the room as related to one another and to classic texts, or at least as related to an artistic intervention. Most guests did so, reading textual traces while they ate. Some participants familiar with the original texts discussed the ways in which peas in surprising formats and textures connected with Woyzeck's experience. Others discussed the relationship of a line from *Miss Julie* or a phrase from Brillat-Savarin with the edible offering atop the text, invested not in the original context but in the resonances between the excerpt and the food. For instance, visitors discussed the significance of the wine gummy's pairing with two pieces of text: Jean's line "You are beautiful, you are refined, nice when you want to be. You are like a fine wine, and your kiss…" and Brillat-Savarin's "We have seen that physical love has taken possession of all the sciences. In this respect it acts with its habitual tyranny." Others focused on the edible offerings' relationships to one another, positing resonances between the desire-inducing characteristics of the aphrodisiac candies and the repulsive qualities of the pea soda. Even when they did not directly engage with textual elements or compare each element to their artistic context, as with some of the small children in attendance, their experiences became a part of the larger aesthetic event. A Büchner expert commented on the textual interpretation of our flavor combinations even as she smiled and nodded at a child devouring a cake ball unaware of its literary significance, enjoying his unknowing appreciation for a foodstuff sprung from a tragedy.

On one hand, PQ Makers highlighted the role of taste as a threshold between past and present. On another, through its performance of labor, PQ Makers also encouraged a more complex temporal doubling as visitors and artists alike invested their time in labor and then spent that time once again in tasting. Visitors and artists alike oscillated between the immediacy of taste as present sensation and the accumulative temporality of taste as distinction, facilitated by the consumption of one another's labor. The prior productions of *Woyzeck* and *Miss Julie* had left the labor of food preparation largely hidden in the backstage space of the production, presenting finished mimetic dishes and menus in order to initiate mimetic recognition on the part of the audience. In combining the processes of creating mimetic cuisine with mimetic eating, PQ Makers brought this previously hidden labor into the foreground and highlighted its potential role in alimentary representation. In doing so, the Makers exhibition demonstrated the ways in which the experience of alimentary performance hinges on the paradoxical conjunction of present and past, the immediate time of sensation overlaid with the accumulated temporality of labor and knowledge.

Contents of an event trace jar (Edible Dramaturgy, Prague, Czech Republic, 2015)

Pea fiber; black pepper conversation hearts; capsaicin floss; garlic marshmallow fluff; wine gummies; toothpicks; fresh peas.

By collecting and displaying a set of material remnants from each performance, PQ Makers also addressed the question of whether taste can exceed the present tense, opening itself for our memory and analysis beyond fleeting sensation or gustatory destruction. As each group completed their session, the artists compiled and left behind a "trace," a glass jar filled with objects representing their performances. As events accumulated, these trace jars filled a small bookshelf near the entrance to the gallery. Most jars brimmed with food detritus, still colorful but perhaps no longer edible or appetizing. *Edible Dramaturgy*'s jar consisted of layers of pulped peas, bright white garlic marshmallow fluff, melting candy floss, and conversation hearts whose messages, written by visitors, had already begun to bleed into incomprehensibility, recording the chaos of the mashup. True, we could not and likely would not choose to taste the contents of these vessels, but glancing at the traces did evoke memories of the flavors of each event, enough to make one salivate or to turn one's stomach. In their combination of familiar and strange objects, these jars seemed to prove the truth but also the incomplete nature of Telfer's and Hegel's aforementioned contentions about taste, time, and permanence. While taste lives only in the present, it depends on and reverberates through our pasts in its connection to memories, texts, social events, skills, and labor. As we translated our edible experiments though the PQ Makers framework, their original pleasures, dangers, associations, and innovations transformed into a chaotic but invigorating moment of incorporation. Taste became a sensory means through which to linger over memory, language, relationships, objects, bodies, time, and knowledge. In creating a platform for food-based performance, the PQ Makers exhibition raised additional questions about the mimetic capabilities of taste. Does taste render self and other, past and present, sensation and knowledge difficult to distinguish, mashed together in an experience of presence that depends on the past? Or might taste in performance reveal the ways in which such distinctions dissolve even as they become apparent?

Mignardises: some thoughts on the future of alimentary performance

This study has aimed not only to better understand the burgeoning trend of culinary mimeticism, but also to advocate for its significance and to promote the continuing development of alimentary performance as a mode of critical, experiential, and often pleasurable meaning-making. Answering the skeptical critique of alimentary representation as a turn toward hedonism, a devaluing of culinary tradition, a degradation of everyday pleasures, or plain silliness, this study demonstrates the ways in which culinary mimeticism opens new horizons not only for understanding cooking and eating, but also for understanding representation and its significance. Rather than a threat to truth or meaning, I propose that the turn toward culinary mimeticism stems from and follows upon an increasing sense of bodies themselves as repositories of knowledge. Accordingly, this embodied knowledge functions differently than one that aspires to a universal truth viewed from a distance. It is multisensory, subjective, and, if not ephemeral, endlessly differentiated by new experience. In *Philosophers at Table: on Food and Being Human* (2016), Raymond Boisvert and Lisa Heldke argue for an alimentary philosophy based in this notion of embodied knowledge. Where the dominant philosophical value of objectivity necessarily banished emotionality, deemphasized individual lived experience, sidelined aesthetics, and relied on schematic, often binary, divisions between different sorts of knowledges and actions, a philosophical practice based in the stomach would hinge on "activities that are necessarily integrative, implicating as they do intelligence, memory, imagination and interaction with the biosphere" (Boisvert and Heldke 2016, 167). The developments in culinary representation chronicled in this book advance a similar view of an integrated intelligence, working on multiple fronts to establish cooking and eating as potential pathways to embodied knowledge.

By reframing the bodily modes in which representation may be experienced, culinary mimeticism provides a generative alternative to the supposed divisions between mind and body, sensation and intelligence, aesthetics and interpretation. The shift in perspective from a representational framework based largely in seeing and hearing to one based in a multisensory alimentary encounter both mirrors and enables a larger shift in ways of understanding human experience and its significance. Similarly, as it elides formerly sharp distinctions between sensation and intelligence, alimentary performance opens new opportunities for bodily thinking which connects intelligence to practicality, aesthetics to everyday life, individual choice to communal experience. Moreover, by asking diners and audiences to deploy their own mimetic faculties in new contexts and modes of experience, culinary mimeticism supports an essential engagement with meaning and significance in a time of deep skepticism of the relationship between representation, truth, and knowledge. As diners and audiences actively make sense through eating, culinary mimeticism, and the versions of alimentary performance it has inspired, reaffirms and repositions the significance of representation as an invitation to struggle with meaning individually and collectively, not at a supposedly objective distance, but intimately, bodily, messily, and even greedily, in activities attended by both pleasure and risk.

The evolution of food as a representational medium continues to proceed frenetically, and as it does so its horizons expand. In keeping with the imaginative, generative aspects of mimesis I have emphasized throughout this study, I close with a glimpse of a few possible pathways for the ongoing development of culinary mimeticism. As with the mignardises that often accompany the conclusion of a tasting menu, I aim to resist the notion of finality and instead gesture toward the future in a few provocative elements to spark the imagination. As this book goes to press, performance artist Marina Abramovic has announced a new partnership with French macaron purveyor Ladurée to create, in collaboration with impresario Raphaël Castoriano, a "pastry portrait" that offers the sweet-toothed art aficionado a chance to consume a macaron that tastes like Abramovic. Rethinking the cannibalistic mimesis of communion, this confection is the material result of a process through which Castoriano aims to "translate her memories and identity into an edible experience" (Rea 2017). Experimental collaborations such as these will surely proliferate and push further beyond the previous boundaries of representation as culinary mimeticism draws artists, performers, and chefs closer to one another in both philosophy and practice. Meanwhile, the continued development of food-based scenographic and dramaturgical practices stands poised to transform experiences of spectatorship in both high art and popular culture. For example, Dog & Pony DC's ongoing project "Sense-Able" remixes sensory hierarchies to create an edible, tactile, olfactory experience of "Shakespeare without Sight or Sound," upending not only hierarchies of meaning but also of ability (2017). Elsewhere, entertainment and food purveyors continue to explore the possibilities of alimentary representation for popular audiences. For example, recording artists the Lost Bayou Ramblers, in a bid to draw attention to the disappearing Louisiana coastline, recently teamed with Bayou Teche Brewing company to release a single on a bottle of "Aloha Golden Meadow" ale, brewed to "augment the sensory pleasure" and the representational strategy of the song that shares its name (Knott 2016). A pineapple-infused Saison hybridized with a Cajun narrative song, Aloha Golden Meadow aims to stimulate, through alimentary and auditory experience, a moment of mimetic recognition of the problem of coastal erosion.

What might it mean to imbibe coastal erosion? To eat in iambic pentameter? To taste Marina Abramovic? Rather than pose an answer to any of these queries directly, I propose that the critical intervention these examples of culinary mimeticism point toward is the pleasurable, confounding, and captivating persistence of these questions themselves. Rethinking the disembodying tendencies of a reductive, illusionistic vision of mimesis, these and the many examples of culinary mimeticism I have explored throughout this volume instead evoke repeated, temporally expansive, embodied, sensed, thought, and felt interaction with representation itself as a literal object of desire. As expansive as a tasting menu or as miniscule as a pea, the dishes, drinks, and performances collected here open onto diverse questions, from the problem of sustainability to the nature of celebrity. Most importantly, rather than reject mimesis as a distraction from truth, these examples of culinary mimeticism allow us to reimagine embodied experience as a space in which we might take pleasure in unpacking and critically considering the relationship between representation and reality. In insisting that the senses, intelligence, and the body not only need not but must not be artificially sequestered from one another in this process, culinary mimeticism offers a rethinking of mimetic experience as not divorcing us from, but connecting us to the very faculties we must hone in order to learn, know, and tell the truth, on our tables, on our stages, and beyond.

Notes

1 Joshua Abrams and I convened 2014's group, "How to Do Things with Food(s)." We convened a similar group with a new theme, "Debating the Steaks," in 2015. In 2016, Susan Bennett joined me to convene a new group, "Transplants: Food/Theatre/Performance." 2017's working group, convened by myself, Abrams, and Megan Marsh-McGlone (a participant in all three prior groups), explored the concept of "Consuming Bodies."
2 Pea foam, pea *pâte de fruit*, and pea ice cream were all cut from the menu, either due to difficulties in scaling the recipe for sixty-five audience members a night or to problems with testers recognizing the product.
3 Audience members received a traditional program with historical notes, biographies, and production credits at the conclusion of each night's performance.

References

Boisvert, Raymond D. and Lisa Heldke. 2016. *Philosophers at Table: On Food and Being Human*. London: Reaktion.
Bolt, Barbara. 2004. *Art Beyond Representation: The Performative Power of the Image*. London: I.B. Tauris.
Brillat-Savarin, Jean Anthelme. 1854 [1825]. *Physiology of Taste; or, Transcendental Gastronomy*. Translated by Fayette Robinson. Philadelphia: Lindsay and Blackiston.
Carter, Paul. 2004. *Material Thinking*. Carlton, Victoria: Melbourne University Press.
Derrida, Jacques. 2000 [1997]. *Of Hospitality*. Response by Anne Dufourmantelle. Translated by Rachel Bowlby. Stanford: Stanford University Press.
Dog & Pony DC. 2017. "Sense-Able." dogandponydc.com/ourwork/sense-able.
Folino White, Ann. 2016. "Tasting the Past: Transhistorical Experiences with Food and Celebrity." Working group presentation. "Transplants: Food/Theatre/Performance." American Society for Theatre Research annual conference. Minneapolis, MN.
Giard, Luce. 1998 [1994]. "Part II: Doing-Cooking." In *Practice of Everyday Life Volume II: On Living and Cooking*. Michel de Certeau, Luce Giard, and Pierre Mayol. Edited by Luce Giard. Translated by Timothy J. Tomasik. Minneapolis: University of Minnesota Press.
Girard, René. 1966 [1961]. *Deceit, Desire, and the Novel*. Translated by Yvonne Freccero. Baltimore: Johns Hopkins University Press.
Ingimundardóttir, Rebekka A. 2015. 'Introduction.' *Prague Quadrennial of Performance Design and Space Catalog 2015*. Prague: Arts and Theatre Institute.
Knott, Karlos. 2016. "Does Cajun music really get better after beer?" *The News Star*, December 18. B1–2. Monroe, LA.
Korsmeyer, Carolyn. 2015. "Can We Taste the Past?" The Humanities Center, Miami University, Oxford, Ohio. October 15.
Marsh-McGlone, Megan. 2014. "How Breastmilk Performs." Working group presentation. "How to Do Things with Food(s): Food as Research/Food in Performance." American Society for Theatre Research annual conference. Baltimore, MD.
Perullo, Nicola. 2016. *Taste as Experience: The Philosophy and Aesthetics of Food*. New York: Columbia University Press.
Rea, Naomi. 2017. "For Frieze Week, Marina Abramović Distills Her Art and Life Into… a Macaron." *Artnet*, October 4. news.artnet.com/art-world/marina-abramovic-macaron-1102277.
Strindberg, August. 2014 [1888]. *Miss Julie*. Translated by Kristin Hunt. Unpublished manuscript.

INDEX

Abend, Lisa 56, 60
Ablutions 106
Abramovic, Marina 157
Abrams, Joshua 49, 61n2, 118, 158n1
Achatz, Grant: Alinea 2, 69–75, 84; Aviary 80–83; at elBulli 68; on e-Gullet forums 69–71; on Homaro Cantu 84; Next 75–81; the Office 82–83; Trio 69
activism, culinary 86–89, 92–93, 121–125
Adrià, Ferran: criticism of 4, 14–16, 55; deconstruction 53–55; Documenta 12 54–58; Elbulli1846 59–60; elBulli foundation 59–60; Heart Ibiza 60; on intellect as "sixth sense" 52; olives 11, 17–18, 34, 54, 59, 130; techno-emotional cuisine 16; theory of creativity 50–56
Alinea 2, 69–75, 84
Alinea Project, the 70
alimentary dramaturgy 141–154
Aloha Golden Meadow Ale 157
Andrés, José 11, 34, 54, 71
anti-mimetic culinary critique 4–5, 14–16, 19–20
Apicius 79, 134–135
appropriation 108, 116–124
Arellano, Gustavo 118
Aristotle 6, 8–10
artificial flavors 25
Athenaeus 22, 79
Aviary 80–83

Baker, Bobby 110–115
Barrymore, Ethel 138–139

Barthes, Roland 77
Bayless, Rick 2, 27, 116–121
Bean Rolls 105
Bender-Wolanski, Helga 57
Benjamin, Walter 4–5, 6, 12, 18–19
Beran, Dave 75
Berrista 87, 92
Birthday Cake lip gloss 21
Blumenthal, Heston 14–16, 36–37, 41–49
Boal, Augusto 9–10, 129
Bocuse, Paul 17, 23
Boisvert, Raymond 156
boundary crossing 14–16
Bread and Puppet Theatre 26
breastfeeding 137–138
Brecht, Bertolt 9–10, 129
Brillat-Savarin, Jean Anthelme 23–24, 145, 147
Brown, Alton 4, 19–20, 40
Byl, Jason 1

Cantu, Homaro: Berrista 87, 92; and culinary activism 86–89, 92–93; and culinary copyright 85; and edible ink 84, 86–87, 152–153; iNG 89–92; legacies 93; and miracle fruit 87–92; Moto 85–86, 88–89; and substitute foods 86–87
Carême, Marie-Antoine 23, 38, 46
Cascabel 118–121
Castoriano, Raphaël 157
Catbird Seat 61n1
Chang, David 13, 20–21
A Change of Harp 149

Chicago, Judy 106
Chicken Sushi 108
Chopped 10
communion 22–23, 114–115, 157
cookbooks as closet drama 83
cooking: and gender 8–9, 99, 26, 112–113; as language 51–52, 111; mimetic 130–131
The Cooking Gene 112
cotton candy 1, 83, 140, 146, 152
Crenn, Dominique 10
Crucial Detail 73–74, 83
culinary activism 86–89, 92–93, 121–125
culinary copyright 85
culinary foam 13–16, 19–20, 40, 49
culinary justice 115–116, 121–124
culinary labor 56–58, 74–75, 106, 111–115, 121–123, 130, 153–154
culinary luddism 20
culinary opera 14–16
culinary theatre 9–10, 14–16

Dahl, Roald 25, 46
Dalí, Salvador 59, 91–92
deconstruction 53–55
Deen, Paula 112
Derrida, Jacques 53, 133–134
Diamond, Elin 28
dining as acting 18
Dinner (restaurant) 47
Documenta 54–58
Dog & Pony D.C. 157
doing-cooking 136
domesticity 9–10, 102–103, 106, 111–115
dramaturgy: alimentary 124, 152–154; of deliciousness 13; of dining 41–46, 61n2, 69
Drawing on a Mother's Experience 110–111
Dudek, Nir 17, 85
Duelli, Aldo 54–55

eating: aesthetic 18–19; incorporative 18–19, 113, 139, 152–154; mimetic 42, 131–134, 137–141; as reading 17
Edible Dramaturgy 152–155
Edible Family in a Mobile Home 111–112
edible ink 84, 86–87, 152–153
edible menu 84
elBulli *see* Adrià, Ferran
El Ideas 93
Elliot, Graham 66, 93
embodied knowledge 18, 54–55, 57, 136, 155–157
ephemerality of alimentary experience 18–19, 56–59, 111, 155–157
epistemology 19, 152

Escoffier, Auguste 24–25, 38, 76–77
Esparza, Bill 118
excess, mimetic 99–100

Fantastical Feasts 46–47
fantasy flavors 25
Fat Duck 14–16, 36–37, 41–46
Fatt 149–150
Finley, Karen 106
flavor-tripping 86, 87–91
Fluxus 101
foam, culinary 13–16, 19–20, 40, 49
Folino White, Ann 138–139
Food and Performance Working Groups 136–141
"Food for Thought" 108–109
food science 19–20, 25
Foss, Phillip 93
Foucault, Michel 58, 76–78
Frankenstein 19–20
French Laundry 68
Fuchs, Elinor 27–28
Futurist meals 17, 38

García-López, Saúl 97–98
Gault, Henri 17, 38
gender 8–9, 99, 26, 112–113
gentrification 80–81
Giard, Luce 136, 143
Girard, René 22–23, 146
Glossier 21
Gopnik, Blake 35–36
Gorgias 7
Gough, Richard 27

Halliwell, Stephen 7
Hamilton, Richard 55–56
Hampton Creek 93
health 4, 20, 23, 29, 38, 47–49
Heart Ibiza 60
Hegel, Georg Wilhelm Friedrich 5, 11–12
Heldke, Lisa 30n4, 156
Hemberger, Alan 83
Hemings, James 123
Henderson, Leigh 145, 148
Heston's Mission Impossible 47–49
heterotopia 58, 76–78
Historic Heston 46–47
hospitality 110, 112–115, 132–133
How to Live 110
How to Shop 114–115
hunger 86–87, 88, 92

Identical Lunch 104–105
imitation 6–8

immersive performance 27–28, 133
improvisation 66–67
incorporation 18–19, 113, 139, 152–154
iNG 89–92
Ingimundardóttir, Rebekka A. 148–149, 150–151
Iphigenia at Aulis 150–151

Joly, Charles 81
Jones, Chris 84, 93
Jouary, Jean-Paul 56
justice, culinary 115–116, 121–124

kaiseki 17, 23, 38, 58, 62n8
Kastner, Martin 73–74
Keller, Thomas 37–41, 68
Kirshenblatt-Gimblett, Barbara 14–15, 23
Kitchen Show 112–114
kitchen table 61n6, 66, 75, 82, 89
knowledge 8–10, 100, 116, 136, 151–152, 155–157
Knowles, Alison 26–27, 101–105
Kokonas, Nick 69–70
Korsmeyer, Carolyn 5, 8, 30n6, 30n12, 138–139
Kurti, Nicholas 19

labor, culinary 56–58, 74–75, 106, 111–115, 121–123, 130, 153–154
Ladurée 157
Last Supper Project 27
Laudan, Rachel 20
lickable wallpaper 25, 46
locavore movement 67
Lopez, Phillip 1
Lost Bayou Ramblers 157
luddism, culinary 20, 86

Maciunas, George 101, 104
Make a Salad 102–104
manifesto cuisine 47–49
Marsh-McGlone, Megan 137–138
Maximin, Jacques 50, 61n5
McGee, Harold 38–41, 42
meaning 11–13, 18–19, 27–28, 39–41
medicine 7, 137–138
memory 18–19, 58, 121–124, 130–131, 136, 145–148
Milk of Amnesia/Leche de Amnesia 107
mimesis: Aristotle on 8–10; Benjamin on 4–5, 6, 12, 18–19; dangers of 7–11; Diamond on 28; excessive 99–100; food as a mimetic medium 11–16, 19–21; and imitation: 6–8; and meaning 7, 11–13; multisensory 42, 47–49, 83, 98–99, 128–130; Plato on 7–8, 12, 20; Taussig on 3, 23, 91, 99–100
mimetic cooking 130–131
mimetic eating 42, 131–134, 137–141
mimetic excess 99–100
mimetic faculty 6–13
miracle berry 87–92
The Miracle Berry Diet Cookbook 87, 89
Miss Julie 145–148, 152–154
Modernist Cuisine 4, 14–16
molecular gastronomy 19–20, 39
Moto 85–86, 88–89
multisensory mimeticism 42, 47–49, 83, 98–99, 128–130
Myhrvold, Nathan 4, 14–16

Next restaurant 75–81
nonsensuous similarity 12, 131
Nouvelle Cuisine 17, 20, 23, 38, 39, 42
Novero, Cecilia 17–19

"Odorama" 26
olfactory design 25–26, 36, 78
olives, spherified 11, 17–18, 34, 54, 59, 130
opera, culinary 14–16

Parks and Recreation 83
participation 130–135, 143–145
pedagogy 67, 72–73
perception 18–19, 41–46, 91–92
Perullo, Nicola 18–19, 136
Petronius 21–22
Phaedo 7–8
pharmakon, food as 8, 55
Physiology of Taste 23–24, 145, 147
Plato 7–8, 12, 20
pleasure 7–9, 11–13, 40–41, 46–49, 52, 56–57
Pliny the Elder 22
La Pocha Nostra 97–98
Poetics 8–10
Pollan, Michael 20
Pont, Fernand 67–68
Prague Quadrennial Makers Event 148–155
Prentice, Jessica 67
Prince, Rose 14–16
proximal senses 7–10, 16
Puchner, Martin 37–38

recognition 10, 12–13, 130–132
Red O 118
remix 131
Republic 7–8
resemblance 7, 11
Ritz, Cesar 76–77

Roche, Ben 86–87
Ruhlman, Michael 4

Santamaria, Santi 4, 55
Satyricon 21–22
scenography 23, 73–74, 77
scent design 25–26, 36, 78
Schapiro, Miriam 106
scratch-n-sniff 25–26
senses: and artistic genres 14–15; and gender 7–8; hearing 27, 45–46, 103, 131, 149; hierarchy of 6, 101, 149; intelligence as sixth sense 52; and meaning 6–11; multisensory mimeticism 42, 47–49, 83, 98–99, 128–130; proximal 5; sight 8–9, 14, 38, 41–42, 73; smell 25–26, 36, 78; taste 5–6, 8, 150–155; touch 132
Serle, Adrian 55
service: and hospitality 67, 113–114, 132–134: as pedagogy 72–73; as performance 74–75, 81–82; and pleasure 43
Sisters Academy 150
Skopec, Rudolf 150–151
Soarin' 26
sound 27, 45–46, 103, 131, 149
spherification 20, 81; *see also* olives, spherified
Square Root 1, 11
"Statement on the New Cookery" 37–40
subjectivity 28, 58
substitute foods 86–87
sustainability 84–87, 157
synsepalum dulcificum 87–92

Taillevent 23
Tasting Notes 149

tasting the past 138–139
Taussig, Michael 3, 23, 91, 99–100
techno-emotional cuisine 16
Telfer, Elizabeth 6, 11–12, 18–19
temporality 18–19, 56–59, 105, 138–139, 154–156
terroir 116–124
This, Hervé 19, 39, 51
Tiravanija, Rirkrit 26, 103
Titus Andronicus 134–135
Tomaska, Jenner 75
Tony n' Tina's Wedding 26
Top Chef 19, 84, 120
Tosi, Christina 21
A Tragedy in Four Acts 150–151
transubstantiation 22
Tropicana, Carmelita 106–110
Trotter, Charlie 66–68
Tuan, Yi-Fu 56–57
Twitty, Michael J. 121–124

Ulterior Epicure 36

Vettel, Phil 77, 80
La Viander 23
Vondrák, Ladislav 150–151

waste 56–59, 60, 86–89
Waters, Alice 4, 20
Waters, John 26
Wells, Pete 71–72
Willy Wonka 25
Womanhouse 106
WOW Cafe 107
Woyzeck 1, 128–129, 141–145, 152–154

Zgheib, Miriane 149–150